Major Philosophers of Jewish Prayer in the Twentieth Century

Major Philosophers
of Jewish Prayer
in the Twentieth Century

JACK J. COHEN

FORDHAM UNIVERSITY PRESS
New York
2000

Library of Congress Cataloging-in-Publication Data

Cohen, Jack, 1919–
    Major philosophers of Jewish prayer in the twentieth century / Jack J.
Cohen.—1st ed.
        p. cm.
    Includes bibliographical references and index.
    ISBN 0-8232-1956-9 (hc)—ISBN 0-8232-1957-7 (pbk)
        1. Prayer—Judaism. 2. Jewish philosophers. 3. Judaism—20th
century. I. Title.
    BM669.C65 2000
    296.4'5'01—dc21   99-049432

Printed in the United States of America
00 01 02 03 04 5 4 3 2 1
First Edition

For
Michal, Jeremy, and Adeena
David, Gail, and Noah

CONTENTS

PREFACE

The subject of this study has given me no rest for the more than fifty years since my ordination into the rabbinate. I expect that it will continue to engage my interest and to disturb me for my remaining years. If I permit myself to bring my thoughts on prayer before the public, despite my inability to answer many of the questions I raise, it is because I believe that the questions themselves should be aired and because I hope that other men and women, more competent than I, will deem my reflections worthy of response. Perhaps they will be able to lead the way to a new era in humankind's problematic dialogue with God.

By and large, I have eschewed references to secondary sources, preferring to confront each thinker directly. It is not that I lack respect for the many scholars who, before me, have conducted their own research into or dialogue with the men and women I have selected for treatment. I have simply wanted to meet each of my subjects face to face. In presenting my approval, reservations, or criticisms of each thinker, I do not doubt that reference to the others who have reacted to one or another person on my list would be useful. However, I had no intention of writing an "academic" book, with a generous sprinkling of references. My purpose was much more modest. It was to see what I could learn from several twentieth-century philosophers of Jewish prayer as I try to resolve my own perplexities. My fellow researchers and critics are another source for me to study. They, too, merit independent consideration. But that, if ever, will have to be another volume. I have read many analytical and scholarly essays and books on the thinkers included in "Cohen's List," but they appear here, for the most part, unidentified—shadowy evidence of my unconscious absorption of their scholarship and thinking.

I apologize also to the unsuspecting reader who might have been tempted by the subject and discovered that I have not written a "popular" work. Nonetheless, I hope that many of both the scholarly community and the serious-minded laity will make the effort to accompany me in my exploration of Jewish philosophies of prayer and in my ruminations on the issues at hand.

My selection of twentieth-century philosophers and philosophies of prayer is, of course, subjective but hopefully fair. Call it a matter of taste. Let someone with a more comprehensive and perceptive mind come along and supplement my list. I shall be the first to welcome such a development.

A theologian today cannot help but trip over the problem of speaking about God in sexist terms. To refer to God only in the conventional He or Him is to court criticism from sensitive semanticists. I agree with the feminists that exclusively male designations for God are no longer acceptable. However, substituting female terminology on an equal basis is also unsatisfactory, for it merely doubles the difficulty entailed in speaking of God anthropomorphically. Furthermore, in the absence of an acceptable new theological language, the balancing act of sexist God-designations becomes rather laughable and stylistically awkward, to say the least. God is not a He or She, and if, nonetheless, I have to use human terms—God forgive me, I do—I take the easy way out and mostly follow convention.

It is easier to find gender-neutral terminology when writing about human beings. Thus, instead of "man," when I mean both sexes, I employ terms like "humankind," "humans," "human beings," or simply "men and women." In quoting, of course, I record the usage of the particular thinker. Most of those quoted use the traditional "man," "mankind," etc.

One has to choose between a uniform way of spelling or quoting passages as the author wrote them, thereby leaving the reader confused as to the "correct" spelling. I have chosen to let each person I cite appear in the form in which his or her words were published.

Rendering thanks is a thankless, endless, and dangerous task. Those who have assisted me in one way or another know how deeply grateful I am to each and every one of them. But there are always several persons who deserve special mention. In my case, I am deeply indebted to the small band of loyal students at Congregation Mevakshei Derekh, in Jerusalem, who for many years have forced me to reflect on the issues covered in this work. I suspect—

and hope—that, if they read what I have written in the coming chapters, they will continue to press me for further clarification and refinement of my ideas.

My friend and colleague Rabbi Harold Schulweis graciously read an early draft of my manuscript and made a number of cogent criticisms and helpful suggestions. I have tried to do justice to his wise counsel. But, as has been repeated by many an author, I am solely responsible for the deficiencies of this study. Harold's reputation remains intact, regardless of the merits or defects of my book.

I thank my beloved wife and beg her forgiveness. I thank her for bearing with me during the years of gestation of my thinking about prayer. I treasure her spirituality, which, perhaps unbeknownst to her, has long made me realize how far I have yet to travel along the road to heightened *kavvanah*. And I thank her for having released me time and again from holding up my end of the household and family chores that we males must begin to accept in this new age of equality of the sexes.

And, of course, I express my indebtedness to Mary Beatrice Schulte and Anthony F. Chiffolo of Fordham University Press for their kind and efficient attention in processing my manuscript and to Debra Hirsch Corman for her skill in spotting errors in my text and proposing improved wording.

Finally, a word of appreciation to my beloved grandmother Bertha Grossman, of blessed memory. She, above all other influences in my life, taught me that in prayer, all distinctions in rank—whether of intellect or social achievement or status—disappear. Before God, we humans are called upon to behave as equal and loving brothers and sisters.

Jerusalem
February 1998

INTRODUCTION
The Crisis of Prayer

PUBLIC WORSHIP is in a chaotic state. In the West, church and synagogue attendance has long been on the decline. The occasional reawakenings make headlines, but they do not change the larger picture. Prayer is not on the agenda of most westerners today. In the rest of the world, there is a wide range between the easygoing, meditative practices of some of the Far Eastern religions, with their tolerance of individual and group predilections, and the rigid traditionalism of Moslem Fundamentalists. The spare liturgy of the Mosque continues to ward off secular influences. The mosques of Saudi Arabia, Iran, Iraq, and other traditional Islamic states are still central to the daily life of the average Moslem. However, modernism has begun to erode the single-minded religiosity of Moslem intellectuals wherever the authority of the mosque has been subjected to secular political control. Nevertheless, as far as I can see, Islam is the exception to the rule insofar as the percentage of worshipers is concerned. But it is often politics or social pressure, rather than the search for God, that influences attendance at prayer services of many a religion.

Numbers, however, are a poor criterion for judging the worth of a spiritual practice or institution. Packed synagogues or churches are frequently a reflection of the success of a charismatic preacher. The crowds come to be entertained and occasionally to be enlightened. But by and large, their presence in houses of worship is not motivated by the urge to pray. Contrariwise, while the widespread aloofness to prayer suggests that something is amiss with traditional and even modern versions of worship, it tells us nothing about whether or not prayer has or should have a place in human fulfillment.

In these chapters, we shall be concerned with efforts of major Jewish thinkers of the twentieth century to provide an acceptable intellectual basis for prayer. Let it be said at the outset that not one of these efforts has reversed the trend away from formal worship; however, they have all made prayer possible for a select group of Jews. That is all we can expect from a philosopher, theologian, teacher, or preacher. For in any intellectual transaction, the effectiveness of ideas is dependent on the background, experience, wisdom, and temperament of both the theoretician and the audience. They are often unable or unwilling to understand or to accept one another.

Furthermore, philosophers and theologians are as subject to their personal idiosyncrasies and the mood of their age when they discuss prayer as they are in their treatment of other theoretical problems. They relate to problems that pique their interest, ignoring other issues that might be more determinative than the subjects of their choice. For instance, most of the thinkers in our study do not attend extensively to the theoretical or practical considerations of liturgical change. The exceptions are Mordecai M. Kaplan and the feminist liturgists, who have attempted serious changes in the content of the prayers while trying to preserve their form. Eugene Borowitz and Lawrence Hoffman endorse the efforts of their Reform forebears to change much of the content of the siddur (prayer book), but as far as I can discern, they do not themselves engage in this aspect of liturgical revival. Most of the other theologians turn to reinterpretation of the traditional liturgy in order to ensure continuity between their sometimes radical theologies and the age-old prayer book, but they pay little or no attention to adapting the wording of the prayers to those theologies. They ignore the possibility and reject the desirability of altering the ancient text. Even Hermann Cohen, who strayed far from Orthodoxy, regarded a balance between Hebrew and the vernacular, rather than alteration of the liturgical content, as the key to the enrichment of public worship. The remaining theologians in this study think that the content of the prayers is basically irrelevant to the human-divine dialogue; traditional prayers can be interpreted to suit the spiritual outlook of each generation and each individual. In other words, intellectual honesty has nothing to do with what one says, only with what one means. What, then, led the Reformists, Kaplan, and the feminists to their liturgical innovations? Is their approach un-Jewish? Is the content of Jewish liturgy less salient than the questions that agitate the other theologians?

Each of the theologians considered in this book took or takes a broad view of prayer. Each had or has enormous respect for the traditional siddur (prayer book), but their reflections often have little to do with its role in worship. Their target is more than the synagogue service, although, of course, they all hope that Jews will return to the pews in large numbers. What are the problems that touch them?

1. They are all troubled by the lack of *kavvanah* in today's worship. *Kavvanah* is a difficult concept to translate or to understand, even in the original Hebrew. It refers to a combination of devotion, concentration on the wording and meaning of the prayers, emotional absorption, intention, self-effacement, and other marks of sincerity that should distinguish the true worshiper from the mere reciter of liturgy—who is known in Jewish circles as a "davener." Prayer without *kavvanah* has been deplored by the sages throughout the ages, while praise has been heaped upon those intent on seeking God in their worship. Typically, R. Eliezer deplored the tendency to routinize prayer excessively, lest it come to lack the sincerity and emotion of supplication that should inform the turning to God (Ber. 29b). On the other hand, we are told that the early pietists would prepare themselves for prayer by engaging in unspecified spiritual exercises and divesting themselves of their worldly concerns (M. Ber. 5:1). Undoubtedly, those exercises included reading passages from the Bible, mainly from the Book of Psalms, a practice that eventually gave rise to what is known as the *Pesukei D'zimrah* (Verses of Song).

All serious theologians understand that no human being is capable of maintaining a consistent level of *kavvanah*. Devotion is more of a spiritual goal than it is a state of consciousness. Hence, perfunctory prayer, such as characterizes "davening," or mechanical recitation of the liturgy, plays an essential role in the effort to achieve concentration and sincerity. Without the formal structure of the prayer service, *kavvanah* would be deprived of its point of departure.

All of our thinkers try to preserve the Jewish prayer tradition and to inspire Jews to invest it with their individual and soulful adjustment to the times.

2. Clearly, the dialogic character of prayer requires every worshiper to adopt a theological position. The *Tannaim* insisted that

everyone who prays should direct his mind to God (Ber. 31a). Such intention is pointless unless the worshiper has some idea of the object of his worship. Yet, the fact is that the average Jew pays scant attention to the meaning of "God." He finds spiritual satisfaction in the negative implication of directing attention to God, which is to say that prayer for him is an attempt to free himself from his ego interests. He rarely takes the trouble to locate the station toward which he wants to travel. No wonder! To conceive of God is an intellectual endeavor that must inevitably lead to different conclusions, depending on the bent of mind of each person. Temperament and education also play their part. In the last analysis, however, do not most persons pray without being too disturbed by their ignorance of what divinity is all about?

All of our thinkers are incapable of such lassitude. They want both to experience God and to be able to communicate the meaning of that experience to others. They feel the need, therefore, to conceive of God in terms that can be made intelligible to their readers. Of course, their conclusions often differ.

We can anticipate a phenomenon upon which we shall touch several times. Theologians and philosophers, like scientists and poets, are frequently forced to employ abstract terminology in designating phenomena. These theological abstractions often conceal ignorance. In this instance, inasmuch as there is no concrete way to point to God, the careful thinker can only try to define "God." The more abstract the word, the less it can tell us about the reality it supposedly designates. God cannot be pointed to; "God," the word, can only be defined or described, and that means to use other terms that can do no more than bring the reader a little closer to perceiving what the writer has in mind. The reader then has to apply the conception he has received to his experience. Manifestly, that is impossible unless the thinker communicates a clear idea of the word "God."

The noted German philosopher Hegel posed the foregoing difficulty with great clarity. He tells us that by itself the word "God" is ". . . a meaningless sound, a mere name; the predicate says afterwards *what* it is, gives it content and meaning: the empty beginning becomes real knowledge only when we get to the end of the statement."[1] Hegel refers to the fact that until we have said something about God that stems from human experience—such as God is love or God is the moral order of the universe or Law-giver or Judge—we have said nothing. Evoking the name "God" is empty of meaning. Hegel goes on to ask, "So far as that goes, why not speak alone of the eternal, of the moral order of the world, etc., or, like the ancients, of pure conceptions such as being, the One, etc., i.e. of what gives the meaning without adding the meaningless sound at all?"[2] One is reminded of the way in which Maimonides hinted at this problem when he stated, "The Holy One, blessed be He, is His attributes, and His attributes are He."[3] Neither of these two great thinkers, however, seems to have drawn attention to the fact that attributes like love, moral order, justice, forbearance, and so on are also normative abstractions. One of our main tasks, then, is to determine to what extent each of the theologians has succeeded in arriving at a communicable God-idea, one that can be illumined by reference to human experience.

3. Theologizing is a function of mind. How much intellect, however, belongs in prayer? Should not the emphasis in prayer be to engender an emotional experience? Must or can worship be turned into another occasion for the exercise of mind? Why should not the synagogue be a place where the heart speaks to God and where the congregation collectively surrenders itself as one to the embrace of God's love? Isn't prayer, after all, a matter of feeling?

This interplay between mind and heart is not unique to prayer, but its role in prayer is probably more germane than in any other endeavor in life. We shall note that all of our subjects assign a major role to both reason and emotion in their philosophies of prayer. Nonetheless, their varied definitions of that role set them apart from one another.

4. Various efforts have been made to define the human differentia. What is a human being, as compared with and contrasted to other members of the animal kingdom? The Bible describes humankind as being formed in God's image. What does this mean? The usual response is to highlight the ability of human beings to think and to distinguish between right and wrong. Unfortunately, we know how humans are prone to error and to moral perversity. It isn't enough to say that a human creature is only a poor image of God. So is a cat, which also has the power,

although limited, to think. Is the cat made in the image of God? Perhaps thinking beasts are just a little lower than humans on the continuum of consciousness, just as humans are "little lower than the angels." The problem is further complicated by the fact that humans differ considerably in their mental capacities. Clearly, the definition of man or woman cannot be a simple description of how humans behave; it must also attend to what they might or ought to become. Our question turns out to be a normative one.

Meaningful prayer has to focus on the question of the ideal person. What should be the character of the man or woman to whose development prayer is expected to contribute? Prayer is as much a matter of anthropology as it is of theology in the narrow sense. Indeed, it is in prayer that theology is seen to entail the ways in which humans reflect on God, humankind, and the cosmos. No theology can be complete without coming to grips with all three dimensions.

5. The list of problems that I have presented thus far is on the agenda of all theologians. The reader will easily discern that the treatment of each of the questions is conditioned by the culture and the intellectual commitment of the writer. All public worship is culture-bound, and some of the most interesting problems in the philosophy of prayer are generated as a result of the unique setting of each religious group. For instance, in Judaism, study plays a crucial role in the synagogue service. What is the significance of this practice for our understanding of the nature of prayer? To what extent is this a Jewish idiosyncrasy? Is it, perhaps, a contribution to prayer that deserves to be adopted in other traditions? Should Jewish worship in the future give greater attention to study and less to repetitious liturgy?

Every religion finds a place in worship for more than verbal expression. In the ancient Temple, for instance, incense was carefully prepared and used to arouse the olfactory sense of the worshipers. Men and women joined in choral renditions. While formal dance does not appear to have been a part of the Temple ritual, body movement was employed in several ways, from bowing and prostration to the waving of the *lulav* (palm branch) and *ethrog* (citron) during Sukkot (Feast of Tabernacles). Touch had its place in the "laying on of hands" during the sacrificial ceremony; and sight, of course, was satisfied by the beauty of the Temple architecture and the magnificence of the priestly apparel and the ritual appurtenances.

With the destruction of the Temple and the evolution of the synagogue service, it was natural that the senses be used differently in Jewish worship. Moreover, the synagogue could hardly be immune to the powerful influences of the surrounding Christian and Moslem cultures. Ashkenazi and Sephardi Jews differ in their use of the senses. In the meeting that is taking place in Israel between Jews who have been separated from one another for many centuries, surely one of the most interesting aspects of their encounter is the mutual influence they are having and will continue to have on their respective esthetic sensitivities. We shall have to see, wherever it is pertinent, how each of our theologians perceived or did not perceive the role of the senses in prayer.

Just as the content and meaning of the words of prayer can become bones of contention among Jews who want to heighten *kavvanah,* so can some of the other practices of traditional Jewish worship arouse considerable controversy. Separate seating for men and women, the honored status of descendants of the *kohanim* (priests), standing or sitting for certain prayers, the direction in which the cantor faces (toward the Ark or the congregation)—these are items of dispute in many a congregation. We shall not expect our thinkers to spend much time on such matters, but the implications of their philosophies of prayer for handling disagreements in practice will be readily perceived.

When we speak of a crisis *of* prayer, we must not suppose that there was ever a period in which there was no crisis *in* prayer. If prayer will not be replaced by a better form of worship, it will nonetheless continue to be plagued by some or all of the problems mentioned above. So it was in the past. The evolution of the basic content of the traditional Jewish prayer book covered at least three centuries of experimentation, creativity, and controversy. Additions, interpretation, and reinterpretation of its liturgical text have never ceased, indicating that in order to enable the hallowed siddur to perform its spiritual task, it must be constantly reconsidered. If not revised, it has at least to be supplemented and its words given new meaning. In recent centuries, the normal problems of change have been exacerbated by doubts about the very relevancy of prayer to the spiritual development of the average person. This is not a Jewish problem alone. All theologians know that the future of prayer cannot be isolated from the general human condition. All of the thinkers we shall review in the chapters ahead had or have their feet firmly planted in the twentieth century, so that their endeavors to contribute to the quality of Jewish prayer are also contributions to the understanding of the universal crisis of prayer.

The Jewish people is distinguished by its success in surviving many traumatic experiences. However, the trauma of our day might prove to be the most difficult to overcome. The Rabbis of old wisely defined the worst trouble confronting the people of Israel as one that bothers the other nations, too. This is the case today. The Holocaust remains a malaise of all humankind. The lesson has obviously not been learned. Moreover, no people has shown evidence of any special ability to equip its members to orient themselves to the new science and technology, to the latest insights into human nature, and to the anachronism of state borders. They do not know how to cope with the pluralism and voluntarism that free men have learned to cherish. The average individual is bewildered, wandering around physically and spiritually, like Cain upon his exile from Eden.

Each people has its own unique form of confusion. The historical successes of the Jews in overcoming the challenges to their spirit cannot guarantee that the strategies of the past will succeed in the future. As we shall see, even the most Orthodox thinkers recognize the need for new methods. Only thus can there be any hope for the reconstitution of the Jewish people and the revitalization of its religious culture. Our study will be confined to twentieth-century efforts to revive synagogue worship. We shall delude ourselves if we think that we can do much more than clarify the problem and perhaps shed some light on the context within which it must be tackled. If I accomplish this much, I shall be satisfied.

NOTES

1. Georg Wilhelm Friedrich Hegel, *The Phenomenology of Mind,* trans. J.B. Baillie (London: George Allen and Unwin; New York: Macmillan, 1949 [revised edition]), p. 84.
2. Ibid.
3. Maimonides, *Shemonah Perakim,* chap. 8.

1
Hermann Cohen

ON A CORNER of the building that houses the Faculty of Philosophy at the University of Marburg is a modest plaque, on which is inscribed: Hermann Cohen, 1842–1918. This tribute to the great neo-Kantian is a reminder of the important role played by Cohen in German philosophical circles for a major portion of his life. To the best of my knowledge, no such tribute has been paid to this distinguished philosopher by any Jewish community or Jewish institution of higher learning. Yet Cohen's magnum opus, *Religion of Reason Out of the Sources of Judaism,* is still mined for its many insights by serious Jewish thinkers everywhere.

Jacob Agus was virtually alone among American Jewish scholars back in 1941 when he wrote glowingly of Cohen, "Out of the goodly number of great Jews in the literary scene of the last generation, there towers head and shoulders above the crowd the giant intellectual figure of Hermann Cohen. He was a great thinker and Jewish to the core; no review of general or Jewish thought can possibly ignore his work. Many will no doubt assert that in his philosophic researches, as in his estimate of Judaism, Hermann Cohen erred. But, none will deny that, right or not, Cohen's thought is laid out in the dimensions of rare genius. On any unprejudiced estimate, Cohen takes his place with the great Jewish thinkers of all times."[1]

What is greatness? Isaiah Berlin locates greatness in a man (or woman) who is in public life and ". . . deliberately causes something important to happen, the probability of which seemed low before he took up the task. A great man is a man who gives history a turn it could scarcely have taken without him."[2] By this standard, Cohen's contribution to Jewish thought was not as great as it was in the field of general philosophy. In the latter, he was the founder of a philosophical school that was in vogue for several decades and is still studied. The same cannot be said about Cohen's role in Judaism. Cohen's philosophy attracts the attention of cultural historians and a few philosophers of Judaism, but it is hard to discern the influence of Cohen on the general Jewish public. Nonetheless, I concur with the assessment of Agus. If Cohen did not cause significant change in Jewish thinking, he did leave us a rich heritage of suggestive ideas that deserve serious examination and application or adaptation. In that suggestiveness lies Cohen's greatness. I shall confine myself to his views on prayer.

Cohen's approach to prayer is consistent with his general philosophical method. Since his starting point is reason, it is to be expected that he would first build the intellectual structure of prayer and only afterward relate it to the historical liturgical tradition. The latter is brought to shed light on and to confirm the philosophy of prayer that has been conceived in a pure act of reason. It is noteworthy that the Jewish sources to which Cohen refers are all taken from the traditional liturgy. None are those of the Reform movement of his day, with which he was connected. Had Cohen begun with a study of the revised liturgy and drawn its lessons for an understanding of prayer, he would have derived a different conception from that which he proposed. But Cohen's method of interpretation is typical of some modern Jewish philosophers, who want to retain their tie with the tradition but who, in one way or another, have abandoned many of the premises of ancestral worship. While they cannot rely merely on recital of the liturgical tradition to express their spirituality, they nonetheless turn to it for emotional support and tend to read into the prayers what, in fact, is not the intent of the original text.

The failure of Cohen to relate to the Reform revisions as a major source of his reflection calls for some explanation. Understandably, Cohen buttresses his philosophy of prayer by examining the classical heritage, but why does he not refer also to the new liturgies that had already gained momentum in his time? Were they not authentic and legitimate expressions of the Jewish soul? Should not a thinker of Cohen's stature have commented on the implications of the Reformist alterations, omissions, and additions to the prayer book? Several possibilities suggest themselves, none of which can be more than speculation.

Certainly, latter-day revisions of a prayer tradition that had evolved over a span of two millenia are unlikely to possess the emotional power of the age-old text. Cohen might have thought that the new liturgy had not yet been sufficiently tested for serving as an object of philosophical interest. New does not necessarily mean better, and Cohen might have sensed that the altered texts of his own day were too shallow and short-lived for his purposes. At the same time, that very fact calls for analysis. If change and experimentation in the contents of the siddur are bound to lack the intellectual depth and emotional conviction of the classic original, must we then assume that Jewish public worship ought to remain untouched by us and by future generations?

Perhaps, however, Cohen confined himself to what he considered the real sources of Judaism, those that have passed the test of time. Authentic Judaism would thus be associated only with the classics and not with with current growth. It strikes me that Cohen's treatment of prayer must inevitably lack the vitality that would come from searching for sources in the flow of present Jewish life, as well as that of the talmudic and post-talmudic past.

Cohen's recourse to the classics, to the exclusion of modern sources, has one exception. He believes that Jews must pay careful attention to the environments in which they live, absorbing what is in keeping with the Jewish spirit and warding off dangers to that spirit. In line with this precaution, Cohen writes: "Prayer . . . must be evaluated and used as a means of education to the content of faith in order to introduce and impress the most important ideas upon the religious mind. For this purpose the original text is necessary; for through translation the Jew would inhale the Christian spirit even in the original biblical idea."[3] It would seem, then, that Cohen does comprehend the important role that current life must play in the prayer experience. However, it is the flux of the non-Jewish environment that catches his attention, rather than the metamorphoses of internal Jewish life and thought. As Agus declares, Cohen was Jewish to the core, and he wanted Jewish worship to be conducted in the spirit of the traditional sources. But his treatment of the language of prayer indicates that it was the vitality of his German background that would be for him a major determinant of Jewish liturgy.

While cognizant of the need for preserving as much as possible of the Hebrew text of the prayer book, Cohen argues that ". . . the viewpoint of the national state one lives in should be normative.

The follower of Judaism should be a modern man of culture, and as such should employ the language of his culture not only for business or for the general cultural use of the mind, with the exclusion of religion, but should also use it effectively in prayer."[4] In this formulation, Jewish culture would seem, at best, to be secondary to or derivative from that of the surrounding majority. Although Cohen argued vociferously for the superiority of Jewish monotheism over that of the dominant Christianity, he did not exhibit the same pride of priority regarding the relationship between Judaism and Germanism. He considered both of these cultures as having been inspired by Grecian civilization and as having developed along similar lines. Cohen's view of the congruence of *Deutschtum* and *Judentum* was a clear and catastrophic misreading of the German mind of the nineteenth and twentieth centuries.[5] However, I am concerned here only with the light that Cohen's political and cultural opinions shed on his philosophy of prayer. Jewish sources play an independent role only as they emerge out of the distant past. Cohen sensed nothing of the need for and the cultural potential of the emerging Jewish nationalism and religious ferment whose signs were already apparent in his day.

Despite this fault in Cohen's vision, his reflections on prayer are essential reading for anyone who wishes to come to grips with the problems of contemporary worship. Cohen's general philosophy is representative of one of several schools of thought that have challenged the historical religions to reexamine the contents and the forms of their liturgies. There is nothing new in this type of challenge to worship. The problem of how to maintain devotion has always disturbed worshipers, and the substitution of new prayers for old, the introduction of new liturgical practices, and the articulation of new insights have never ceased. Behind all these adjustments have been philosophical considerations that have either stimulated the changes or reflected the atmosphere in which they occurred. The current crisis, however, is revolutionary; it stems from a radical change of intellectual mood. In the past, Jewish philosophers and theologians discussed prayer with a view to strengthening the devotion of regular worshipers. In the twentieth century, much of the thinking has sought to inspire Jews to return to worship in the synagogue. It seems to me that Cohen's effort had much to do with his own desire to regain the ability to participate sincerely in worship services. For long years, he had been estranged from the synagogue.

Many readers will point to the peculiar phenomenon of large numbers of Jewish intellectuals who have found their way back to the synagogue and who consider theologizing about prayer to be irrelevant. They do not expect prayer to be an intellectual concern and come to the synagogue for emotional release and inspiration, something that is more effectively acquired through the traditional siddur than through its modernization. This is a phenomenon that deserves psychological analysis. However, such analysis must be accompanied by reckoning with the latest scientific insights into the nature of man and the cosmos. Equally important is the need to take into account the current experiences of the Jewish people. Let us examine how Hermann Cohen saw the challenge and how he responded to it.

Cohen's German patriotism inevitably distanced him from Zionism. He could not appreciate the significance of and the need for a creative Jewish national revival. This should not be construed as a rejection of the need for some kind of Jewish group solidarity. Cohen found an answer in the congregation. On the one hand, he deemed prayer to be essentially a function of the individual. At the same time, Cohen saw the individual as a cell of a larger unit—first, of a historic people and ultimately of humanity as a whole. It is the duty of the individual to serve as a mouthpiece for the entire human race and to contribute to its salvation. Therefore, Cohen writes: "Solitude can only be a transitory state of the human mind. Man is the carrier of mankind. For this purpose he must first of all assemble into a community. The totality of mankind must be his final goal, but for this totality he must first achieve the unity of plurality. The unity of plurality is the congregation."[6]

The congregation is thus the medium through which the apparent contradiction between the inwardness and personal character of prayer and its role as the expression of universal humanity can be overcome. Prayer is the means by which the individual establishes his connection with God and His Kingdom. But it is only in the congregation, whose function it is to pray for the coming of that Kingdom on earth, that the individual can properly pursue this objective. "Prayer," says Cohen, "belongs not so much to the individual as to the congregation."[7]

Hence, prayer is the efficient cause of the formation of a congregation. Through the congregation, prayer also molds the individual, to the extent that he or she is at one with the other members of the group. Cohen reaches this conclusion by reference to the *Alenu* prayer, which proclaims the messianic advent of God's universal Kingdom. In this concluding prayer, in which the Jewish service reaches its climax, the congregants as one dedicate themselves to the furtherance of a united humankind. Each worshiper attains his true humanity as a member of the God-seeking collective. The Jewish people, in Cohen's vision, is a religious entity that is formed by its dedication to this common ideal.

Cohen oversimplifies the prayer process. Congregations are organized by groups of people who have several common interests and purposes, only one of which is prayer. If only prayer is held in common, the group cannot become a congregation in the sense in which Cohen conceives it. In order to attain a unity of mind and soul, the members of a congregation must share other interests in addition to those of the *Beth Tefillah* (House of Prayer). Cohen himself hints at this fact when he argues that worshipers must study together if their prayer is not to be shallow. However, he fails to see that the unity of a congregation is hewn out of shared experiences and interaction of the members in other affairs of life beyond the confines of prayer or other purely mental exercises. It is more appropriate to state that congregations are the basis of prayer, rather than the other way around. Or, at least, it would be more pertinent to observe that while the desire to pray together might motivate men and women to form a congregation, they already have a sense of togetherness before the thought occurs to them to unite for public worship.

Our criticism of Cohen's understanding of the sociology of the congregation should not blind us to his suggestive remarks about the theology of prayer. As we have seen, Cohen views prayer as a step in the moral improvement of humankind. As such, it must be based on truthfulness, a virtue that is clearly demanded in the pungent teaching in the early part of the synagogue service: "At all times let a man revere God as well in private as in public, express the truth, and speak the truth in his heart." This calls for utmost concentration and devotion *(kavvanah),* intellectually and emotionally, so that "the correlation of man with God is adapted in the prayer to man's turning inward to his most profound moral powers."[8] Moral power has to be cultivated in the course of and as an ineluctable part of the search for God. Hence, we must examine Cohen's approach to the God-idea.

Cohen associates the term "God" with the concept of truth. Truth, in turn, ". . . is the law of the necessary connection of the knowledge of nature and the knowledge of morality. . . . Truth is the accord of theoretical causality with ethical teleology. This accord of both kinds of lawfulness had been from of old the philosopher's stone. It is the original problem of theoretical philosophy, but it is also the fundamental meaning of the idea of God."[9] Finding the law by which the "is" and the "ought" can be harmonized is the meeting ground of religion, science, and philosophy. Indeed, it is only in the idea of God that humans can hope to attain a measure of truth, for it is only this idea that can unite the various forms of knowledge.

Despite the abstractness of Cohen's definition of God, it is obvious that it emanates from and has concrete bearing on human experience. It is humans, after all—and particularly ethical humans—who realize their self in relation to God. Without God, the human career has no focus, no purpose, and no possibility of fulfillment. It is readily seen, therefore, that prayer is one of the main instruments by means of which humans establish their relationship to God and infuses it with emotional force. As Cohen puts it, prayer establishes ". . . the relationship between religious knowledge and religious action, and at the same time between religion and morality, in general."[10]

Prayer transposes the correlation between humans and God from the realm of intellect alone to that of purposive action. This does not mean that the mind is excluded from the prayer experience or that its presence is obtrusive rather than germane to worship. Quite the contrary. Trust in God is both a stimulus to and a result of prayer. But how can such trust be attained without the confidence in God's reality that can find support in knowledge of the universe? And knowledge is the business of intellect and reason. Therefore, when worshipers enter the synagogue to pray, they must bring their minds with them.

What happens in the prayer experience? Cohen declares that "for all spiritual, for all moral action, the mind needs to withdraw into itself; it needs the concentration of all its inner forces and prospects."[11] Such concentration is essential for the difficult reconciliation with God that constitutes redemption for mortal humans. Men and women are in constant need of moral improvement, an objective that Cohen believes is unattainable without confidence in the presence of a good God. This confidence is the emotional outcome of successful prayer. To reach this point, individuals have to be able to distinguish between themselves as subject and object. As worshipers, they reach out to God, so that they might see themselves objectively and honestly. They need God in order truly to repent. Thus, prayer, in Cohen's formulation, requires an abundance of intellect. Indeed, it is hard to see the connection between the traditional repetition of the formal liturgy and the internal dialogue that characterizes the mental state of the worshiper. As Mordecai M. Kaplan points out, ". . . with prayers that are formalized and repeated three times a day year in and year out . . . it is impossible to expect the average person to exercise *kavvanah*."[12] It would seem that for Cohen, the ideal prayer would be a form of meditation, in which an attempt is made to spell out the divine-human correlation. Clearly, that correlation is a product of "pure thought," rather than observation, imagination, or some other possible way of seeking knowledge.[13] In other words, prayer is a conscious act of cogitation that would seem to have little to do with human emotion.

Cohen is quick to deny such an allegation, both psychologically and theologically. In the first place, humans come to prayer out of a deep yearning. They are ever in search of redemption, and they are consumed with longing for God. These are goals of an essentially emotional thrust. This deep feeling never departs from human beings, for the quest is and must be eternal. Longing for God is compared by Cohen to the emotion experienced by a lover as he or she seeks the presence of the beloved. The desire of a lover is ". . . based on the substitution for presence of the distant image, which it paints with the glow of its heart. Longing, therefore, holds fast to its distant goals without which it cannot accomplish the activity of approaching the beloved. . . . Love is the longing for the essence, which is not present in perceptible actuality, and should not be, insofar as it is being longed for. So also is the prayer's longing for God, who should not be desired as a perceptible actuality; as such he cannot be sought for in knowledge, and therefore also not in love."[14] Prayer, in this sense, is perpetual emotion, eternal longing, whose satisfaction lies in the feeling itself.

This eternal longing is the emotional vector that is formed out of two opposing tendencies of the soul—doubt and trust. Cohen writes: "Man's heart knows no greater conflict than that caused by doubt, that is, by the suspicion that his belief in the superior power of the good may be nothing but delusion and that all hope in the eventual triumph of truth may, in the end, prove vain. It is here that prayer can enable us to scale the heights of moral confidence and trust; for God is the rock to which all hope must cling. Yet the struggle of the two souls within us, the realistic, skeptical soul and the soul which believes that the idea is reasonable after all—this, too, constitutes prayer."[15]

The longing that eventuates in prayer and is, at the same time, prayer itself can best be understood in the perspective of man's love of God. Even in human love there is a sense of a new beginning at every moment. True love is a continuous discovery or rediscovery of the beloved. Or, stated differently, it is a consuming desire to achieve an intimacy of release with the one person who holds the key to one's fulfillment. Similarly, love of God, which Cohen describes as the longing for redemption from the burden of the feeling of guilt, is expressed in never-ending prayer. Each moment is a new revelation of God's saving power. The worshipers' love is aroused by their confidence that this divine power is available to them if only they will pursue it with the necessary devotion. Prayer must, therefore, be ever fresh. God must be approached again and again with the excitement of adventure. The hope is always present that the quest will succeed, but the worshipers know that their success can be only proximate and that they will always have to renew their pursuit of the Beloved.

While Cohen thinks about prayer as quintessentially intellectual, he argues that it must not be only such. That is so because love, which is a psychic state, transcends intellect. The love relationships between God and humankind—humans' love of God, God's love of humans, and humans' love of other humans—grow

out of the primal sense of pity that is common to both the divine
and the human correlates. The worshipers recognize God's love
for humankind. Out of their own capacity to feel pity for their
fellows, they learn to match God's love for mortal creatures with
their own love for one another. The experience of human love
enables the worshiper to turn to God with total trust. It is this
trust that drives humans to pray, but it is the intellectual determination of the meaning of God that validates the act. Were prayer
only a matter of intellect, most men and women would be unable
to understand its role in their lives or to persist in the habit of
worship. Were prayer to be only a function of feeling, its content
would be misdirected or haphazard.

The question might still arise that love of God, as portrayed in
Cohen's theology, is too abstract to allow for prayer. Cohen's God
can be construed as essentially an idea and therefore not capable
of being addressed. Cohen responds forthrightly. He writes: "The
power of the idea to realize itself is nowhere so clear as in the love
for the idea. *How is it possible to love an idea?* To which one should
retort: how is it possible to love anything but an idea? Does not
one love, even in the case of sensual love, only the idealized person, only the idea of the person?"[16]

Humans' love of God is thus the love of a moral ideal or arche-
type, on which moral action can be established. True love always
has to be expressed in action, which takes the form of humanitari-
anism and of prayer. Interestingly, both types of action embody
the human search for knowledge, but neither is itself knowledge.
In the love of one's fellows that leads a person to humanitarian
behavior, there is the constant pursuit of the ideal human being.
But he or she is always beyond us. That is so because we can never
know what perfect humanity is meant to be. Meanwhile, we know
that we are imperfect and must follow the lead of love. The beloved draws us on and inspires us to loving action. If the latter
ceases, it is a sign that love has come to an end. Similarly, although knowledge and the search for it are indispensable to
prayer, it is the ceaseless yearning for God that is its cornerstone.
According to Cohen, this is the spirit of the Psalms, in which God
is never described. Instead, it is the heart of poets or worshipers
as they express their yearning for God's goodness that is bared in
these paradigms of prayer. It is not God who is desired; God can

never be reached by a mortal soul. It is only in God's action that humans can experience divine love; it is God's saving grace that worshipers seek to activate in their prayer. However, the success of the prayer is dependent on its *kavvanah* and continuity and not on the divine response.

So once again we return to devotion, to sincerity, and to as much understanding of what we are about as it is possible to acquire. Cohen relies heavily on the knowledge of and dedication to moral goodness. Perhaps intuition would be a better way of identifying the apprehension of goodness; but in any case, worshipers aim in prayer to gain, to restore, or to preserve their moral purity. Hence, in repentance or atonement we might gain insight into the proper mood of prayer.

Atonement is essentially an individual act, just like sin, whose effects on the individual repentance is designed to overcome. Even though sin is committed almost always in a social context, it is the "I," the individual, who is its cause. Sin cannot be treated simply as a violation of socially accepted morality.[17] The key to humans' self-improvement lies in the awareness and acceptance of responsibility for behavior—whether toward oneself, one's neighbor, one's group, or humankind as a whole. Nevertheless, moral conscience arises in society, and society is molded by the collective behavior of its individual members. Religion, then, is a synthesis of individual and group morality. Religion differs from pure ethics in that it highlights the dimension of individuals and their ultimate responsibility for their actions.[18] In contrast, there is a tendency in theorizing about social ethics to attribute sin to the group. Cohen would have us recognize the role played by society in creating the conditions that generate sin, but he insists on tracing its cause to the individual.

Cohen's individual, however, is not just one of the persons who constitute the group. He or she is an "I," an independent and responsible being who, along with other "I"s, gives the group its character. In other words, Cohen seems to assert that while the individual is to be sought in a social setting, he or she must always be seen and treated as totally independent. But how do these independent creatures arise in a group in which they and their fellows are all interdependent? And if all humans are interdependent, in what sense can sin be attributed to the individual and atonement be considered a matter of individual self-transformation?

It was Ezekiel, according to Cohen, who provided the answer to these questions. In contrast to his prophetic predecessors, Ezekiel located sin in the individual rather than in the group. The other prophets had defined sin in social terms, as a violation of justice, which is, of course, an immoral act committed by one or more persons against others. So defined, the individual recedes into the social framework. Insofar as individuals are concerned, their moral responsibility is absorbed into the morality of the group. Ezekiel, however, observed that an unjust act is a sin against God, thereby forcing the individual to stand alone before a tribunal from whose judgment he or she cannot hide. Even though an act of injustice might have been perpetrated by a group, each member is called before the heavenly court. The I stands alone before God. The I alone must seek escape from the burden of sin. It is at this point that the I comes into focus and repentance becomes possible. Individuals are able to separate themselves from the mass and to accept full responsibility for their freedom and their use or misuse of it.

In acknowledging their sin, individuals accept the need and duty to pay a penalty for their misdeed. Ezekiel sees in punishment not primarily an act of authority or retribution but a divine stimulus to repentance. The punishment need not be actualized in order for repentance to take effect. Atonement is itself a symbolic form of punishment. However, penitence and the punishment that accompanies it cannot be accomplished in private; sinners might then succumb to the danger of mere verbalization. In order that sinners confront themselves as in need of punishment, they must confess in the presence of the community, in an act that bears public testimony to their guilt. As Cohen explains, for the step toward self-renewal, the sinner ". . . must be joined to a public institution; it cannot be actualized in the silence and secrecy of the human heart. It is the meaning of all moral institutions that they support the individual in his moral work."[19] In Ezekiel's day, this meant offering a sacrifice in the Temple. In our time, prayer and confession in the midst of a congregation are the media for repentance. In a congregation, a community of like-minded and warm-hearted men and women, the individual finds the support needed for confession. The presence of other "I"s, all of whom share in human failings and eagerness to overcome the common sense of guilt, enables individuals to stand before their conscience and God and admit their sins. In this way, their repentance loses its abstractness and becomes a matter of public record. Surrounded by their fellows, the sinners renew and equip themselves to begin a new life. While Cohen develops these thoughts in connection with the theology and the ritual of Yom Kippur, the points he makes apply to prayer in general.

In several ways, Cohen's analysis bears witness to his effort to think organically about the purpose and conduct of prayer. As we have learned, one of the main issues that bothers Cohen is the dialectic of the individual and the group. On the one hand, prayer is always an expression of the individual. On the other hand, as exemplified in the sinner's need for a communal venue for his or her confession, prayer is a profoundly social enterprise. Cohen is clearly aware of the impact of the group and its cultural heritage on the molding of each person's character. This accounts for his reference to the Jewish heritage as the source for an appreciation of prayer. What is lacking, I repeat, is the sense of the worshiper's participation in a living and creative people. The vitality of prayer cannot be measured only by the degree of impact of tradition on the present generation. Worship, both in form and content, has to express the concerns and aspirations of the living, and they too have to be observed in their social milieu. Of course, Cohen sought to ensure Jewish survival, but his rejection of Jewish nationalism could lead him only to a truncated Judaism, confined to the synagogue and oblivious of the spiritual energy of a people resurrected on its own soil.

It is pertinent to add another comment about Cohen's assertion that the purpose of prayer is to improve the moral stature of the individual. One could accept this assertion more easily had Cohen qualified it by mentioning the many prayers that petition God for sustenance, wealth, health, protection from enemies, freedom from having to rely on the favors of others, and mention of other wants and needs of everyday existence. Instead, Cohen assesses prayer from a highly idealized perspective. He claims that ". . . in prayer and through prayer the individual is to be turned away from all eudaemonism. Only that which connects man with God is to be the content of prayer. Prayer is to further only the impetus to man's infinite task. Therefore, besides the moral, only the spiritual, the knowledge, and the study of the Torah were made the concern of the individual in prayer."[20] Again, we miss here the sense of a pulsating vitality that can come only from the life of a people engaged in fashioning a complete civilization. Equally, human individuals have more than moral needs; they also have to attend to the biological, social, and psychic aspects of their makeup. Prayer must help each person to gain a wise perspective on all these needs.

Cohen handles with great depth the problem of the God–human correlation in prayer. Humans' address to God is easily understood, since each individual articulates what is in his or her mind and heart. Indeed, it is only through God's being addressed by men and women that divine holiness becomes manifest. Cohen explains that "God is not determined as holy through the secrets of his essence. And, generally speaking, not through knowledge does he become the holy God, but only through the act of sanctification; his holiness is effected through action, which man has to accomplish."[21] Thus, humans' turning to God is a manifestation of their nature and of their need to feel that their hope of coming near to God is not blind self-assertion but one pole of a cosmic design—the other end of which is the divine morality. But how are we to know God's response?

Cohen's answer is to deny the relevance of the question. Whether or not God will help the suppliant should not be the latter's concern. Prayer is the duty of individuals who need to express their concerns and who know that they can depend on a good God. That faith is itself the answer they seek. "My soul," writes Cohen, "achieves the innocence of belief in the good God. Therefore, I pray to him. My prayer becomes my belief. So intimately does the prayer connect me as an individual with my God, with the God who in this prayer more than ever becomes my God."[22] The circularity of this formulation needs no elaboration. Cohen relies on his concept of correlation to minimize the force of his reflexive association of God and humans. Each pole of the correlate has meaning only in the light of the other. But the ploy is only partially successful. God in human consciousness has no greater standing as a product of imagination than any other idea. This is no derogation of the importance or validity of the God-concept. The actuality of that to which the term "God" refers may or may not be a fact. But in Cohen's description of the act of prayer, humans are not only the crucial and initiating factor. They determine or mediate God's response, as well. It is hard to see, therefore, how Cohen can escape the conclusion that prayer is really an exercise in the ability of men and women to transcend themselves. They can never know whether the perspective from which they perceive themselves in prayer is correct or not, but at least they refuse to rest satisfied with themselves and their fellow human beings as they are.

In a partially analogous way, scientists have constructed visions of space that, for long periods of time, could not be confirmed by experience. Only when they were able actually to explore outer space could they witness the behavior of the earth and other celestial bodies in the way they had imagined. Similarly, worshipers hope to rise above themselves. In prayer, however, men and women want not only to observe themselves, but to use their new power of observation to change themselves or supply what is lacking in them. In the end, we cannot help concluding from Cohen's theorizing that prayer is, after all, meditation and that God is never to be understood except as an inference of the intellect. The longing for God will remain and impel us to pray. But given Cohen's premises and analysis, it seems that while prayer is directed to the Holy One, blessed be He, it also seeks to uncover the deeper self of the human person that can be reached only through the strenuous and honest self-examination that is required in prayer.

Thus, Hermann Cohen has carried intellect a long way into the caverns of prayer. He has probably failed to satisfy those who thirst for the kind of emotional experience that goes beyond all contact with cognition. But in compensation, he has opened up new vistas for anyone who wants to pray honestly and profoundly.

NOTES

1. Jacob B. Agus, *Modern Philosophies of Judaism* (New York: Behrman, 1941), p. 57.
2. Ramin Jahanbegloo, *Conversations with Isaiah Berlin* (London: Peter Halban, 1992), p. 201.

3. Hermann Cohen, *Religion of Reason*, trans. Simon Kaplan (New York: Frederick Ungar, 1972), p. 57.

4. Ibid., p. 390.

5. Hermann Cohen, *Juedische Schriften*, vol. 2 (Berlin: C.A. Schwetschke und Sohn, 1924). See Cohen's two essays on "Deutschtum und Judentum," pp. 237–318. I refer the reader also to the perceptive study by William Kluback, *Hermann Cohen: The Challenge of a Religion of Reason*, Brown Judaic Studies (Chico, Calif.: Scholars Press), 1984.

6. Cohen, *Religion of Reason*, p. 386.

7. Ibid., p. 385. Cohen finds much Rabbinic support for his view on prayer as a group exercise. See, for example, Rabbi Yohanan's statement that a person who prays at home (instead of in the synagogue) is to be compared to one who builds an iron wall around himself (T. Yer. Ber. 5:1). But note, too, the fact that the talmudic Sages would often absent themselves from synagogue services, fearing that they would be detracted from their preoccupation with study.

8. Ibid., pp. 380–381.

9. Ibid., p. 420.

10. Ibid., p. 410.

11. Ibid., p. 370.

12. Mordecai M. Kaplan, *The Purpose and Meaning of Jewish Existence* (Philadelphia: Jewish Publication Society, 1964), p. 228.

13. See the essay "Joseph B. Soloveitchik on Hermann Cohen's Logik der reinen Erkenntniss," in *Torah and Wisdom*, ed. Ruth Link-Salinger (New York: Shengold, 1992), particularly pp. 147–149.

14. Cohen, *Religion of Reason*, p. 374.

15. Hermann Cohen, "The Concept of Reconciliation," in *Juedische Schriften*, vol. 1. The quotation is taken from the translation by Eva Jospe, in *Reason and Hope* (New York: Norton, 1971), p. 202.

16. Cohen, *Religion of Reason*, p. 160.

17. Ibid., p. 180.

18. Kluback (see note 5) describes the journey of Cohen from his early, Kantian-grounded, abstract theory of ethical responsibility to his later trust in God as the ground and source of all reality and values. In this transition, reason continues to play its central and essential role; but it is trust in the existence of God, and not the dictates of reason, that now arouses the individual's sense of responsibility. God calls upon man to repent. Henceforth, prayer becomes the language of man's love for and intimacy with God (Kluback, *Hermann Cohen*, p. 53.)

19. Cohen, *Religion of Reason*, p. 196.

20. Ibid., p. 383.

21. Ibid., p. 110.

22. Ibid., p. 378.

2

Franz Rosenzweig

FRANZ ROSENZWEIG (1886–1929) was one of the major philosophers of Judaism who sprang from the ranks of German Jewry during the last half of the nineteenth century. After thinking seriously of converting to Christianity, he decided to deepen his ties to the Jewish people and to explore the treasures of Judaism. He wrote his masterpiece, *The Star of Redemption,* while serving in the German army during World War I. Shortly after the war, he fell victim to a progressively worsening disease that left him totally paralyzed. The remarkable way in which he continued his creative thinking during the last years of his life remains one of the finest examples of courage in the annals of the human spirit.

Rosenzweig's achievement in conferring meaning on life, despite the eclipse of his body and his slow, agonizing approach toward death, might be attributable to his ability to concentrate life in thought. Even before his illness incapacitated him, Rosenzweig had already lived in a world of intellection. We have seen how Hermann Cohen, Rosenzweig's mentor, endeavored to derive his conception of God out of pure thought. Although Rosenzweig departed from Cohen's approach and evolved his own theology, he was equally cerebral and was thus able to find satisfaction in the kind of contemplative existence that fate had thrust upon him.

For Cohen, we should recall, the apprehension of the "I" marks the first step in prayer. It is the redemption of the I that prayer purports to accomplish. Cohen regards pity as an additional catalyst that brings about self-recognition and the realization of sin and the need for atonement. The ultimate aim of prayer is to enable all humans to merit the redemption toward which they must strive through repentance.

Rosenzweig, too, sought to extract the individual from the general salvation that was the hallmark of the Hegel-inspired idealism of the time. However, instead of *pity*, Rosenzweig assigns to *love* the role of enabling individuals to discover their neighbors and, through them, their own I. With this discovery, prayer gets into high gear.

The discovery and release of the I are essential in prayer, because it is only the free, altruistic individual who can address God in truth. The others, who are stimulated to piety by the realization that it can do them no harm and might do them good or who are placed in a plight in which the appeal to the Redeemer seems to be their only outlet to fulfillment, want God to act in an ungodly fashion. If God responds favorably to the prayer of the unfree, that is, those who turn to God for selfish reasons, then favor is bestowed on the undeserving. If God denies the requests of those who have not been blessed with the ability to become free, then divine kindness is silenced. In both instances, God is tempted to act in response to human misconception or misbehavior, rather than out of spontaneous divine will. Consequently, God desires only the prayer of the free soul, for that expression emerges out of a disinterestedness and a will that resemble God's own. And that means that humans have to pray out of love. God, says Rosenzweig, in His own act of love, ". . . freed the soul for the freedom of the act of love, just as he gave creation the power to grow vitally within itself."[1]

What are the characteristics of love that are so vital to prayer? In a sense, human love of God is irrelevant to God's action. For God acts out of His own love and not as a reward or quid pro quo for the reciprocal love from humans. True love is always unconditional and independent of the response of the beloved. This applies both to the love of humans for God and their love of neighbor. Both forms of love are commanded, but they are equally spontaneous. This spontaneity is the essence of freedom. Freedom is commanded by the very nature of humans, but it is a virtue that must be discovered, cultivated, and rehearsed. Once possessed, it must be relearned and practiced anew at every moment.

If the path of true love is never smooth, how much more difficult is the path of our romance with God? A woman who has many suitors wants to be certain of their characters and motives; she tests them all with her aloofness or challenges their sincerity and determination by withholding her acceptance even of her favored one. Inevitably, only one of the suitors will reach the goal. His rivals will have to learn that love is a hazardous emotion, which has to be unconditional. Often, its only reward is the love itself. We should not be surprised, therefore, that God does not make easy our access to Him. On the contrary, notes Rosenzweig, in order to sift the sincere lovers from the self-interested worshipers, God not only denies them His help; He must harm them or ". . . hide his sway from man: he must deceive him about it. He must make it difficult, yea impossible, for man to see it, so that the latter have the possibility of believing him and trusting him in truth, that is to say in freedom."[2]

Rosenzweig's employment of the analogy between human love and the love of humans for God is suggestive but breaks down at crucial points. In the first place, a distinction has to be made between platonic love of neighbor and the erotic love of men and women, even when the latter love is crowned with spirituality, mutual respect, and selflessness. The former can be all-inclusive and unite many persons in bonds of eternal friendship; the latter is exclusive and confined to a single relationship. As soon as erotic love loses this exclusivity and incorporates another love object, the original relationship loses its redemptive quality. The new relationship might, and often is, a redemptive replacement for the first. But that occurs only when the new tie, in turn, takes on the exclusiveness of what had been lost. *Amor dei,* too, is exclusive in the heart of every worshiper and is potentially common to all humans. However, those who abandon God for another divine love object are lost to idolatry. Their new love can only condemn them to damnation.

Prayer, although it comes to consciousness in the lonely heart of individual persons, owes its form and content to the experience of a group. Rosenzweig, like Cohen, seeks in the traditional Jewish liturgy the content that is born of the love between humans and God, but this content is a social creation aimed at conditioning how the individual should learn to love God and to give expression to this emotion. Against this background, one must ask whether group worship and its liturgical structure have any real bearing on the individual's love of God. Traditional prayer, after all, predates the urge of any person to seek God. Group prayer, if sincere, might enhance some persons' love for God, but it is unlikely that it can generate this sentiment in most worshipers. Maimonides understood long ago that love of God is stimulated by the sublimity of nature and the wonders of the cosmos. And the authors of the Jewish prayer book were men who not only responded to nature, but who also felt it necessary to find meaning in the tribulations of the Jewish people. This prayer book is expected in every generation to heighten the Jewish worshiper's love of God. It seems, therefore, that public worship involves a spiritual heritage and social and communal considerations that antedate and are often more primary in the prayer experience than the spontaneous love of God. It is generally assumed, for example, that most Jews in the Diaspora attend synagogue out of a desire to identify as Jews, while the bulk of worshipers in Israel participate out of a sense of duty or out of habit. The motivation for prayer turns out to be not *amor dei* but the desire to connect with one's fellows and with a noble tradition.

Rosenzweig does recognize that the analogy between love of neighbor and love of God has to be posited with circumspection. In loving another human being, one relates to an object of flesh and blood, whom one can experience both sensually and spiritually. True, even love of one's fellow can never be static and necessitates a continuous pursuit of an elusive ideal. But the loved one is never out of potential sight, and his or her actuality is always manifest. Not so the divine object of human love. Even when worshipers are overwhelmed with what they describe as love of God, they cannot say more than this. Presumably, God can be felt emotionally, but declarations about divine attributes are always inferential. This conclusion, however, must surely cool the ardor of the worshiper. How can one pray to an inference? Rosenzweig has an answer, which he derives from his analysis of the I and the other.

The I, according to Rosenzweig, is discovered in the act of seeking the Thou. He writes, "Where is there a Thou altogether? This inquiry for the Thou is the only thing that is already known about it. But the question already suffices for the I to discover itself. By the very act of asking for the Thou, by the Where of this question, which testifies to its belief in the existence of the Thou even without the Thou's coming into its purview, the I addresses and expresses itself as I. The I discovers itself at the moment when it asserts the existence of the Thou by inquiring into its where."[3] In this typically convoluted argument, Rosenzweig draws upon the psychological experience of humans, in which self-consciousness arises when a person becomes aware of the existence of another being. One observes this phenomenon in an infant, who passes from consciousness to self-consciousness at the moment when he or she is able to recognize others. Rosenzweig concludes, therefore, that awareness of the I is a correlative of awareness of the Thou. The reflexive process continues when the I or the soul ". . . makes acknowledgment before God's countenance and thereby acknowledges and attests to God's being; therewith God too, the manifest God, first attains being: 'If ye acknowledge me, then I am.' What then is God's answer to this 'I am thine' by which the beloved soul acknowledges him?"[4] This experience precedes the intellectual apprehension of God's existence. And it is this instinctive recognition of a reality not oneself that enables men and women to pray. Just as they strive to fathom the depths of the neighbor, so they seek to relate to the eternal Thou.

Psychologically, however, prayer is a response to God and not to a human initiative. For it is stimulated, says Rosenzweig, by God's call, the command of the divine lover, who demands that man requite His love. "The commandment to love can only proceed from the mouth of the lover. Only the lover can and does say: love me!—and he really does so. In his mouth the commandment to love is not a strange commandment; it is none other than the voice of love itself."[5] Rosenzweig realizes that the divine Lover is a hypostatization of a human being's sense of having to obey the call of conscience. But there is no escape. Once one has uttered the name of God, God must be obeyed. Humans have to answer God by declaring God's presence. That is the genesis of prayer.

Of course, prayer is more than a consequence of God's revelation to the worshiper or, as Rosenzweig suggests, of the coming to self-consciousness of the I and the eternal Thou. Once the I has been released to freedom in and by God's love, it seeks the redemption in whose attainment it now has confidence. For prayer ". . . is an overflow of the highest and most perfect trust of the soul. There is no question here regarding the fulfilment of the prayer. The prayer is its own fulfilment."[6] However, redemption is elusive, and its quest can never cease. "The prayer for the coming of the kingdom is ever but a crying and a sighing, ever but a plea."[7]

Prayer is its own reward, but it is always directed to hastening ". . . the coming of the kingdom. God once descended and founded his kingdom. The soul prays for the future repetition of this miracle, for the completion of the once-founded structure, and nothing more."[8] When did this first founding take place? Was it in the antedeluvian era, before mankind corrupted the earth? Was it at Sinai, when God's revelation conferred upon man all that he needed for establishing the kingdom? Or was this Rosenzweig's reference to "the future repetition of this miracle," a scarcely veiled reference to the Christian contention of a second coming? Whatever be the meaning of this assertion, the main point holds true—the effort to effectuate God's kingdom extends into a future without a foreseeable end.

For Rosenzweig, God's kingdom, the outcome of the messianic process, is more than an inspiring idea, as it seems to be with Cohen. Hence, the appeal of the worshiper for its consummation is no mere verbal exercise. How does prayer work? We have already noted that the I is aroused to consciousness and self-consciousness by God's love. The soul is commanded by God, the lover, to love Him. In one sense, redemption occurs the moment the individual responds wholeheartedly to that command. As Rosenzweig observes, "It is only in being loved by God that the soul can make of its act of love more than a mere act, can make of it, that is, the fulfillment of a—commandment to love."[9] Or, as he adds, "Only the soul beloved of God can receive the commandment to love its neighbor and fulfill it. Ere man can turn himself over to God's will, God must first have turned to man."[10] The act of prayer is thus initiated by God. This, however, is only the ontological side of prayer. Of greater importance to humans is to understand it psychologically.

Psychologically, as we have observed, prayer starts with the self-awareness that stems from love of one's neighbor. This experience, which is and must be renewed, lest it lose its vitality, seems paradoxically to be the very antithesis of prayer. For love of neighbor has no purpose other than love itself. It is entirely of the moment. Yet we have said that prayer is directed to the future—a call for the redemption of the human species. And so it is, Rosenzweig tells us. Love of neighbor is not self-generated. We are commanded to love the neighbor (Lev. 19:18). Love can easily end in the solitary blindness to the surrounding world of both the lover and the beloved, who are robed in the ecstasy of the moment—exemplified in the passionate Liebestod of Wagner's *Tristan and Isolde.* The soul in this state is oblivious to reality. Both the lover and the beloved lose their own identity. Their union is a consummation but, at the same time, also a loss of the self and the object of one's love.

What I have described just now is the height of the esthetic experience. The playing of a musical composition can be said to have reached the peak of virtuosity when the audience is drawn into the music, when the listeners lose consciousness of their surroundings and themselves, and when they and the music become one. Something similar happens when an observer is overwhelmed by a painting and, as it were, enters into the work of art. Such moments, of course, are rare, but once experienced, they are sufficient to inspire us to continue the search for the beautiful. The objective of prayer is altogether different. The self is not to be lost or extinguished in a moment of mystic rapture. To experience God or to imagine one is experiencing Deity is one thing; to become one with God is a dangerous supposition. For then, the unsuspecting man or woman can easily be captured by idolatry. In responsible prayer, individuals retain their self-awareness, indeed seek to heighten it, even as they attempt to respond to the love that they feel is offered to them by God.

Love of neighbor mediates a person's love of God, as it does of his or her love of the world. Rosenzweig declares: "Love goes out to whatever is nighest to it as to a representative in the fleeting moment of its presentness, and thereby in truth to the all-inclusive concept of all men and all things which could ever assume this place of being its nighest neighbor. In the final analysis it goes out to everything, to the world. . . ."[11] True love is observed here to be accidental and outer-directed. The presence of the neighbor is fortuitous. It could have been anyone else, but since it is this one, the command to love him or her applies. On the other hand, says Rosenzweig, the closest neighbor, the representative of all humankind, must not consume one's whole attention. Beyond the neighbor are other neighbors and the entire created world. These, too, await the redemption that only love can bring.

The meaning of salvation must always be problematic, inasmuch as redemption is ever in the future. In this, Rosenzweig follows Hermann Cohen. But Rosenzweig, we repeat, cannot rest satisfied with a mere ideal. Somehow redemption must become real and actual, and to this end prayer must contribute its share. As we have seen, it is the human soul that makes the connections between the three actors in the drama of redemption—God, man, and the cosmos. Of course, the roles of the actors are incommensurate, but it is the function of the soul to piece them out and to conduct its search accordingly. Its first step is to seek out the neighbor, although the search is guided by the accident of nearness. The action of the soul ". . . heads for the future, and the neighbor sought by the soul is always 'ahead' of her and is only anticipated in the one who just happens, momentarily, to be ahead of her. . . . The soul's action, wholly turned toward the neighbor in deed and consciousness, wants to anticipate, in so doing, all the world. And the kingdom's growth in the world, hopefully anticipating the end at the next moment—what is it waiting for at this next moment if not for the act of love."[12] Rosenzweig is telling us that redemption emerges out of the interaction of the acting, willful soul and the uncalculating, growing cosmos. Redemption, then, occurs in this world, but it is nonetheless always in the future. For although human beings and the world interact, they cannot redeem one another. The cosmos changes at its own pace, although it is affected to a small extent by human action. Were it only to wait for humans to act, the world would have no impact on human action. And were it not, in some sense, to wait for such action, it would deny humans their role in the scheme of redemption.

Thus, Rosenzweig concludes, man and the world ". . . cannot deliver themselves by themselves from each other; they can only be delivered together with each other—delivered by a third one, delivering one on the other, one by means of the other. Besides man and the world, there is but One who is third; only One can become their deliverer."[13] God's creation of the world and His revelation to His human creatures generate the interaction of the two other poles, but it is only He who can provide the redemptive connection between them; it is only God who can synthesize Creation and revelation. What can one make of this obscure analysis of reality?

Rosenzweig is intent on overcoming the paradox of deliverance in an endless future and in a cosmos that grows in ways that defy pursuit. The answer according to Rosenzweig has to lie in the will of a good God who expresses His goodness in love for both. Rosenzweig illustrates the impact of God by distinguishing between two types of sentences. When a parrot is trained to deny that two times two are four, it can say so, and the sentence is untrue, ". . . for what is mathematics to a parrot?"[14] On the other hand, even were the parrot to be trained to deny that God is good, the sentence "God is good" would remain true, because the parrot, too, is God's creature and the object of His love. The distinction, I believe, is misleading. Rosenzweig asks, what is mathematics to a parrot? He could equally have inquired, what is divine love to a parrot? Then too, while the parrot's denial of the truth of two times two equals four is untrue, this is the case only from the perspective of the mathematician, not from that of the parrot. Similarly, the parrot's denial of God's goodness would still be true to it, even though untrue in the eyes of the person who trained it to utter the blasphemy. Nevertheless, Rosenzweig's observation casts light on the need for a bridge between humans and the confusing world of which they are both a part and from which they are apart. They have to find some way to harmonize their relationship to this world. For that, humans need God, to whom they must turn in mind and heart. One step in this direction is prayer.

Prayer, let us remember, is not a solo. It can occur only when the I has been aroused by the Thou, when the individual has found the neighbor, and when they, together with their other neighbors, have formed a community. Salvation comes to the individual only through the harmony of a chorus. Only when a people has been created can God be praised (Ps. 102:19). The language of prayer is the language whereby neighbors communicate with one another. It is the language of men and women, but it is also the means whereby the mute world is brought into the scheme of redemption. Nature, too, is called upon to praise God, but it is humans who articulate what the growing universe seems to imply in its orderly procession from one stage to another. God mediates between humans and the world, but in prayer, humans try to interpret the terms of the mediation. For "the kingdom of God is actually nothing other than the reciprocal union of the soul with all the world."[15]

However, since both humans and nature are processes that transcend the individual and the world at any given moment, prayer must express both the accumulated wisdom of the past and the hopes of the two poles of Creation for the future. Like all human culture, prayer has to reckon with the heritage transmitted from previous generations, even as it projects its light into what lies ahead. Rosenzweig, like Cohen, looks to the tradition to illumine the way, for the experience of the forebears has prepared the ground for today's prayer. Yet, it is not only the heritage that equips humans to address God. The world also plays its role. It is here, in the place where we are born, live, and die, that the kingdom of God is brought about. For it is here that the soul is united with the rest of Creation. Again, Rosenzweig's message is unclear but nonetheless suggestive. Just what is meant by the union of the soul with the world? Rosenzweig seems to declare that this occurs when the soul expresses its thanks for what the world is. Thus, the natural and cultural endowments of man combine to provide the ingredients for the fulfillment of "every conceivable prayer."[16]

The prayer described above is communal prayer. Individual prayer has its place, but when conducted in isolation, it is not a step in the path to the kingdom. Individual lament and plea may be uttered only within the context of the community, especially in one that has a long history behind it. Such a group has accumulated experience in comprehending the world and has learned to appreciate it as the locale and agent of redemption. Rosenzweig therefore concludes, "This union of the soul with all the world occurs in thanksgiving, and the kingdom of God comes in this union and every conceivable prayer is fulfilled. Thanks for the fulfillment of each and every prayer precedes all prayer that is not an individual lament from out the dual solitude of the nearness of the soul to God. The community-wide acknowledgment of the paternal goodness of God is the basis on which all communal prayer builds."[17] The union between humans and the world is made possible only by God's love and goodness. Thus, when we perceive the harmony between the world's seemingly indifferent flux and our own aspirations, we sense God's presence and pour forth our thanks in prayer. Paradoxically, prayer is answered before it is uttered, but psychologically, we know that the harmony is momentary and that we must project ourselves into an uncertain future. Together with our neighbors, we now utter prayer in the language of appeal for the coming of the kingdom. As members of a community, we have caught a glimpse of what salvation might and can be like, but it is only that—just a glimpse. Even as thanks, prayer is still future-directed.

Although the community is the foundation on which prayer is based, the individual and his or her neighbor begin the redemptive process that binds the whole community and ultimately all mankind. The whole, it is true, is greater than its parts, but the whole needs the parts. And the latter must fulfill their roles if the whole is to become complete. Rosenzweig tells us that the plural of things must everywhere bear the mark of singularity.[18] Prayer turns out to be a complicated dialectic. The individual—and all prayer is articulated by the single person—discovers himself or herself only as he or she is able to see and to love the neighbor in the person who happens to be close by. The resulting mutuality enables both souls to look beyond one another and to embrace other fellow humans and to be embraced by the cosmos. The union with other humans and the world leads us to a chorus of worshipful song, which has been prepared for us in the liturgy of a historical community. Nonetheless, the individual is not absorbed into extinction in this inexorable process. On the contrary, the individual remains a dynamic force at the vortex of this cosmic integration. However necessary it is that prayer be cast in the plural, it is the single ones who declare the glory of God. They must do so in unison with their neighbors, but they are conscious at all times that theirs is the obligation to praise God. And although they derive the power to pray from the community, each of them endows the latter with his or her unique singularity.

Rosenzweig is fully cognizant of the accidental nature of so much of human experience. We have already described how the discovery of neighbor arises by force of unforeseen circumstance. The same applies to the formation of community. It, too, is a matter of chance. And yet, is it not also an enterprise of will? In the case of Rosenzweig himself, it is well-known that both considerations entered into his decision not to convert to Christianity but instead to become a devoted Jew. Once having made the decision to accept the fact of his birth as a Jew, it was to Jewish tradition that Rosenzweig turned in order to search for the words to articulate his love of God. As far as I can discern, he did not deal with the problem of how people were to orchestrate a symphony composed of the motifs of the separate Jewish communities and their cultures. However, once having opted for Judaism and its firm rootage in Jewish group solidarity—described by Rosenzweig even in terms of biological continuity—he left it to the other nations to find their own way to address God. Out of those efforts, he assumed, there might eventually be a point of intergroup symbiosis.

In the Jewish liturgy and the ideology of the Jewish holy days, Rosenzweig found the way to express the yearnings of his soul for God's kingdom. Among the elements of tradition that proved helpful to him was the factor of time. Prayer, after all, is deeply concerned with time. The suppliant is eager to advance toward redemption or to draw it closer to himself or herself, but the rate of movement cannot be faster than has been decreed by God but not yet revealed. Therefore, the worshiper must not appropriate time in ways that are unsuitable to the divine plan. We must neither tempt God by pleading to Him to change His will nor miss the moment when our prayer is proper and likely to prove effective. The Hebrew calendar sets forth such a schedule, which enables the Jewish worshiper to experience the blessedness of eternity within the present moment, without thereby being guilty of exerting undue pressure on God to establish the divine kingdom before its time.

Rosenzweig formulates the problem of prayer as one in which worshipers seek to eternalize the evanescent moment when they catch a glimpse of redemption. Of course, while eternity might be encapsulated in a moment, the moment itself can be but a passing flash of light. For this disappointment, posits Rosenzweig, there can be but one solution, in that ". . . the moment which we seek must begin again at the very moment that it vanishes; it must recommence in its own disappearance; its perishing must at the same time be a reissuing."[19] In the Hebrew calendar, Rosenzweig perceives the rhythmic occurrence and recurrence of the redemptive moments. Such moments are rendered uniquely in the liturgy of the synagogue service and in the ritual order of each holy day in the Jewish calendar.

Although based on the cosmic order, the succession of day and night and the changing seasons, the divisions of time—second, minute, hour, day, week, month, and year—are all human inventions and conventions. In marking off time, man, as it were, seeks to grasp the brass ring as the carousel of life continues to whirl uninterruptedly. Humans capture a piece of eternity by infusing into each of the divisions of time significance of their own invention. Thereby, they pull eternity into the orbit of their aspirations. In prayer, worshipers give voice to this perception of eternity. "The cycles of the cultic prayer are repeated every day, every week, every year, and in this repetition faith turns the moment into an 'hour,' it prepares time to accept eternity, and eternity, by finding acceptance in time, itself becomes—like time."[20] The point made by Rosenzweig is clearly enunciated in Jewish tradition in the concept of the *Kiddush* (sanctification). The Jew is called upon to introduce each Sabbath and festival with this benediction. It is the Jew, not the natural passage of time, who sanctifies the special moment. It is humans—in this case, the Jews—who determine when the year is to end and when it is to begin anew. In so doing, they ensure the continuity of the redemptive moments. Time is converted from a mere linear passage of no human significance into a drama of eternal salvation.

Again, individuals pray together with their fellow humans. The prayer of the congregation is directed to the distant, yet near, kingdom of God and not to their personal fate. The congregational prayer ". . . is addressed not to the personal fate but directly to the Eternal, that he might prosper the work, not of my hands or thine or his, but of 'our' hands, so that He, not 'I complete it.' "[21] Each of the cultic occasions illuminates a distinctive aspect of salvation, and each of these is incorporated and recaptured in the yearly cycle.

Shabbat (Sabbath), for instance, focuses human attention

upon Creation as an ongoing process in time. "Just as the world is there, and wholly there before anything at all happens in it, so the order of the Sabbaths precedes all the festivals which commemorate events, and completes its course in the year, undisturbed by other feasts. And just as creation is not contained in the fact that the world was created once, but requires for its fulfillment renewal at every dawn, so the Sabbath, as the festival of creation, must not be one that is celebrated once a year, but one that is renewed throughout the year, week after week the same, and yet week after week different, because of the difference in the weekly portions."[22]

The annual cycle of the reading of the Torah is the center of the Shabbat service in the synagogue. It is prayer par excellence, in that it marks the common acceptance by the congregation of Jewish tradition as the warrant for their addressing God. The reading itself and the exegesis by the preacher are rooted in the silence of this acceptance and are designed to deepen that silence and the communal unity that it represents. Each Shabbat is thus different; each is nonetheless a symbolic link in the chain of Creation that binds the revelatory and redemptive occasions of the year. Rosenzweig describes the twenty-four-hour regimen of each Shabbat as a miniature of the whole divine scheme of Creation (Shabbat eve), revelation (the morning service), and redemption (the afternoon service). But we need not enter into the details of his analysis here. Suffice it to say that the Shabbat liturgy lifts the worshipers out of the mundane affairs of daily life and raises them to an experience of fulfillment. The magic of the day lies in the fact that it is renewed. When Jews are not experiencing Shabbat, they anticipate it. Their redemption, as Rosenzweig sees it, is always present, either in the content of their prayers or in the confidence that the prayers guarantee that the kingdom will eventually come.

Before leaving Rosenzweig's discussion of Shabbat, of which I have given a bare introduction, I call attention to the highly subjective and vague quality of his view of salvation. In treating Shabbat as a day of rest, Rosenzweig comments that ". . . the rest is intended to signify redemption and not a period of collecting oneself for more work."[23] I can agree with Rosenzweig in declaring that the day of rest should be conceived as more than that and not merely a period of re-creating oneself. His view of re-demption, however, would seem to favor the elimination of work as an indispensable ingredient of the full life. Rest, it seems to me, should be conceived not as the reward or the culmination of creative work but as part of the rhythm of life. In fact, with the advance of civilization, it has become abundantly clear that rest cannot be confined to a single day. It must be included as an essential part of daily existence. While the Shabbat should con-tinue to be a day on which a passive view toward the natural proc-ess should be adopted and men and women should refrain from gainful employment or engage in their weekday acts of exertion, the traditional categories of what constitutes forbidden work need to be overhauled. When they were formulated in the biblical and talmudic eras, it was premature to consider the possibility that certain kinds of work and creative endeavor could be re-demptive. That possibility, as in the making and enjoyment of art, is now a reality. Under this circumstance, the task of prayer be-comes more difficult than ever. It must now take on the responsi-bility of helping humans to utilize their native skills both for their own broad fulfillment and for the benefit of society as a whole. Accepting Rosenzweig's suggestive agenda of the Shabbat, we must adapt the liturgy to the new set of perceptions and problems that affect our understanding of Creation, revelation, and re-demption.

And so it is with the other sacred days of the Jewish calendar. Each holiday offers its own glimpse into eternity, and each estab-lishes for Jews the values that are to govern their life individually and collectively. Each year, the holiday prayers remind the con-gregation of these values and evoke new insight into their content and implications. The three pilgrimage festivals—Pesah, Shavuot, and Sukkot—are depicted by Rosenzweig as embodying the di-vinely ordained vocation of the Jewish people, to be the bearers of revelation throughout history. "This vocation is shown in three stages: the people are created into a people; this people is en-dowed with the words of revelation; and, with the Torah it has received, this people wanders through the wilderness of the world."[24] Rosenzweig stresses that the celebration of these feast days must not be mere commemoration. All Jews must project themselves back into the historical moments of the exodus from

Egypt, the theophany at Sinai, and the trek through the desert. They must try to repeat for themselves the experience of their ancestors. They must see themselves as being with their forebears in all these revelatory moments. The Pesaḥ seder, which raises the family meal to an act of worship, and the liturgies of the other two festivals carry the Jew repeatedly through the eternal moments of Creation (both of the world and the people), revelation, and redemption. Each is a moment in history, but each moment is experienced by the worshipers as if they had entered the kingdom of God. Such, opines Rosenzweig, is the power of prayer. Of course, this consummation is not permitted to last. The moment passes and redemption reappears, as it must, as a hope for the future. The cycle must begin again. The prayer and its accompanying rituals must be repeated.

The full significance of prayer is to be found in the services of the *Yamim Noraim* (Days of Awe), when the plea for redemption is brought into the present. The blowing of the shofar, the ram's horn, on Rosh Hashanah, heralding the day of judgment, and the prostration of the suppliants on Yom Kippur convert the hope for God's kingdom symbolically into acts in which each individual Jew confesses his or her sin and is forgiven. In so doing, they act not only for themselves and their people; they pray for and exemplify in their actions the redemption of all humankind. Rosenzweig insists that the ". . . 'We' in whose community the individual recognizes his sin, can be nothing less than the congregation of mankind itself. Just as the year, on these days, represents eternity, so Israel represents mankind."[25] This universal thrust at the height of the Jewish holiday calendar is characteristic of Jewish prayer, in general. The *Alenu*, the concluding prayer of every service, expresses the hope for the unification of all humankind under the sovereignty of God. For Rosenzweig, this plea becomes actualized during the Days of Awe.

It is hard to know how to deal with Rosenzweig's approach. Are we to take it as pure symbolism? Or are we expected to concur with Rosenzweig's claim that the hoped-for future can actually be experienced in the present, if only for a moment? Both conclusions as to Rosenzweig's intent, it seems to me, are plausible. But then, redemption remains a state of mind. Is this another example of Rosenzweig's adaptation of Christian theology to Judaism? Or should his opinion be understood as a this-worldly view of the *olam haba* (the world-to-come)? Rosenzweig is after high stakes. Redemption, it is true, is a goal, an anticipation. But if it is of this world, it must somehow become a reality for the person of faith. So Rosenzweig wants to eat his cake and have it. He accepts the fact that human life is never completely fulfilled; yet, at the same time, he describes prayer as having more than symbolic significance.

Given the foundations of Rosenzweig's thinking, we should not be surprised at its outcome. Rosenzweig's ambivalence about prayer stems inevitably from the view that he had of the Jewish people. He related to the people mainly as an ecclesia, a spiritual collectivity, whose continuity would depend on its ability to define and put into compelling prayer and ritual a set of theological convictions. He wanted to preserve the connection of the people with its heritage, but, like Hermann Cohen, he did not see as an essential part of that heritage the vital elements of an autonomous national existence in a native land. Even the Hebrew language was to continue as the sacred language of prayer and scholarly study, but it was not important that it be the means of daily communication for a large section of the people. Rosenzweig feared the consequences of Zionism—although late in life he seems to have acquired greater respect for its possibilities. As a result, Jewish public worship, in his conception, eschews attention to the spiritual concerns of power and responsibility for the conduct of a pluralistic society. He would want the Jewish people to avoid having to face the dilemmas of sovereignty and of war and peace. However, it is only out of the matrix of such a full life, at least for a major part of the Jewish people, that a spiritual creativity can be developed that might enhance the heritage of the past. The Jewish neighbor must be not only the object of recognition and love. He must also be a partner in the work of creation. Prayer can contribute insight and determination to the making of a better world. Its effectiveness, however, depends not only on its wording but on its social setting and the wealth of relations that bind the members of the congregation.

Notes

1. Franz Rosenzweig, *The Star of Redemption,* trans. William W. Hallo (New York: Holt, Rinehart and Winston, 1970), p. 267.
    2. Ibid., p. 266.
    3. Ibid., p. 175.
    4. Ibid., p. 182.
    5. Ibid., p. 176.
    6. Ibid., p. 184.
    7. Ibid., p. 185.
    8. Ibid.
    9. Ibid., p. 214.
   10. Ibid., p. 215.
   11. Ibid., p. 218.
   12. Ibid., pp. 227–228.
   13. Ibid., p. 228.
   14. Ibid., p. 231.
   15. Ibid., p. 233.
   16. Ibid.
   17. Ibid.
   18. Ibid., p. 235.
   19. Ibid., p. 289.
   20. Ibid., p. 292.
   21. Ibid., p. 294.
   22. Ibid., p. 311.
   23. Ibid., p. 314.
   24. Ibid., p. 317.
   25. Ibid., p. 325.

3

Avraham Yitzhak Hakohen Kook

TRADITIONAL WORSHIPERS are often viewed by their critics as devoid of the tension that is attributed to the "seekers." This stereotype has no basis in fact. We need only point to the figure of HaRav Avraham Yitzhak Hakohen Kook in order to disprove this assertion.

Kook (1865–1935) was the first chief rabbi of the Ashkenazi community in Eretz Yisrael, holding this post from his election in 1921 until his death. However, it was not the authority of his office that conferred on Kook the enormous spiritual influence that he exercised during his life over most sections of the Yishuv. Long before he began to function as chief rabbi, he had acquired a reputation as an outstanding halakhic scholar and a daring and original thinker in a wide range of Jewish concerns. That reputation persists to this day, and no treatment of the problem of prayer in our time can overlook Kook's contribution to the subject.

In order to understand the deep tension that characterized Kook as a worshiper, we have to distinguish between his complete subservience to the halakhic routine of prayer and the search for God that transcended any and all of his habitual practices. As a traditionalist, Kook observed the mitzvot without challenging their authority or his duty to obey them in every detail. There is no evidence in Kook's behavior or in his writing that he ever questioned the obligation of every Jew to pray according to the dictates of the Halakhah. In this respect, one might be justified in saying that Kook's prayer lacked tension. However, there is much testimony by those who observed Kook at prayer that he did not engage in mere recital of the formal liturgy, at least when his concentration did not affect the tempo of the congregational service. When he had the chance to follow his own pace, he is said to have lost contact with his surroundings and entered a realm of utter devotion, known as *devekut*—all this, apparently, still within the sphere of the prescribed prayers.[1]

Thus, anyone who dismisses traditional prayer as lacking the capacity to arouse devotion ignores the notable souls, including Kook, who succeed, during their repetition of the ancient liturgy, in scaling heights of ecstasy. Nonetheless, Kook's spiritual thirst could not be slaked by habitual worship alone. Orthodoxy—or perhaps more exactly, Orthodox persons—should not be accused of spiritual sanguinity. For many of the most observant Jews, the inherited tradition is only a springboard to spiritual depths and to the greater insights into man's place in the universe that they seek. Clearly, HaRav Kook was such a restless soul.

In Kook's eyes, prayer is part of a cosmic process struggling toward unity. In keeping with the kabbalistic myth of the universe as having been created by God's ineffable act of self-contraction, Kook sees the perfection of all existence in the restoration of the original state of unity. According to the well-known view of the Lurianic school of Jewish mysticism, God's self-contraction gave rise to the material world with its many defects. These faults can be corrected only by the scrupulous performance by Israel of all the mitzvot. Israel, however, plays a double role. On the one hand, it bears the major responsibility for repairing the world *(tikkun olam)*. On the other hand, the Jews are but one link in a cosmic effort of all matter and spirit to draw closer to God. As Kook states, "Prayer is the ideal of all worlds. All existence yearns for its source . . . longs for the treasured completeness of its supreme, living, holy, pure and mighty origin."[2] On its part, the human soul engages in ceaseless prayer in order to establish its place in the cosmos and to elevate and unify all of reality with the Source of blessing and life.

Given such a conception of prayer, it is readily understandable why Kook could not find in the mere repetition of the traditional liturgy a complete answer for what he was seeking. Kook's version of prayer calls for a more profound employment of intellect and feeling than that which characterizes the most sincere attention we can give to the content of the ancient liturgy or any of its modern revisions.

It is not surprising, therefore, that Kook should confer a more extensive role upon intellect than one might expect from so confirmed a traditionalist. While not denying the emotional impulse that leads to prayer, Kook insisted that in true prayer, it is necessary for intellect to be active more pervasively than feeling, so as to enable the worshiper to bring ever fresh content to his supplications and meditations.[3] Kook sided with those early Sages who opposed the tendency to have prayer become a mindless recital of a rigid, habitual liturgy. That type of prayer obviously depends on the desire of the worshiper to fulfill a duty or on an emotional urge to approach God through a sanctified procedure. Indeed, the predominance of emotion over reason and wisdom abounds in human consciousness, and Kook sees this as a weakness to be overcome. He declares that ". . . feeling should be founded on the fundamentals of wisdom and on sound intelligence. There is greater worth to emotional declarations that emerge from a heart filled with wisdom than to declarations that express deep feeling but come from a heart devoid of wisdom and cultivated intelligence."[4]

On the other hand, Kook cautions against exaggerated intellectualism in prayer. Inasmuch as reason is less spontaneous than feeling and therefore requires conscious effort, a person can easily become so involved in intellection as to lose the inner emotion that inspires piety and constitutes the aura of prayer. Moreover, for all the importance that Kook assigns to reason and reasoning in the conduct of prayer, the synagogue is not a substitute for or the equal of the *Beth Hamidrash,* the house of learning.

Kook does not tell us forthrightly what is meant by *sekhel,* reason, or *regesh* or *hergesh,* emotion. These are the two essential components of complete prayer. Certainly, he would insist on the rational study of Torah as a prerequisite to worship, for prayer is designed to inspire the Jew to implement the lessons of the Torah. Torah study is essential in order that each individual should know the spiritual and moral values he or she is expected to implement in his or her life. If this were all, then reason's job would be to set the stage for the operation of emotion. The latter, however, brings humans a step closer to action than does abstract intellection. Thus, Kook puts traditional study, *Talmud Torah,* into an organic setting. Rational grasp of Torah leads to the emotion that bursts forth into prayer. This interpretation of Torah study might seem to be self-evident. But Kook was no ordinary traditionalist.

It would take us far afield were we to try and describe fully Kook's philosophy of education. However, I cite an important point in his approach that casts light on our question as to what Kook means by *sekhel* and its role in prayer. In a brilliant but oblique discussion of three levels of the human mind, Kook outlines his philosophy of education.[5] At the bottom of this sequence, he places the traditional method of absorbing as much as possible of the wisdom of the past and reflecting on its message. The result is a positive will, but only in a weak form. From such an education, nothing of great consequence can be expected—only a continuation of tradition. A rung above such schooling is the exercising of reason not confined to the parameters set by the Torah. Such reason can be implemented in action by what Kook calls *yekholet,* the ability to activate and implement ideas and to concretize the abstract. This combination can produce what Kook designates as *ratzon kabir,* a powerful will. Unhampered intellect, coupled with the capacity to act on the possibilities it reveals, leads to novelty and creativity. Neither of these approaches is to be denigrated, and any system of education will necessarily have recourse to both of them. But the highest stage in Kook's educational ladder is what makes his thought so distinctive among traditionalists.

Reason together with *yekholet* can surpass even the creation of a powerful will. The combination, when functioning in consonance with the flow of experience, eventuates in a dynamic life. Reason here is not abstract thought; it is rather the mind's working on natural events, seeking to perceive relationships and exploring their meanings for an understanding of how humans might best draw near to God. Thus Kook tries to bridge two worlds of thought. He never departs from his belief in the authority of divine revelation, as adumbrated in Torah and its extension in Halakhah. On the other hand, he comes amazingly close to John Dewey in viewing life as open-ended growth rather than as directed to a divinely appointed end. This is the burden of the following remarks by Kook: "The Creator, blessed be He, has instilled in the soul of all existence a love of life because it is good. Life is undoubtedly good, because it is the means chosen by the beneficent God to favor His creatures. The essence of life is the perception of its reality. It follows that the more a [conscious] entity senses quantity and quality beyond itself, the more life it will possess, inasmuch as the basic focus of its life is the apprehension of its existence. Therefore, its rise and growth depend on the amount and the quality of what it is able to experience beyond itself. The greater the amount and excellence of what is experienced, the more exalted life will be."[6] While Kook does not say that the purpose of life is growth, he does suggest that *Talmud Torah,* the study of the traditional texts, is not all there is to life. Indeed, in the course of the passage we are examining here, he remarks that while, for the present, God has given Israel the Torah, in the future He will grant it life.

Were Kook to base his philosophy of prayer solely on the foregoing considerations, he would have to advocate a constant reconstruction of the liturgy. A life-accompanying liturgy would require continuous reaction to the flow of life. Ideals would take on new content, emphases, and forms of expression. Traditional prayers would have to undergo reinterpretation, change of wording, or elimination. "God," "man," and "world" would take on new meanings. But for all his imaginative vision of reality, Kook was no modernist. He believed that he could give free rein to his thoughts without having to step out of the bounds of tradition. To a considerable extent, Kook succeeded in this endeavor. He was aided by the enormous richness of the Jewish prayer literature, which lends itself to a variety of interpretations. He found support in the openness of the synagogue to the vicissitudes of Jewish experience and by the relative freedom of thought in Jewish tradition (as compared to the restrictive nature of its ritual practice).

Kook paid no attention to the inconsistencies between his theorizing and the content and wording of the classic prayers. In this respect, he did not differ from the type of modern intellectual mentioned above, who is comfortable with the old prayer book despite its obvious anachronisms and views that contradict the standards of modern ethics and cosmology. Such individuals, I emphasize, deliberately underplay the intellectual ingredient in prayer, preferring to emphasize its emotional origin and purpose. They posit that when they enter a synagogue, they must leave behind them their secular existence and surrender themselves to the embrace of an aged, loving, and beloved tradition with which one does not argue. One's relationship to one's parents and grandparents is not measured by their ability to keep pace with the advancing knowledge of the younger generations.

Kook, however, was not as simple-minded as those who manage consciously to live in two disparate and often contradictory worlds. He brought all of existence into his conception of prayer. As I have suggested, he was able to do so without undue inner disquiet about the possible effect of his method on the conduct of synagogue worship. He took full advantage of the art of interpretation and reinterpretation to discover in the liturgy and in the entire halakhic approach ways of accommodation to the demands of contemporary thought. Moreover, he was able to elicit from the vast Rabbinic literature many valuable insights not yet appreciated by so-called modernists. I maintain, in other words, that Kook was able to convince himself that Judaism could cope with the latest knowledge and that its system of prayer could be interpreted so as to give free play to advanced intellect. Of course, as must be emphasized again, Kook's conception of reason and intellect lacks the experimentalism that characterizes the scientific method and ends at the point where its conclusions would lead to the denial of the absolute truth of Torah. The urge toward growth intuited by Kook must remain within the confines of revealed tradition. Nevertheless, the confines of Torah are broad enough for Kook to engage in far-reaching flights of imagination. Let us examine several of those flights so as to capture the mood of Kook's philosophy of prayer.

Prayer is addressed to God, but its purpose is to effect change in man and the world. Kook declares: "Prayer intends to change nothing in God. . . ."[7] He stresses that ". . . prayer must be so conceived as to eschew any idea of producing change in the Blessed One's will or intended action. Such an idea of godliness is false and damages human completeness."[8] On the contrary, prayer is intended to improve man and his environment. Kook insists that ". . . every worshiper must understand that prayer is a remarkable law promulgated for the cosmos by the Holy One, Blessed be He, for the purpose of perfecting His creatures in every way, particularly as regards their moral completeness. . . ."[9]

Thus, a worshiper ". . . must keep in mind that our intention is to remove evil and darkness from the world and to increase goodness and light. . . ."[10]

Admittedly, Kook does not always depart from the common view of prayer as influencing God's treatment of man. For instance, he informs us, "The prayer of the righteous causes God to abandon His attribute of wrath in favor of His quality of mercy. Philosophy, which posits the absence of change in God's will, cannot rise to this exalted level."[11] In line with this thinking, Kook explores the psychological foundations of the daily morning, afternoon, and evening prayers.

At the outset of the day, humans are blessed with an abundance of spiritual energy, which enables their prayer to prepare them to withstand the pressures and temptations that are bound to weigh upon them during their normal activities. Therefore, classical Judaism calls upon all males, before they set out to engage in the affairs of life, to pray and fortify themselves with an abundance of moral strength. (It should be obvious that Kook, in keeping with halakhic tradition, regards women as possessing a psychological orientation of their own that imposes on them a separate regimen. We cannot engage here in an analysis of this important issue.)

In late afternoon, as individuals are about to cast off the cares of the day, they can reflect on their experiences and ponder the new spiritual assets that they have acquired and that now have to be integrated into their personality. The *Minhah* service, says Kook, is the appropriate time for the prayer that can work this effect.

At night, the mystical element of prayer comes to the fore. Humans are more passive then than they are during the rest of the day. The body and soul relax and are susceptible to the spiritual impact of thoughts that are not consciously generated. Nature seems to recede, and ineffable forces are free to penetrate the soul. The *Maariv* service is the only one that is designated as *reshut* (voluntary). Presumably, it was recited in ancient days from sundown to midnight, at any time fitting the convenience and the spiritual mood of the worshiper. This timing of *Maariv* still holds true today, except that its recital under the Halakhah is now obligatory.

In all of these instances, we should notice the attention that Kook gives to psychological preparedness. Unless individuals are fully aware of the potential of their state of mind as they set out to utter the prescribed liturgy, they will fail to elicit from the prayer what it is meant to accomplish. In traditional Judaism, the recital of the liturgy is to be undertaken whether or not the individual is in the mood to do so. From this perspective, psychological readiness is totally irrelevant. Nevertheless, we should be mistaken were we to see this disparity as an inner contradiction in Kook's approach. Undoubtedly, a major aim of the formal liturgy, whether recited alone or in a group, is to draw Jews closer to God. Moreover, the traditional prayer book has the added sanctity of having evolved during and from the long history of the nation. Its recital confers merit on the worshiper, even if he or she does not attend to its message. The average Jew, loyal to this age-old habit, is thereby able to experience a kind of spiritual satisfaction that is denied to anyone who fails to find a home in the siddur (prayer book).

However, in addition to being a traditionalist, Kook was a mystic, who could never be satisfied with mechanical or haphazard worship. Yosef Dan has described mystics as ". . . individuals who seek their own, profound communion with God, in an intensely personal and unique manner."[12] Kook was such a person, but he was evidently able to approximate that communion by making the text come alive through the passion of his spiritual determination. The siddur, far from being a block to his search for God, served as a catalyst for his ecstatic moods. Tradition played a more significant role for Kook than that assigned to it by Professor Dan. The latter sees mysticism and tradition as ". . . two different levels of religious and spiritual experience, divided from one another as the common is divided from the unique."[13] It would be more accurate to describe Kook's view of the distinction between the mystical and traditional approaches as one of a relentless effort of the mystic to evoke from the traditional text its power to effectuate *devekut*, the union of the human and the divine. I must, however, qualify this assertion. Kook was a complicated thinker, whose mysticism and rationalism counterbalanced each other. As I have mentioned above, although one can scarcely doubt that Kook achieved moments of great emotion during communal worship, I suggest that his quest for communion was conducted mainly in isolation, when he was free of the distractions of other men and when he could step beyond the bounds of the liturgy without disturbing the congregation.

Kook wrote many poems in which he expressed his longing for God, an obvious indication that his need to express his spiritual aspirations and frustrations could not be satisfied by resort to the prayer book alone.

The following outpouring by Kook illustrates the intensity of his spiritual yearning:

> I pine
> For the supernal light,
> For the light infinite,
> For the light of the God of truth,
> The God of my life.
> The living God,
> Who sustains the universe.
> My longing consumes my strength
> Of body and spirit.
> I am not endowed with the knowledge
> Nor have I been prepared
> To still this great longing.
> I prostrate myself profusely
> Before the Sovereign of all worlds
> Whose hand is open
> To satisfy every living thing with favor.
> Grant my desire,
> Grant me the light of Your revelation,
> Satisfy my thirst for Your light,
> Illumine me with Your light,
> And I shall be helped.[14]

Kook, I have claimed, was also a rationalist, who, as might be expected, explored in depth the intellectual dimension of prayer. I have intimated that he differed from other halakhic loyalists in the extent to which he applied his mind to life experiences beyond the study of Rabbinic texts. Consistent with this view of intellect, Kook interpreted Torah in terms reminiscent of Maimonides. The latter broadened the scope of Torah by including in it philosophical speculation and the investigation of nature. Basing himself on this vision of reason, Kook widened the range of prayer beyond the formal liturgy. He wrote, for example, "Prayer, concerned with mundane life, serves to draw all Torah and all worship, all wisdom and all phenomena into a natural setting and a mental state of fixity. That is to say, prayer vitalizes each moment, causing it to confront eternal life and to draw sustenance from its abundance. Torah, however, is eternal life, transcending nature. Where nature operates fully, the importance of miracles is extremely great, but when nature functions in weakened fashion, miracles are identified as annoying God and as defacing the order of Creation. . . ."[15] If prayer is not a way of bypassing or overturning nature but a step in the accommodation of human interests to a healthy, vigorous natural environment, then the worshiper must keep pace with the accumulation of knowledge about nature. This conclusion, however, is never fully explored by Kook.

Although prayer starts with human needs and aspirations, its primary aim is not to satisfy them but to cause humans to perceive what in their human concerns and hopes corresponds with God's will. Thus, the success of prayer is predicated on the degree to which worshipers are able to devote themselves to the study of Torah. For it is this occupation and not research into nature that equips the worshiper to seek God. Torah engages man in trying to weave together the realms of above and below, to appropriate for natural existence the treasures of the divine intellect. Again, although the vector of prayer is projected from earth to heaven, the lesson of Torah is always in the reverse direction. Therefore, tradition proclaims, humans learn about their obligations from God's revelation of His will in Torah. The employment of intellect in the study of nature can be useful mainly to illumine obscure items in the Torah and to give added force to its contents, but it cannot be looked upon as an independent, adequate source of truth.

In his exposition of the respective roles of Torah and prayer, Kook writes: "The Torah always supplies man with rational perceptions that constantly engender new ones and derive existential, eternal truths from eternal life, the Source of Truth."[16] Prayer, on the other hand—and here Kook seems to contradict himself—does not proclaim new knowledge. Rather, it purports to recall and reinforce well-known, established knowledge with emotional power, in order that the moral functioning of the soul be strengthened.[17] The soul, says Kook, is the consciousness of the body, so that the content of prayer is tied not to eternal, divine truths but to the perceptions related to the accidents of the body and of mundane life.[18] Obviously, Kook argues, it will not do to abandon eternal life—the study of Torah—for the passing life of bodily existence. Study takes precedence over prayer. But the matter is not to be resolved in this hierarchical manner. The Jew must both study and pray. Nonetheless, since the Sages declared that a person should study what the heart dictates, the body and its needs and wants play a crucial role in the spiritual curriculum of the traditional Jew. All this is in keeping with Kook's insistence that intellect and emotion are inevitably involved in serious prayer.

It would seem, then, that prayer should be construed as a matter of individual predilection. Were this point to be pressed to its logical conclusion, group worship would, indeed, be difficult, if not impossible, to sustain. Kook responds by indicating that in this instance, the interest of the group as a whole takes precedence. There is a time for study and a time for prayer, and the hours of prayer are established as a rule. It is up to individuals to internalize this commandment, so that timing too becomes part of the very content of their prayer.

We are still left with the problem of the specific role of Torah in the prayer process. Here Kook is quite clear. In order for worshipers to channel the emotional drives that generate or are generated by their prayer, they must be guided by knowledge of Torah, for this knowledge directs them in the paths of justice. Like other traditionalists, Kook looks to the Torah to discipline stormy emotions and to prevent spiritual aspirations from remaining abstract or becoming destructive. Prayer, even though it might be in search of Heaven, can become a stumbling block and do harm ". . . if it does not receive divine rational instruction."[19] Once individuals have acquired moral competence through the instrumentality of Torah study, their emotional resources can then be employed in prayer to convert the ideals into acts. Prayer is never complete until it has taken on the flesh of moral deeds.

When I examine Kook's efforts to harmonize his broad view of reason and intellect with the traditional concept of Torah and its application in the halakhic way of life, I cannot but suspect that he was not altogether at peace with his method of resolution. Kook was well aware of the reluctance on the part of several talmudic Sages to abandon their studies in order to pray with the congregation at the appointed times. Kook himself cites the well-known example of R. Simeon bar Yohai, who, it is reported, studied Torah with his disciples without their ever halting their scholarly concentration in order to pray. Bar Yohai is justified in the Talmud by the claim that "his Torah was his craft." That is to say, his study was of such a nature as to require no additional spiritual exercise such as prayer to effectuate its conversion into deed. Or, to be less charitable, R. Simeon b. Yohai was so wrapped up and so skilfully engaged in Torah, that prayer was to him a distraction.[20]

However one interprets the case of Bar Yohai, I suggest that HaRav Kook was a kindred soul, at least in the sense of finding the study of Torah to be so soul-satisfying and challenging as to make the repetitive recital of the liturgy in the synagogue something of a problem. Nonetheless, he never questioned the need to obey every jot and tittle of the laws of prayer. Nor, as we have indicated, did he permit himself to fall into mindless and emotionless "davening." All evidence indicates that Kook found tremendous spiritual satisfaction and inspiration in daily prayer, particularly prayer recited while wearing *tallit* (prayer shawl) and *tefillin* (phylacteries). Yet the inordinate and profound emphasis that he placed on Torah and intellect in prayer suggests to me that there was one part of Kook that could not be satisfied by the traditional synagogue approach. I admit that this is speculation, but if I am wrong about Kook, the issue itself is a real one. Can the practices of the Jewish prayer tradition continue to capture the hearts of any Jews except the minority that are still convinced about the validity of the halakhic universe of discourse? Many inquiring Jews, it appears, are troubled by the concerns that bothered Kook but are unwilling, as he was, to turn to the synagogue as it is, even in its various versions of adjustment.

Although a halakhic Jew like Kook will not tamper with the traditional liturgy, his imaginative intellect forces him to attend to other facets of the prayer experience that do not bear on altering the liturgical content. Some of his thinking on these matters illustrates his psychological insight. For example, Kook was keenly aware of the rhythmic nature of human consciousness and of the limits of attentiveness. He never lost sight of the fact that the body and soul are intertwined and that the unconscious drives of the former sometimes overwhelm the intentions of the latter. The Rabbinic concept of *tirha detzibbura* (burdening the congregation) spoke to his heart. There is a pace to be followed in public worship that should eventuate in a compromise between those who are deliberate in their recitation of the prayers and those who tend to a speedy rendition. We observed above that Kook himself, although tending to thoughtful consideration of each word, eschewed delaying a group service by excessive deliberateness.[21]

Some deliberateness, of course, is essential if prayer is to be meaningful and sincere. Kook realized that the effort to attend to the meaning of the prayers could easily convert worship into a totally intellectual exercise. To avoid this eventuality, he argued that Torah and its accompanying ideas must be prepared prior to worship. In a sense, the suppliants have already accomplished their purpose before they enter the synagogue. Their soul has attained its spiritual potential; the prayer then comes to reinforce and to activate the willing soul.

Another important aspect of the prayer experience that engaged Kook's attention is the question of the answer that the worshiper hopes to receive. Whether the prayer be one of supplication, affirmation, or glorification of God, worshipers want to experience the effects of their prayer. We know, however, that there is no one-to-one relationship between prayer and God's response. Often, a person is completely disappointed; the worshiper's words elicit only cosmic silence or, equally disheartening, denial. At other times, the response is inscrutable. An answer is given but not understood. Kook handles this uncertainty by recommending that if the response is slow in coming or is unsatisfactory, the worshiper should repeat the prayers again and again. One must not expect immediate satisfaction. In the final analysis, prayer is essentially hope or, as Kook states it, "Hope itself is a measure of fulfillment."[22] (See Ps. 27:14, where the point is made never to lose hope.) Kook's realism is evident in his description of fulfillment as relative to the background of the individual. The effect and effectiveness of prayer, therefore, are dependent upon the manner of coordination between a man or woman's scope of understanding and breadth of vision and the wisdom of their aspirations. Again, we note that Kook does not refer to the obvious gap between repetition of traditional liturgy and the type of prayer that is motivated by the concerns of the individual. That problem remains open in his system.

The philosopher of prayer has to deal with another complicated issue—the network of relationships that obtain or ought to obtain between the individual and the group. Public worship is group worship. What is or should be the impact of the group on the individual? Must individuals submerge their independence in favor of the interest of the congregation? Can the congregation stand apart from the people as a whole? These and other questions are taken up throughout Kook's efforts to ensure both the Jewishness and the universalism of synagogue worship. We can present here only the general direction of Kook's reflections on the subject.

Every liturgy arises in a distinctive cultural setting. The personality and character of individuals are educated in that environment and conditioned by its cultural ambience. However, there is an important difference between conditioning and determining. The will of every person is circumscribed to a greater or lesser extent by the breadth and power of the native culture, but there is always an area of freedom within which the mind of each person expresses its independence and individuality. Perforce, tensions between the congregation and the single worshiper often arise. These tensions, says Kook, can be assuaged by two steps. The first is for individuals to make certain that while their prayer is always aimed at serving God and meriting God's favor, they will accept gracefully even God's negative verdict, no matter how pressing their own urges seem to be. The second step, expressed symbolically by facing Jerusalem and the location of the Temple Mount, is for the congregants to feel intensely their participation in Jewish nationhood. This emotion ". . . prepares the heart for worshiping God and also heightens one's realisation of the worth of the *mitzvot* and of the need to perform them with love."[23]

Basic to Kook's affirmation of Jewish nationalism as a positive factor in Jewish spirituality is his certainty that the Jewish people possesses inherent qualities of mind and soul that are embodiments of God's wish for human character. These qualities can be construed as biologically inherited or culturally induced as a result of many centuries of education from generation to generation. Clearly, the entire presupposition is questionable. One can believe in the validity or worth of Jewish views on morality or spirituality at a given time without attributing them to any biological heritage or permanent cultural excellence. Nonetheless, Kook properly points to the fact that behind the Jewish liturgy hovers the presence of the Jewish people with its value-laden culture. In one way or another, we have to come to terms with the ideals of Jewish tradition and the present-day goals of the Jewish people. Whereas Kook felt that the acceptance of Jewish nationhood in and of itself equips Jews with the moral and spiritual tools that they need to help them become fully human, the more open-minded among them are likely to adopt a more self-critical view of the nation—precisely because they love their people and want to be worthy of the good in its past and the universal ideas of its future.

Prayer is man's way of addressing God. Interestingly, Kook always assumes God's availability to the worshiper, but he neither tries to define God or say anything of a substantive nature about the Deity. This is in keeping with his fear that such endeavors would be pure hubris. In no uncertain terms, Kook proclaims: "Any definition of God leads to heresy. Definition is spiritual idolatry. . . ."[24] Kook is even worried about the traditional names assigned to God, because names, too, are a form of definition. He sets aside this doubt by explaining that everyone understands these designations as mere hints of something beyond our ability to perceive. In the final analysis, theology must not be pressed beyond the context of a commitment to the traditional form and content of prayer. Kook refused to theologize about God; he could only worship Him and long for Him. To delve too deeply into the workings of the cosmos and to draw theological conclusions from them, other than to recognize them as God's deeds, would have been too dangerous.

One other facet of Kook's philosophizing should be mentioned. Kook's entire system is an interpretation and reinterpretation of Rabbinic or halakhic tradition. There is scarcely a sentence in his entire corpus that lacks a quotation from the *Tan-*

naim, Amoraim, or later halakhic authorities or that does not utilize their phraseology or contain an open or veiled reference to
their ideas. Kook was a true disciple of the great masters of the
halakhic heritage. Nevertheless, he was an innovator from within.
The new light that he cast on every facet of Jewish life was often
very radical. For this "sin," he was reviled by the extreme rightists
of his day. At the same time, he was conservative enough to stop
at the brink of breaking with traditions that had lost their relevancy or spiritual authority over the mind-set of many enlightened Jews. Today, over sixty years after his death, Kook continues
to stir Jews who are capable of inhabiting two universes of discourse. In one, that of halakhic Judaism, they are sufficiently at
peace emotionally to be able to repress the occasional discomfort
they might have with it intellectually. In the other, they are sometimes intellectually attracted but dissatisfied with the disruption
that it causes in their cherished way of life. There is nothing new
about this state of mind. It is to be found in every generation. In
Kook's vision, prayer enables the Jew to travel without too much
discomfort between these two opposing forces.

NOTES

1. For example, one of Kook's fellow students at the Volozhin Yeshi-
vah, Rabbi Ephraim Teitelbaum, recalls that in addition to studying sixty
pages of Gemara every day, Kook would pray with great concentration
on every word. Teitelbaum claims that many a prayer would be accompanied by Kook's tears. (Moshe Zvi Neriah, *Tal HaReiyah* [Kfar Haroeh,
1985], p. 65.)
2. Avraham Yitzhak Hakohen Kook, *Olat Reiyah* (Jerusalem: Mosad
HaRav Kook, 1962), vol. 1, p. 13. In a similar vein, Kook writes: "Prayer
embraces all of life, in its entirety and in the depth of its natural
essence. . . ." He goes on to describe prayer as the "inner desire of the
soul to be drawn to the Source of all life" (Avraham Yitzhak Hakohen
Kook, *Orot Hakodesh*, [Jerusalem: Mosad HaRav Kook, 1966], vol. 3, p.
60).
3. *Olat Reiyah,* vol. 1, p. 15.
4. Ibid., p. 348.
5. *Orot Hakodesh,* vol. 3, pp.106–107.

6. Avraham Yitzhak Hakohen Kook, *Musar Avikha* (Jerusalem: Mosad HaRav Kook, 1971), p. 66.

7. *Olat Reiyah,* vol. 1, p. 16.

8. Ibid., p. 14.

9. Ibid.

10. Ibid., p. 16.

11. Avraham Yitzhak Hakohen Kook, *Arfillei Tohar* (Jerusalem: The Institute in Memory of Rabbi Zvi Yehudah Kook, 1983), p. 75. See Berakhot 7a (top of page) and my comment in chapter 12 on the divine attributes of mercy and justice.

12. Yosef Dan, "Prayer as Text and Prayer as Mystical Experience," in *Torah and Wisdom,* ed. Ruth Link-Salinger (New York: Shengold, 1992), p. 34.

13. Ibid.

14. "I Pine," trans. Ben Zion Bokser, in his *Abraham Isaac Kook* (New York: Paulist Press, 1978), pp. 184–185.

15. *Olat Reiyah,* vol. 1, pp.19–20.

16. Ibid., p. 20.

17. Ibid.

18. Ibid.

19. Ibid., p. 21.

20. See the listing by Kook of Sages who hastened their praying because they were too busy with studying or fulfilling communal responsibilities (Avraham Yitzhak Hakohen Kook, *Iggerot Reiyah* [Jerusalem: Mosad HaRav Kook, 1965], vol. 2, p. 70).

21. See also his reference to the habits and practices at prayer of R. Akiva (*Olat Reiyah,* vol. 1, p. 28).

22. Ibid., p. 25.

23. Ibid., p. 30.

24. Avraham Yitzhak Hakohen Kook, *Orot* (Jerusalem: Mosad HaRav Kook, 1963), p. 124.

4

Mordecai M. Kaplan

ONE OF THE GAMES played by scholars is that of classification. This thinker is a neo-Kantian, that one a realist, a third is a pragmatist, and a fourth a disciple of Lurianic mysticism. Having categorized the thinkers, it is then more or less possible to understand them and to subject their thought to the criticism that their schools evoke. In this way, one is able to ignore the contradictions, the changes of emphasis, the reexamination of long-held views, and the uncertainties or tentativeness that characterize many a philosopher or theologian.

To be fair, it must be stated that for the most part, serious and creative thinkers do tend to organize their system around a central intuition or vision, such that anyone who wishes to grasp what they are trying to get at is justified in concentrating on that point of departure. Thus, both followers and critics of Mordecai M. Kaplan can be upheld for focusing their attention on his naturalism, of which they respectively approve or disapprove. However, when disciples or opponents interpret Kaplan solely in the light of this single intuition, they miss the complexity of his thought—for our purpose, Kaplan's views on prayer.

Mordecai M. Kaplan (1881–1983) lived through a century of enormous upheavals, social and political, intellectual and esthetic, religious and secular. Without the aid of a balancing intellectual gyroscope, it is hard to see how any seeking mind could navigate safely in that stormy sea of relentless surge. It is equally hard to imagine how anyone could emerge unscathed from such a journey without sensing the uncertainties that accompanied him and that would affect others who ventured on a similar odyssey. Kaplan was guided by his conviction that there is a distinction between *belief* in God, which he held to be common to all humans who think that the cosmos is available to their quest for fulfillment, and *concepts* of God, which vary with the many differences in knowledge and intellectual ability that mark people off from one another. Belief or faith in God, as defined by Kaplan, is an intuition or emotional response to life, a disposition, if you will, incapable of proof and subject to the vicissitudes of each person's experience. Thus, even so-called believers can become atheists in times of extreme doubt or sorrow. At such moments, life can lose all meaning. Our emotional despair puts to nought the entire intellectual structure that we have built with so much care.

Kaplan's naturalistic conception of God was far removed from what might have been expected in the light of his early training. The traditionalism of his childhood years would not lead one to expect that almost all of his professional career would be marked by a break from the supernaturalist strands in Jewish theology. Kaplan tells of an incident that occurred when he was about six years of age. He found himself on a street far from his home when a thunderstorm broke out, accompanied by much lightning. To calm his fear, Kaplan recited the blessing that tradition decrees for such an occasion, making sure that within the four ells around him there was no sign of dung. One may not utter a benediction except in purity. Even in those years, though, Kaplan, according to his own testimony, saw ritual observance not as a way of meeting or addressing God but as an expression of what is expected of a Jew.[1]

Some of Kaplan's critics are misled by the heavy sociological emphasis in both his character and his philosophy. They underestimate the breadth and seriousness of his theology. His attempt to place religion in its social context has led several critics to accuse him of sociolatry.[2] However, Kaplan cannot be dismissed in this cavalier fashion. His theology and his conception of prayer, it is true, are off the beaten path of most philosophers of religion, and it will take time for conventional thinkers to see the merit of his innovations. But, if I have read Kaplan correctly, his questions, if not all his proposals, merit careful attention.

Kaplan did battle not only with the various kinds of traditional theism. He also had to combat secularists whose critical barbs were of the kind implicit in the question "When did you stop beating your wife?" Kaplan would have had a field day with the following judgment of a well-known Israeli journalist: "Every time I see kippot-wearing Jews reciting prayers at the site of one of the extermination camps . . . I rise in protest. True, Jews may pray wherever they wish, but I suggest that they conduct their worship of God outside the confines of a concentration camp. For the simple reason that when a third of the Jewish people was exterminated, God was not there."[3] This comment by Yoel Marcus represents a widespread view that appears in all kinds of combinations and permutations, in the writings of professional theologians and secularist philosophers, and in the conversations of sophisticated and unsophisticated laypersons. They all assume that the only way to describe God is as a supernatural Being who rules the world by His inscrutable will. In this view, either God does not exist or must be held responsible for the Holocaust.

Kaplan rejects this alternative, because it presupposes either a cruel God or humans who are incapable of distinguishing between good and evil. Assuming that God is willful, Marcus is correct in his denunciation of prayer in the horrible setting of the Nazi camps and, by implication, wherever a crime against humanity is committed. On the other hand, if it be argued that we must not judge God, since our minds are incapable of understanding His thoughts and ways, we then commit ourselves to moral ignorance or incompetence. Kaplan, who had a strong sense of justice, wrestled ceaselessly with the problem of evil. Truly pious persons, he said, are doubly tormented when others suffer. First, they ". . . participate in their neighbor's suffering and, secondly, they are tormented by the wound to their faith in God."[4]

Kaplan was troubled mainly about natural evil. Specific moral evils could at least be attributed to the failure of humans. In this respect, although Kaplan was devastated by the horror of the Holocaust, he reasoned that it was not a theological problem. While others argued that God had been eclipsed, Kaplan maintained that what the Nazis had done was explicable by recourse to moral, psychological, and political analysis. The whole complex of German behavior and the world's pathetic response was, of course, unprecedented, and Kaplan never claimed that the human sciences have already perfected the tools necessary for accurate explanation of all phenomena. But he clearly rejected attributing the Holocaust to God's will, eclipse, or passivity. Moral evil is always humanly caused. Men and women, sometimes individually, sometimes collectively, are the agents of social evil. The real theological issue is the existence of natural evil.

For all his forthrightness, Kaplan was a modest theologian who accepted the limitations of human intellect. Regarding evil, he writes: "The question of why evil exists is one to which the human mind should never expect to find an answer. It seems to be a necessary condition of life which we accept as part of existence. . . . But *if the existence of evil is part of the mystery of the world that baffles human understanding, the existence of the good is no less a part of that mystery*"[5] (Kaplan's italics). The question to be asked by a theologian is not why evil exists but whether or not it can be overcome or mitigated and whether the universe is so constituted as to respond to the corrective efforts of humans. The success of such striving implies a positive answer to the question and presupposes an orderly universe, in which human effort makes sense.

In the last analysis, belief in the possibility of our achieving fulfillment is, as Kaplan claimed, an expression of natural emotion. It is unfortunate that in the polemics surrounding Kaplan's naturalism, he is often criticized for being a cold, unfeeling rationalist. This is a total misreading of Kaplan's character, theology, and view of prayer. Consider the following: "Who in his right senses ever claimed that he could afford to ignore the role of the emotions, the non-rational, the irrational or the mystical aspects of reality? Who ever attempted to base disinterested love or loyalty on pure reason?"[6] This attitude was embraced by Kaplan in regard to prayer, as well. He understood the difference between thinking *about* God and praying *to* God. But emotion, mysticism, and nonrationalism must not be permitted to cruise beyond the control of reason into the outer space of irrationalism. The heart should be free to roam where it will; but if it loses touch with the mind, it will lead humans into dangerous regions. For example, some prayers that are loaded with the emotional power of the ages prevent Jews from maturing. The idea of sin as violation of outmoded rituals, the insistence on the chosenness of Israel, and the hope for the restoration of the sacrificial system are among the prayers that Kaplan identified as satisfying the emotional wants of many Jews but that deter them from clear and honest thinking.

The following is a touching example of Kaplan's profound awareness of the need to express emotion while keeping it in tow by standards of reason and ethics: In the *New Haggadah,* which

Kaplan and his colleagues published in 1941, they omitted the famous passage, composed of verses from Psalms and Lamentations, that begins with the words "Pour out Thy wrath upon the nations that know Thee not" and asks God to wipe them off the face of the earth. This cry for punishment of the defiant and cruel nations is readily understandable against the background of Jewish suffering throughout the ages. However, in Kaplan's theology, it is for the repentance of humankind and its humanization that prayer should appeal, and not for punishment. This is obviously a rational and educational consideration. Yet Kaplan, emotionally, was at one with the sentiment of *Shefokh Hamatkha* (Pour out Thy wrath). In one of his diary entries, in the midst of the Nazi era, Kaplan writes in large block Hebrew letters: "Alas and alack! What a miserable people we are! Would that there were someone to whom to pray to pour out His wrath upon the nations."[7]

Kaplan looks upon prayer as a natural form of consciousness. He states: "To say, 'I believe in praying' sounds to me as absurd as to say, 'I believe in thinking'. The question whether prayer is effective is only a special form of the question whether thinking is effective."[8] In other words, thinking and praying are two functions of the same instrument, the human mind—just as throwing a ball and hammering a nail can be performed by the same hand. In the same entry in his diaries, Kaplan provides an interesting analogy that casts light both on the way in which the mind thinks and prays and on the desirability of maintaining creative contact between traditional views of intellect and worship and the modern need for self-expression in both of these areas. He writes: "And just as we make use of the best thoughts of others in order to channel our own thinking into the surest and most beneficent effectiveness, so should we make use of the most noble and sincere prayer of others to channel our prayers into a life of the greatest nobility and sincerity. . . . Unfortunately, we Jews have limited prayer to the deadening routine of reciting the few meager passages which make up our official prayer book. If I had [had] anything to do with prescribing the rules of prayer . . . I would have insisted that the vast storehouse of religious poetry be drawn upon continuously. . . ."[9] By the time he wrote these words, Kaplan had embarked on the implementation of his opinion. Today, resort to expressions of Jewish spirituality throughout Jewish tradition is commonplace in the siddurim of the Reform, Conservative, and Reconstructionist movements.

Once Kaplan had committed himself to naturalism, he tried persistently to refine his position and to fill in the inevitable gaps. He knew very well that he was breaking new ground and that his approach to prayer would be difficult to implement. How can one pray to a Kaplanian God? He articulated the problem as a twofold one. Was his use of the term "God" legitimate, and what should worship to such a Deity be like? The questions are manifest in this relatively early reflection by Kaplan on God and prayer: "In the past, religion was based upon the conception of God as an identifiable being. In the future, religion will have to be based on the conception of God as a particular attribute of Reality or the Universe. From an intellectual standpoint, there is an unbridgeable gap between Reality or the Universe as an attribute or creation of God and God as an attribute of the Universe; but from an emotional and volitional standpoint, there is enough in common to justify the use of the term God and of the traditional manner of personal address to Him in prayer."[10]

This is not the place to polemicize about the validity of Kaplan's theology. Our purpose is merely to indicate its radical departure from the generally accepted scope of Jewish theology and to follow Kaplan's thinking in regard to its implications for the future of prayer. In continuing the just quoted statement of his basic theological position, Kaplan remarks about prayer: "The creative principle in human life, especially in the manifestation of intelligence, courage and good will, can best be called into play through that self-conscious act for which there can be no better name than worship." Reading a passage of this kind should enable us to perceive several points of agreement along the spectrum of the wide range of Jewish views about prayer.

For example, if we compare Kaplan's conception of prayer with that of HaRav Kook, who stands at the opposite end of the theological spectrum from Kaplan, we are struck by their common recognition of the different roles to be played in prayer by reason and emotion. Both Kook and Kaplan acknowledge that intellect is indispensable in formulating the aims and content of worship. The mind must not dominate the heart once the worship service is under way. However, Kook and Kaplan agree that before engaging in prayer, the worshiper should develop as clear an understanding as possible of the God whom he wishes to address.

Both Kook and Kaplan see emotion as the force that impels the worshiper to put into action the ideals espoused in prayer. Without such feeling, prayer would remain an intellectual exercise of no practical consequence. Intellect gives direction to prayer; emotion supplies the energy needed to stimulate the worshiper to embark on the journey. Furthermore, despite the distance between them, Kook and Kaplan are reticent about exaggerating the ability of reason always to be right in its perception of truth. They are equally reluctant to permit emotion to take on cognitive functions that it is unequipped to handle.

More surprising is the agreement of the two representatives of supernaturalism and naturalism on the heavy weight placed upon the worshiper in the prayer experience. Neither Kook nor Kaplan envisages prayer as essentially petition by humans for things of the body and the mind that they cannot acquire by their own devices. Both men reject crude supplication, although they find merit in the kind of appeal that arouses worshipers to awareness of their true needs. They consider prayer to be a means of transforming men and women into better human beings. Whether such transformation is to come about by God's intervention or by an act of self-transcendence of the worshiper is a matter of debate between the two theological visions, but it is of extreme interest that the two thinkers are in accord that the function of prayer is to enhance the quality of the human spirit.

In conceiving of God as an attribute of the universe, Kaplan does not mean thereby that He is to be sought only as an immanent Presence and as having no quality of transcendence. Kaplan's readers are sometimes misled, because he criticizes the ways in which many theologians use the term "transcendent" as a synonym for supernatural. Reading a passage like the one in Kaplan's *Judaism without Supernaturalism*,[11] one gets the impression that he is a total and uncompromising immanentist. Such, however, is out of keeping with Kaplan's organic and correlative approach to every phenomenon. In order to understand an experience of an immanent event, one must see it against the background of that which transcends it. This is evident in the assignment of names to things, to values, and to abstract ideas. To make sense of the meaning of these words, one has to acknowledge that they point to a reality beyond themselves. Every particular item is meaningless unless it can be connected to other immanent realities under an all-embracing, transcendent scheme or Gestalt.

In Kaplan's system, then, transcendence can be described in several ways. To a scientist, it is natural law or some method of relating physical phenomena to one another in an orderly, causal fashion. The law is hypothetical, and it is often mistaken and has to be replaced by other explanations. But scientists must have recourse to more than what is available to their senses if they are to conduct their search for knowledge about the physical universe and its occupants. To artists, transcendence is in the vision of the whole that provides the Gestalt of their creation. The whole of any work of art is greater than its parts, individually and collectively. Without such a transcendent objective in mind, all that an artist does would amount to doodling. To a religionist, transcendence is the presumed orderliness of the cosmos, which enables humans to continue to hope and strive for salvation and which serves as a constant corrective to their arrogance and pride. Humans can make use of the world of their immanent experience, but they had better realize that they can never exhaust the transcendent reality. The cosmos preceded the appearance of human creatures on earth and will outlast them and all their successors. In all these and other instances of transcendence, Kaplan opposes both those who identify transcendence with supernaturalism and those who see no rhyme or reason in Creation. Immanence is a necessary corollary of transcendence but not of supernaturalism.

The bearing on prayer of this version of transcendence is obvious. Prayer continues to be a reaching out to the realm of transcendence, but it no longer means addressing a supernatural being. To whom, then, is prayer addressed? Kaplan explains: "The human self is not a monad, but a duad, consisting of actualized and potential parts. The actualized part is rooted in the body with its biological needs and a complex of habits, attitudes and ideas bound up with those needs. The potential part represents the operation of those universal forces in the environment with which the individual must cooperate to achieve his maximum. That part operates as truth, when, as reason, it elicits from man the knowledge of reality. It operates as goodness, when, as conscience, it elicits love."[12] In both instances—in reasoning and in appealing to conscience—individuals engage in a dialogue between their present state and a more satisfactory condition of mind or heart that they hope to attain. This dialogical quality of consciousness characterizes prayer, as well.

As Kaplan describes the worshiper, ". . . that part of him which is the actualized element in him addresses itself to that which is potential. It is then that one's entire personality is implicated. When one's personality is entire, it necessarily includes something of the divine that transcends it."[13] Note Kaplan's reference here to transcendence. The divine transcendence is the vision of the whole personality, always greater than the immanent soul, always pulling the individual toward becoming a more complete and better person than he or she now is. Kaplan is not advocating a dualism of body and soul. The two facets of the human being are functions of the same organism expressing itself in mutually dependent ways. Nor does Kaplan suggest a two-story universe, a lower one of immanent appearance and an upper one of transcendent Spirit. Here, too, the cosmos is an organic unity, in which two qualities of existence implicate one another.

Worshipers, therefore, according to Kaplan, must understand that they are engaged in bringing to consciousness a process of change, to which they want to give direction. As long as a human being lives, his or her body and mind undergo ineluctable metamorphoses, for better or worse. An unchanging person is dead. Now, while change is relentless, its vectors can be altered. Humans have several ways of contributing to this process—for example, haphazard manipulation, technology, and art. Prayer is another such means, whose purpose, as is manifest in the diverse theologies mentioned in this study, is to bring the worshiper closer to moral and spiritual perfection. "Public worship," Kaplan declares, "should concern itself mainly with the improvement of character and conduct in the individual and in society."[14] Kaplan would have us conceive of prayer as a method of self-improvement, in which the immanent self strives to attach itself to some desirable potential that awaits it, if only it can be apprehended. In traditional prayer, the fulfillment of the potential is left to the will of a listening God. In naturalistic prayer, the answer comes from the ability of the worshiper to apprehend or comprehend ever more accurately the physical and moral laws that govern the universe. This understanding is a product of intellect prior to worship.[15] In prayer, individuals try to connect emotionally with their understanding and to relate honestly to what they know to be the truth about themselves and the physical and social reality of which they are a part.

It is this state of mind, characteristic of the prayerful mood, to which Kaplan refers when he writes: "... *God must not merely be held as an idea; He must be felt as a presence, if we want not only to know about God but to know God.* ... Religious souls have never been satisfied with an awareness of God merely as an intellectual concept. They always craved a religious experience in which the reality of God would be brought home to them with an immediacy akin to our awareness of objects through the senses, and with an overpowering emotion that stirred every fibre of their being"[16] (Kaplan's italics). The awareness of God's presence, for Kaplan, is equivalent to a sense of certainty that the cosmos does operate according to physical and moral laws, by means of which humans can achieve a large measure of fulfillment.

This version of prayer can easily be misconstrued as anthropocentric. However, a closer look at Kaplan's intent will set the record straight. He tells us the following: The workings of our universe can be grasped only by imaginative probes into its as yet unknown realms of time, space, and human creativity. Conceptions of cosmic orderliness must be validated before humans can use them legitimately for their purposes. Creative acts of human beings, in turn, must be subjected to the tests of confirmed moral and physical law before they can be accepted as constructive additions to human culture. These acts of intellection ennoble humans with the power of discovery and prediction. However, prayer is designed to place humankind in perspective. Kaplan acknowledges that humans are the *measurer* of their experience; but they are not the *measure*. The measure always transcends our grasp. We are ever in pursuit of truth, goodness, and beauty, but we always falls short of completeness and certainty. Prayer is a check on hubris, but it also fosters hope that if the rules of the cosmic game can be more thoroughly known and if a deeper and more honest awareness of the self can be achieved, we will be able more readily to find meaning in our life. People must always subject themselves to their better self. That can happen only if they realize that their present self is deficient. The self they hope to acquire will become legitimized only if it accords with the real laws of the universe and not with their often misguided perception of them. Again, the interactive nature of transcendence and immanence, of ideal human beings and humans as they are, of the ideal world and the actual world is what Kaplan stresses. He explains his position by means of the concepts of polarity and organicity.

Kaplan maintains that all phenomena in the universe have a reciprocal relationship. Everything is both the cause and effect of everything else. This is ". . . the universal law of polarity whereby everything in the universe, from the minutest electron to the vastest star, is both self-active and interactive, independent and interdependent"[17]. Polarity is a fact of nature. If this is so, there is no need to have recourse to supernatural explanations of cosmic behavior. "The freedom and responsibility of which human nature is capable are the natural manifestations, on a self-conscious level, of the cosmic principle of polarity. Freedom expresses the pole of selfhood, and responsibility the pole of otherhood, or cooperation."[18] Implicit in Kaplan's vision is the belief that humans can improve themselves into as yet unknown beings. This open-ended belief has always been at the core of faith in God. Whatever else "God" has been meant to express, says Kaplan, ". . . it has always had the connotation of man's responsibility for what he does and his freedom to choose between right and wrong, good and evil".[19] Prayer is one of the ways in which we humans employ our freedom better to apprehend and to fulfill that moral responsibility.

The polarity of freedom and responsibility is the core of the larger reality of cosmic organicity, the term that Kaplan applies to the processes of nature, ". . . whereby totalities act upon each of their parts and each part upon the totalities."[20] In prayer, worshipers seek to attach themselves to these processes, knowing that despite their miniscule role in the evolution of the universe, they are nonetheless responsible for their share. Moreover, by becoming more sensitive to the organic character of reality, they identify the Source of their powers of self-transcendence and self-improvement—all this within a naturalistic or, as Kaplan was wont to state, a transnaturalistic perspective. Prayer is thus declared to be an act of self-transcendence in the presence of a reality of inexhaustible potential.

Kaplan realized that a congregation is not composed of theologians who have a single conception of God. He said time and again that theological agreement is a far-fetched hope. People are too different in their mental abilities and temperaments to be able to reach a theological consensus. Nor is it necessary that they do so. Public worship is based on an urge to find meaning in life, accompanied by confidence that the universe is so constructed as to make that objective potentially attainable. That emotion can be satisfied by any number of different theological views. What, then, lies at the basis of a congregation and the ability of diverse personalities to worship together?

Kaplan finds that public worship in the midst of a congenial congregation serves a number of vital purposes. Being in a congregation not only helps individuals to feel close to their fellows; it enables them to feel at home in the world. Our social environment is often unhelpful or even hostile. In a congregation at prayer, however, we are together with our fellows who share common ideals and who gather to support one another. We gain strength from the knowledge that we are not alone. Kaplan adds that such companionship stirs us to become aware of support that is available to us in the universe at large. "Man is not alone." The common effort to seek answers to shared human needs helps all worshipers to focus attention on the cosmic Source of their hope, which they identify as God. Even though worshipers are wrapped up in their own concerns, the congregational surrounding, the awareness of the joys, sorrows, and worries of their neighbors aids them in preventing personal needs and wants from becoming all-consuming egotism.

Kaplan elaborates on the power of group worship by declaring that it arms the members of the congregation with a kind of immortality. "For death cannot rob our life of significance and value to us so long as we are interested in passing on to our posterity a heritage of culture and ideals. The past before we were born and the future after our death are a part of us, and every moment is eternal that embraces them. . . . It is as though by surrendering our souls to God, we admit God into our souls and partake of His infinity and eternity."[21] Needless to say, this is an idealistic account of what should occur in public worship but rarely does.

The content and form of prayer, like many other facets of human culture, are the products of group experience. The principle of polarity operates here to describe the setting within which the individuals express their peculiar needs. It serves as an outlet for the accumulated and accumulating aspirations of one's group. The language of prayer, like the language of interhuman communication, is socially conditioned.

Society is formed out of the interaction of individuals. Prayer cannot be bodiless tradition, passed along untouched from generation to generation. It has to live along with the worshipers and has to give voice to their knowledge, convictions, and longings—in brief, to their experience. Therefore, Kaplan insisted, the siddur has to be more than an anthology of the spiritual past; it must be more than a series of quotations from the accumulated wisdom of the people. He saw no escape from the responsibility of bringing forward what is relevant and inspiring in the tradition, eliminating what is unworthy of mature Jews, and creating new prayers to satisfy and to challenge the souls of the living.

Kaplan constantly deplored his inability to express himself poetically. Nevertheless, he considered poetic articulation to be so essential to prayer that he tried his hand repeatedly at composing just such emotion-stirring meditations. He sought an esthetically effective way to give emotional force to his reading of reality. Here is a short passage from a prayer that Kaplan entitled "God the Life of Nature":

> Our Fathers acclaimed the God
> Whose handiwork they read
> In the mysterious heavens above
> And in the varied scene of earth below,
> In the orderly march of days and nights,
> Of seasons and years,
> And in the checkered fate of man.
>
> Meantime have the vaulting skies dissolved;
> Night reveals the limitless caverns of space,
> Hidden by the light of day,
> And unfolds horizonless vistas

Far beyond imagination's ken.
The mind is staggered,
Yet soon regains its poise,
And peering through the boundless dark,
Orients itself anew
By the light of distant suns
Shrunk to glistening sparks.
The soul is faint,
Yet soon revives,
And learns to spell once more the name of God
Across the newly visioned firmament.[22]

This hymn to God and nature indicates Kaplan's desire to infuse prayer with modern conceptions of reality. This same desire motivated him also to introduce revisions into the traditional liturgy. Kaplan was not the first Jew to revise the prayer book. This is not the place to review the long and fascinating history of the evolution of the traditional text—more accurately, texts—the various formulations of the main prayers, the additions to be found in the siddurim of different countries, and the unique customs that clothe the recitation of the liturgy.[23] Pluralism has always existed. Nonetheless, Kaplan can be credited with attempting more consistently than almost anyone else in the twentieth century to coordinate what he prayed with what he believed. Other theologians have confronted the questions of petitionary prayer, the good and omnipotent God and the fact of evil, the autonomy of nature, the unusual and miracle, and the other perplexities that are likely to disturb honest worshipers. The committees on liturgy of the Reform and Conservative movements have made their respective changes—the result of compromise between the differing wings of their denominations. Kaplan, however, was theologically the most far-reaching.

I have touched on several of the major theological difficulties with which Kaplan wrestled in his attempt to reconstruct Jewish prayer in keeping with his naturalistic convictions. But he was dissatisfied with many of his conclusions and practical recommendations. For example, although he acknowledged that prayer and poetry are intimately related, he could not reconcile himself to a poetic liturgy in which theological fudging was brushed aside by the argument that certain prayers are poetic expressions that can be reinterpreted to meet modern standards. Thus, in trying to maintain contact with the tradition, he and his colleagues included in their liturgical works prayers that could be justified by them only as quotations of what our ancestors once believed. It is their piety, not their theology, that is celebrated in those ancient prayers that are retained. Kaplan was always torn whenever he felt compelled by other considerations of a practical nature to maintain the continuity of worn-out tradition. He was uncomfortable whenever he had to pay the price of intellectual inconsistency or weakness. Emotionally, his attachment to tradition compelled him, before discarding an ancient prayer, to try and justify its retention.

Kaplan felt that the accepted language of prayer was inadequate, but he was unable to find a satisfactory substitute for it. Bearing in mind his declaration of man's need to experience God, Kaplan accepted the universal formula of addressing God in the first person. On the other hand, since he rejected the concept of God as a Being, he toyed with the idea of creating a liturgy in which God becomes the object of meditation in the third-person mood—blessed be He, rather than blessed art Thou. He also wanted to place the emphasis in prayer on a certain kind of study. In preparation for prayer, he urged people to examine the meaning of salvation and the idea of God. One gets the impression that for Kaplan, true prayer is to be found in study and reflection, rather than in the recitation of a fixed or even flexible liturgy. He felt that the traditional form of prayer could not effectuate its purpose of human improvement. Participation in public worship has never been proved to be a builder of character. So Kaplan sought other methods, even while he practiced the popular norm. Scattered throughout Kaplan's writings, and particularly in his diaries, are reservations about his own conclusions. However, to pursue this line of investigation would take us far afield.

As we have indicated, Kaplan knew that there are and will remain vast differences between the praying of intellectually gifted individuals and that of persons with lesser cultural background and mental capacity. The problem of the former is more complicated. As Kaplan indicates, "The greater one's mental development, the more subject one is to contradictory tendencies, and the more susceptible to mutually exclusive influences. The more intelligent a man is, the more likely is he to be engaged continually in making peace between reason and impulse."[24] Since all congregations include men and women on these varying levels of intellect, it is obvious that no worship service can be more than a compromise. Nevertheless, Kaplan was convinced that compromise is essential. The most enlightened intellectuals must be able to find a place in the synagogue service even though it might not meet their standards of probity and taste. The mental capacity of gifted persons places them under the strain of self-consciousness. Such individuals need an outlet in order to recharge their spiritual energy. Such need, of course, is universal, but for the mentally gifted, the strain is more severe. Therefore, it is vital that they find a community in which they can be united with others in a spirit of love that enables them to transcend their doubts and to kindle their sympathy for all humankind. It is by group worship, more than by any other instrumentality, that human beings can discover their transcendent unity.

As with our other thinkers, Kaplan has much more to say about prayer than can be contained in a brief essay. I mention, however, three more points. One is Kaplan's emphasis on the connection between prayer and the involvement of the worshiper in the total life of the Jewish community. Without loyalty to the Jewish people and knowledge of and participation in its interests, it is unlikely that a Jew can be touched by or find meaning in a synagogue service. Lacking attachment to his or her people, the individual Jew is like those who find themselves alone in a crowd of foreigners whose language they do not speak and of whose culture they are ignorant.

Concerning another item of preparation for worship, Kaplan writes: "Before worship can have any genuine spiritual influence upon us, before it can reveal God to us, we must qualify ourselves by an arduous discipline in deeds of self-control, honesty, courage and kindness. . . . Communion with God is a reward of holy and righteous living."[25]

Kaplan's proposals for worship are likely to attract tough-minded intellectuals before they can become available to the masses. That such individuals are few accounts partially for the fact that a radical theologian like Kaplan had to make many compromises in the liturgy he contemplated. As an educator, he knew that he could not hasten too far ahead of the masses. As it was, however, even the pace that he considered restrained has proved to be too rapid for most Jews.

And finally, I mention the relationship between worship and the arts. Kaplan was one of the few Jewish theologians who considered the arts to be of religious import. (Lawrence A. Hoffman, whom we shall meet in a later chapter, spells out this point far more completely than Kaplan.) Most Jewish thinkers have been locked into the long-standing bias that the esthetic dimension is somehow fraught with the danger of paganism. Kaplan was fully conscious of the distorted use to which art in all its forms can be put, but this is true of the other dimensions of the true and the good, as well.

Kaplan saw the positive features of the arts, and he endeavored to apply them to the prayer experience. His position is stated most clearly in one of the entries in his diaries: "It is questionable whether the arts have reached the same sublime heights since they have been leading a life apart from worship. . . . The foremost question which those who organize public worship should ask themselves is, 'What art forms, what poetry, what music, what song, what drama, and even what dance and movements are best calculated to produce in us the cosmic mood'?"[26] Kaplan stated the case and encouraged the implementation of these thoughts in the conduct of the services in the synagogue he founded. But for the most part, his vision is for future generations to capture.

One of Borowitz's major dissatisfactions with Kaplan's theology is what seems to him to be the lack of transcendence in the latter's concept of God. But Borowitz, like other derogators of Kaplan, simply ignores the many declarations in Kaplan's published works and in his diaries to the effect that transcendence is an ineluctable quality of deity. Borowitz fails to deal seriously with Kaplan's effort to comprehend transcendence as the correlate of immanence rather than as a distinct, supernatural realm. Borowitz writes: "A concept of God that makes direct address to God infantile or denies that God can be of help to us to meet the varied experiences of life stumbles against a theme of divine approachability unbroken in Jewish religious experience over the ages" (*Renewing the Covenant* [Philadelphia: Jewish Publication Society, 1991], p. 60; subsequent citations from Borowitz are from this volume). Borowitz's own theological position as delineated here raises a flood of questions. But this chapter is not a rejoinder to him. My only purpose in citing his critique of Kaplan is to set the record straight about what Kaplan said and the probing nature of his reconstruction of theology. Not only did Kaplan argue that God, in His essence, is transcendent; he suggested a way to conceive of transcendence as a category of a naturalistic but spiritual theology.

In describing Kaplan's understanding of prayer ". . . as essentially communion with oneself at one's best" (p. 124), Borowitz believes that he has dealt a lethal blow to Kaplan's philosophy of prayer. However, is not traditional prayer itself laden with reflections of just such meditativeness? What is the recitation of the confession of sins if not a reaching out to the better self that each of us seeks to become? In so doing, do we not seek to bind ourselves to a Reality that we can hope to perceive only to the extent that we can transcend our present, limited selves? Borowitz would have us leap over our natural capabilities and potential to a direct appeal to God. How are we to know what kind of persons God wishes us to be unless His will can be refracted through our conscience? Kaplan provides a more acceptable answer to that question than those who view addressing God as parallel to communication between humans.

Borowitz correctly attributes to Kaplan belief in a non-omnipotent God. Kaplan does have a thick humanistic thread in his theology. Borowitz also attacks Kaplan for viewing God as finite, for this becomes ". . . *simple* [italics mine] humanism in which we put our real trust in people and their goodness, a confidence made dubious by the Holocaust and much else in human conduct" (p. 124). What, however, is faith in man, if not trust in his potential? Neither Kaplan nor any other serious Process theologian should be accused of believing in other than the possibility that humankind is capable of improvement. Believing in our ability to rise above our animal ancestry makes sense only as a corollary of faith in a transcendent process that we call "God." Humankind is only the beneficiary of that process and not its creator. In praying, worshipers try to define the goal of their maturation and to gain insight into how they and their fellows might achieve it. The independent role of humans in this endeavor naturally raises doubts about God's infinity and omnipotence. Even if one rejects Kaplan's opinion on these questions, the description of God as infinite and all-powerful stumbles on the matter of natural evil.

Borowitz has much more to say about Kaplan's philosophy of prayer, some of which is a misreading. I hope that this chapter on Kaplan will serve as an initial response to some of Borowitz's strictures and those of other critics. However, the chapter is designed to introduce the reader to Kaplan's thought and not to be a full exposition of his position. Indeed, although I express my opinion freely about certain facets in the positions of all the thinkers discussed in this book, my ultimate purpose is to provide a respectful introduction into their views on prayer. In the chapter devoted to Borowitz, I shall present more directly some of my reservations about his own interesting theology.

NOTES

1. Mordecai M. Kaplan, "The Way I Have Come," in *Mordecai M. Kaplan: An Evaluation,* ed. Ira Eisenstein and Eugene Kohn (New York: Jewish Reconstructionist Foundation, 1953), p. 286.

2. A glaring example of this genre is the chapter on Kaplan in David Hartman's *Conflicting Visions* (New York: Schocken, 1990). Eugene B. Borowitz criticizes Kaplan with greater fairness and objectivity. While I cannot deal here with the full extent of Borowitz's observations, it is worth mentioning a few of them in order to elucidate some of the disagreements at stake between naturalistic and more common types of theologizing.

3. Yoel Marcus, "Seven Comments on the Situation," *HaAretz,* 23 April 1993, sec. B, p. 1. In his reference to *kippot,* Marcus speaks of *kippot* beanies worn by male Jews while praying and by traditional Jews at all times. Fundamentalist Jews are accustomed to wear an additional head-covering, called a *shtreimel.*

4. Mordecai Kaplan, *The Future of the American Jew* (New York: Macmillan, 1949), pp. 232–233.

5. Ibid., p. 235.

6. Mordecai M. Kaplan, Diaries, 17 April 1955.

7. Diaries, 4 April 1937.

8. Diaries, 21 May 1933.

9. Ibid.

10. Diaries, 17 December 1929.

11. On transcendence and supernaturalism, see Mordecai M. Kaplan, *Judaism without Supernaturalism* (New York: Reconstructionist Press, 1958), pp. 21–24.

12. *The Future of the American Jew*, p. 184.

13. Ibid., pp. 184–185.

14. Mordecai M. Kaplan, *The Religion of Ethical Nationhood* (New York, Macmillan, 1970), p. 55.

15. Note, for example, the statement by R. Elazar: "A person should always put his prayer in order [that is, understand its meaning and intent] and only then recite it" (R.H. 35a).

16. Mordecai M. Kaplan, *The Meaning of God in Modern Jewish Religion* (New York, Reconstructionist Press,1963 [first printing, 1937]), p. 244.

17. *The Religion of Ethical Nationhood*, pp. 34–35.

18. *Judaism without Supernaturalism*, p. 27.

19. Ibid.

20. *The Religion of Ethical Nationhood*, p. 79.

21. *The Meaning of God in Modern Jewish Religion*, pp. 248–249.

22. Mordecai M. Kaplan, *Sabbath Prayer Book* (New York: Jewish Reconstructionist Foundation, 1946), pp. 383, 385.

23. The classic work on the history and structure of Jewish prayer is that of Ismar Elbogen, now available and updated in English: *Jewish Liturgy*, trans. Raymond P. Scheindlin (Philadelphia: Jewish Publication Society, 1993).

24. *The Meaning of God in Modern Jewish Religion*, p. 255.

25. Diaries, 18 August 1929.

26. Ibid.

5

Aaron Rote (Reb Arele)

IF ANY EVIDENCE were needed of how disturbing the discipline of prayer can be even to the most pious person, we need only turn to R. Aaron Rote,[1] more popularly known as Reb Arele. Rote (1894–1944) was the founder of a small Hasidic sect in the Meah Shearim quarter of Jerusalem. The synagogue that he established is noted for the ecstatic mood generated among his followers who worship there. In his magnum opus, *Shomer Emunim,* Rote describes the attainment of devotion in worship as so elusive as to necessitate the employment of all the spiritual skills that a man can exercise. (It is the prayer of the male that concerns R. Arele, inasmuch as it is upon him that tradition confers the duty and the privilege to fulfill most of the mitzvot of worship.)

Every authentic philosophy of Jewish prayer, of course, must reckon seriously with classic Jewish tradition. Those who regard that tradition as authoritative—and Arele was so minded—must accept as a categorical imperative that recital of the prescribed prayers is inviolable. At the same time, the more pious traditionalists cannot be satisfied with mechanical worship. For them, every prayer must have a meaning and evoke in them the most profound experience of God's presence. Here is where Arele located his challenge.

As a mystic, Arele believed that each day of our life we have the opportunity and the duty through our prayers to redeem sparks of divinity that had been separated from God during the act of Creation and that lie scattered in our imperfect, material universe. However, Arele writes, "In every prayer there are different sparks to be elevated. Not a day has passed since Creation which resembles any other. Nor is there a prayer that is like any other, as indicated by our teacher, R. Isaac Luria, may his memory be blessed, who, referring to R. Moses Cordovero, may his memory be blessed, declared that no man is like his neighbor. Every man and, indeed, every creature, is born to fulfill a unique need, except that we do not know what that need is."[2]

What, however, does it mean to say that each prayer is different? Are we to assume that every time we repeat the words of the traditional prayer book we must, through interpretation and reinterpretation, interpolate into them or extract from them new ideas? Or perhaps Arele is hinting at the necessity of initiating new prayers, more relevant to the needs of the moment than the prescribed formula? He probably holds both views, but he devotes more of his treatment of prayer to exploring some of the byways of his more daring proposals.

Novelty in prayer can stem from both objective and subjective circumstances. For instance, it happens frequently that a person simply cannot pray. Whatever be the reason for such incapacity—psychological upset, intellectual confusion, or physical disturbance—Arele faces such situations with rare candor and courage. On the one hand, he tells us that the distinctiveness of each prayer is no excuse for evading the obligation to address the challenge of every new situation. He states that ". . . no man should say that today it is hard for him to pray sincerely; tomorrow, he will have to pray an entirely different prayer. . . ."[3] Thus, the absence of a prayerful mood is no excuse for not trying to acquire such a mood. The worshiper will never have a chance again to confront the need of the moment, since he or she will always be faced with a unique circumstance.

Even more daringly, Arele explains that there are occasions when it is both impossible and improper for a person to pray. Citing the Baal Shem Tov, Arele claims that ". . . if a man is troubled or is in danger, God forbid, it is advisable that he utter no prayer but rather try to strengthen his confidence in God. Such behavior is virtuous. And if a person, without praying, succeeds in increasing his trust in God, it is evident that he no longer has the requisite power to pray. He resembles a little child who does not know what to seek."[4] Arele compares the spiritually incapacitated adult to the weaned infant. Such a comparison is suggested in Psalm 131:2: "Surely I have stilled and quieted my soul; / Like a weaned child with his mother, / My soul is with me like a weaned child." God's mercy rests both on the totally innocent and on those who might not deserve His kindness but who nonetheless trust in Him. In the case of those who cannot pray, silence is a meritorious response to their plight, provided that they retain faith in God's grace.

In these seemingly contradictory declarations, we find evidence of R. Arele's ambivalence. He wants to pray honestly and with fervent devotion. Yet he is powerless, at times, to overcome the accidents of normal human existence that deprive him of the ability to approach God in words of the tradition or in expressions of his own. The contradiction is not an intellectual one. Arele's theology leaves no room for doubt concerning God's absolute sovereignty or of the Jew's obligation to worship Him in accordance with the dictates of Halakhah. Nonetheless, his own spiritual character gave him no surcease. He could not find satisfaction in mechanical repetition of the words of the siddur. Nor could he rebel against the traditional content. He had to seek a way of finding or cultivating inspiration without abandoning one iota of that heritage of worship.

At this point, we might ask ourselves whether Arele, by justifying silence and refraining from prayer, has stepped beyond the bounds of legitimate options within the tradition. Our answer will depend on how we interpret Arele's problem. If, by prayer, Arele refers to the daily recital of the three prescribed liturgies, then we can observe him relating positively to those special individuals who are so spiritually skilled and so occupied in exercising their special talents that they are exempt from the halakhic regimen of prayer. In this regard, as is to be expected, Arele, like other traditionalists before and after him, also mentions the well-known example of R. Simeon bar Yohai. According to the Sages, total concentration on Torah was Bar Yohai's true spiritual vocation and method of worshiping God. He had no need to pray in the usual sense.

Arele belongs to that honored and honorable tradition of halakhic-minded Jews who were ready to go beyond strict adherence to the letter of the law in order to achieve a moral or spiritual state that uncompromising *din*, strict application of the law, had to ignore. Halakhic literature abounds in examples of acting in what is known as *lifnim mishurat hadin*, making compromises with the law in order to take account of cases in which insistence on its full implementation would be unfair to innocent individuals or those in need of special treatment. The principle of *lifnim mis-hurat hadin* also applies to a situation, such as that to which Arele refers, in which strict construction of and obedience to the law would do violence to one's intellectual or spiritual integrity. For instance, there is a famous action by R. Moses Isserles who, in order to prevent embarrassment to a young orphaned woman, performed her marriage ceremony after the advent of the Sabbath. In more recent times, we are told concerning the renowned R. Yisrael Meir HaKohen (affectionately known as the Hafetz Hayyim) that once, when HaRav Kook came to visit him during the days between the first and ninth of Av (when it is forbidden to eat meat or drink wine), he ordered a sumptuous feast to be prepared in honor of his guest. The Hafetz Hayyim defended his startling departure from the unanimous halakhic practice by claiming that when one wishes to honor the Torah—and Kook, in the eyes of the Hafetz Hayyim, embodied Torah in his very being—one should do so with gracious celebration.

R. Arele was so intent on heightening the *kavvanah* of worship that his book *Shomer Emunim* can virtually be interpreted as a disquisition on just that subject. He credits the success in prayer of his ideal model, the Baal Shem Tov (the Besht), to the latter's enormous sincerity and devotion.[5] We shall see, however, that *kavvanah* has less to do with the content of the prayers than it does with the state of mind and the emotional concentration of the worshiper.

Arele laid great stress on the psychological readiness of the individual for prayer, as we have already noted. It follows that sincerity in worship demands appropriate response to changing moods and to the steps that sometimes have to be taken in order to prepare the person for prayer. There is nothing new in Arele's attention to this fact about the prayer experience. The Sages of old, in prefacing the daily communal liturgy with excerpts from the Psalms and other biblical and talmudic sources, did so in order to enable the congregants to calm the disturbed souls they had brought with them into the synagogue. By means of such preliminary readings, they were enabled gradually to slip into a spiritual state conducive to addressing God with concentration and sincerity. Arele regarded this problem of preparation as crucial.

A typical example of Arele's psychological insight can be found in the following passage: "A number of zaddikim [Hasidic mentors] sang before Him, may His Name be praised, in jargon [Yiddish]—for example, our holy teacher, the Baal Shelah [R. Isaiah Hurwitz], who published his melody in his siddur, *Allmaechtiger Gott* . . . and our teacher from Kosnitz, may his merit protect us, whose custom it was always to sing in Polish or Russian. There was also our holy teacher from Kalov who was known always to have sung in the language of the stranger or in German. Moreover, there were many zaddikim who sang before the blessed One in Polish. Among the ancients were some who sang to words in Arabic. In solitude, they gave full vent to their desire for and love of God, thereby elevating [to sanctity] ordinary, secular utterances. . . ."[6] Undoubtedly, although Arele carried out the halakhic requirements of worship, the prayer that touched him most and to which he aspired was that which came spontaneously and naturally from the heart.

Arele was a product of Eastern European Jewish culture. Although steeped in the Hebrew of Rabbinic Judaism, Hebrew was not his native tongue or his natural language of communication. For him, then, prayer is most profound and emotionally satisfying when it arises in and out of ordinary speech. As he puts it, ". . . the heart is more effectively stirred to enthusiasm out of the customary language of speech. . . . In regard to acts of worship and the expression of one's most innermost feelings about God, it is advisable to speak in mundane words in order to arouse the soul from its slumber. . . ."[7] It is difficult for the disinterested observer of this phenomenon to judge just how far Arele wished to lead his followers. As we shall see, he certainly was not asking for a rejection of traditional prayer. At the same time, he realized that for many persons, the hallowed liturgy could not meet some of their spiritual needs or stimulate them to more profound and honest expression of their passion for God. That passion had to find an outlet outside the bounds of habitual prayer. In the mere attention that Arele gave to the limitations of traditional practice, there arises the danger of doubt about the efficacy of synagogue worship. It is made to appear that while Jews should continue to worship in the way that has been sanctified for two millenia, true prayer is that which is highly personal and intimately related to individual experience.

Let us not oversimplify Arele's perception. As a halakhic loyalist he had no intention of abandoning traditional prayer, but as a pietist he strove to infuse enthusiasm, concentration, and full awareness of the content and implications of each word in the siddur. This brings us to a major element in Arele's treatment of the liturgy. The title of his major work, *Shomer Emunim,* can be translated as "Keeper of the Faith," "Trustworthy Guardian," or "Faithful Guardian." The simple meaning is thus a reference to those who believe firmly in God and observe Jewish tradition without reservation. Arele's usage is based on Isaiah 26:2. In keeping with the prophetic spirit, Arele has more in mind than obedience to the Law. He wants wholehearted devotion and sincerity on the part of every worshiper. Such qualities of prayer are inherent or at least more easily attainable when a person voices his felt needs. In communal, repetitive worship, special effort has to be made in order to reach *kavvanah.* One of the steps in this direction is for the worshiper to concentrate on every word of the siddur, whether that word be uttered by himself or by the *hazzan* or lay leader of the service. He must always be alert to the response *Amen* that is expected of him at the conclusion of any of the benedictions that abound in the course of every service. Hence the *shomer emunim* is to be construed as the person who is meticulous in responding *Amen* at all the appropriate places in the service. Arele's pun dramatizes the serious problem of concentration and sincerity in prayer.

Arele devotes many pages to the rules and regulations that have to be followed in order to have the recital of *Amen* become the fulcrum on which sincerity in prayer must rest. For example, he remarks that the worshiper is most severely tested early in the morning service. The worshiper recites or listens to the reader chant a list of benedictions. If there is a minyan (quorum), the reader chants the blessings, and after each one, the congregation responds *Amen.* Arele warns his disciples that they must be so attentive to what the reader recites as never to call out *Amen* before the conclusion of one blessing or after its successor has been begun by the reader. This exactitude is clearly a challenge to the worshiper's power of concentration, which is precisely what Arele demands.

The achievement of *kavvanah* is a complicated matter, particularly in public worship. The service is led by a cantor, whose rendition of the prayers is designed to inspire each member of the congregation to complete devotion. The *hazzan*'s rendition, however, is often disturbed by the natural tendency of the other worshipers to lose contact with the chanting, for shorter or longer moments. The mind wanders. How can such a common lapse be forestalled? Furthermore, there is rarely a connection at any given moment between the thoughts of the liturgy and the concerns of the worshiper. How is the halakhic obligation to repeat the prescribed service to be made sincere? Arele's answer to these questions is unique.

We must preface his reply by reference to his Hasidic orientation. His model, the Besht, was noted for his loving attention to the ignorant, the indigent, and the masses of Jews who were never able to ascend to the ideal level of toraitic scholarship but who aspired, no less than the fortunate, intellectual elite, to draw near to God. The Baal Shem Tov sought every opportunity to enable the disadvantaged to enjoy the salvation and the respect that are the birthright of every Jew. Arele writes at one point: "It is common knowledge and reported in countless anecdotes how lowly and despised persons, by virtue of their honesty and lack of guile, split all the heavens, forced open the upper channels, and caused the suspension of evil decrees—all this, because there can be no haughtiness before God, before Whom the small and the great are equal."[8] Indeed, the very essence of prayer is the equality of the worshipers. The learned and the ignorant, the rich and the poor, men and women, the old and the young, the saint and the scoundrel—before God, they are of equal weight. Recognition of that fact, implies Arele, must be spelled out in the conduct of public worship. In the challenge and opportunity it offers to each individual, we become cognizant of our role as equal partners with all others in the work of Creation. For this reason, Arele argued that answering *Amen* at the appropriate spots in the service should be seen as the great leveler. While there can be only one *hazzan*, every person has the capacity and, if sincere, the will to express faith and confidence in God by following the prayers and answering *Amen*, "So be it."

The next logical step toward sincere prayer is the avoidance of any act that might interfere with concentration. Arele fought vigorously against the prevalent habit of conversing during the service, particularly during the recital of the blessings at the beginning of the morning service and the repetition of the *Amidah* prayer by the cantor. He declared that anyone who answers *Amen* while he is engaged in conversation with his neighbor is dishonest. Such an *Amen* is to be considered an "orphan *Amen*"; it is unclear to which blessing the response belongs. A person of this kind ". . . cannot possibly know to which benediction he is responding; nor can he even intend that his *Amen* be directed to the simple content of the blessing. . . ."[9]

We can now understand Arele's obsession with *Amen*, "So be it" or "So may it be." This is the response that everyone in the congregation is called upon to recite when he or she hears the *hazzan* recite a blessing. Arele goes so far as to credit the one who recites *Amen* with greater merit than is granted to the one who recites the blessing on behalf of the congregation.[10] For in order to qualify for the right to answer *Amen*, one has to listen avidly and sincerely to the benediction. It might happen that those who make the blessing are deficient in their own *kavvanah*, but this need have no bearing on the involvement of the listeners. Their sincerity is to be judged only by the *kavvanah* of their listening and answering. Thus it is that Arele lashes out repeatedly at those who converse during the prayers. "Whoever engages in conversation while the prayer leader repeats the *Amidah* aloud is a sinner. His transgression is unbearable, and he must be reprimanded for it."[11]

The matter, of course, is not as easy as it might seem at first blush. Even the simpleminded person is called upon to accept the rigors of spiritual discipline. For instance, as the cantor prepares to chant the *Kaddish*, each member of the congregation is expected to give thought to four positive mitzvot: the extinction of Amalek (interpreted by Arele as resistance to the evil impulse, the *yetzer hara*); enhancing God's renown; seeking communion with God in utter devotion; and walking in God's path by observing the mitzvot.[12] The pronouncement of *Amen* is thus a kind of mnemonic device to remind the worshipers of the depth of the act in which they are presumably engaged. Arele feels that this psychological prod is an effective way of preventing slothfulness in worship. However, it is evident that the device can work only with those who are equipped with adequate erudition and mystic skill, to say nothing of intellectual capacity and emotional predisposition. How to gain the ability to say *Amen* in the way in which Arele would have us all proclaim it is itself a difficult problem. As much as we should want to have prayer enable all humans to recognize their equality in God's eyes, there is no easy method of reaching that goal.

The obstacle just mentioned looms larger to a modern, rationalistic mind than it does to the kabbalistic mentality of an Arele. Relying on the potency of a doxology like the *Kaddish* in trying to bridge the chasm between the mundane and the heavenly realms, Arele's techniques are more readily attractive to the mystic who remains within the Halakhah. For him, Arele's whole system of spiritual concentration is both a stimulus to *kavvanah* in the congregational response during the recital of the different versions of the *Kaddish* and the reward for such devotion. The peak of prayer, according to Arele, is reached in the *Kaddish* when the worshiper utters the words *Amen, y'hei shmei rabba mevorakh* (So may it be, may His great Name be praised). To each of these words and, indeed, to the entire vocabulary of the *Kaddish*, Arele attaches a special spiritual connotation and message. The words *y'hei shmei rabba* are to be said or chanted while concentrating on the determination to overcome Amalek or the evil impulse that is found in every human. The response unites God's transcendence and immanence, as the worshipers dedicate themselves to glorifying God and Israel.[13] The word *mevorakh* is directed to arousing the worshiper to complete devotion to God, to the point of self-effacement and self-sacrifice. In these and other *kavvanot*, as such references are called, Arele presents a mystical theology in which God's transcendence and immanence are within our power to unite by our adherence to the mitzvot and by sincere and intense prayer. Persons who are fervent believers in the efficacy of this vision and of Arele's prescription for fulfilling it will be undisturbed by the doubts of even the mildest skeptics. The rest of us might find Arele's mentality somewhat bizarre, but of absorbing interest.

One of the consequences of Arele's insistence that every word of prayer be meaningful and sincere is that the length of a service be indeterminate. If one must understand each word and its context in the prayer as a whole, it stands to reason that the timing of a service will be subject to many unpredictable circumstances. Of course, factors of practicality play their roles, and even Arele himself had to acknowledge that human nature and needs force limitations on the most pious people. The reader should try to sense the spiritual urge that drove Arele. The following is one example, demonstrated in an anecdote concerning the Besht: "Once, the Besht's in-law, the holy Gaon [Sage] R. Gershon of Kitov, asked him why he prayed at such length. The Besht replied that during his worship, thousands of souls come before him, asking that he help correct their failings or satisfy some needs. [R. Gershon] asked why these souls do not also entreat him. Whereupon, the Besht said that he would send some of these souls to R. Gershon. He did so, along with special formulas [*yihudim*] for dealing with each case. When [R.Gershon] came to the prayer for the resurrection of the dead, thousands of deceased appeared before him. He fainted out of fear, for at that time, he had not yet become accustomed to the experience."[14] Arele and his followers relate to such an incident with utmost seriousness, but rationalists, without attributing magic powers to the Besht, can nonetheless also extrapolate important lessons from this charming tale.

Underlying the supposed reason for the tendency of the Besht to pray at length,[15] we detect an overwhelming concern for the unfortunates for whom salvation seems to be a distant or unattainable goal. Many bring their misfortune on themselves, but there are also those who, by virtue of bad luck or inability to cope with the complexities of existence, are doomed to misery. Certainly, prayer that lacks sensitivity to the plight of our fellow humans can hardly be dignified as worthy of decent men and women. Prayer should aim at qualifying every worshiper to contribute to extending the borders of salvation for all.

Furthermore, Arele, in citing this anecdote and in other passages throughout his work, challenges us to overcome the rigidity of much of our formal worship. Although we might not be able to be as relaxed as were the Besht and his disciples about the time to be devoted to worship, we should be able to open ourselves to occasional departures from the prescribed liturgy. Even without surrendering the long-standing pattern of public worship, we should be able to take account of surprising and unusual events that deserve our attention. It is not only the timing of prayer that is of concern but the objectives that we ought to have in mind. Those objectives, in turn, will naturally affect the length of time devoted to the prayer service as a whole and to its parts. Arele has opened the way to a much more fluid approach to our synagogue services than is the current practice.

Motivating Arele's daring and creative approach to prayer is a profound sense of urgency. He perceived that ". . . genuine, sincere prayer has ceased and that as a result of our sins, God is hiding Himself more and more. . . ."[16] Arele's pessimism about the state of Jewish spirituality was and is shared by many professional and lay Jews dedicated to Jewish survival. However, what makes Arele unique, at least in traditional circles, are his awareness of the need for radical measures and his readiness to take them. The stake for which Arele plays is no less than the restoration of faith in God and confidence in His providence. He would have been horrified to think that the spiritual exercises described above were no more than that—another form of behavior bearing no relationship to the purposes for which they were designed. Whether or not he was successful with his little group of followers is a subject for psychological and sociological study. But successful or not, Arele's innovative methods suggest that faith is more than a state of mind. It is a disposition that has to be sustained not only in thought but in action, as well.

Arele understood that action and consciousness are inseparable. Therein lies one of the knotty problems of worship. Consciousness is both active and receptive. A person may embark on prayer and in the midst of his devotions suddenly be struck by some thought having nothing to do with the thrust of his praying. The stimulus to the new thought might be a pure one—a passage from the Bible or from a Rabbinic text that suddenly emerges out of the recesses of memory, a concern about a friend, or a reminder of an important event—but for Arele, again citing the Besht, this is a sign that the worshiper is being driven from the upper spheres. Unless he is able to divest himself of these extraneous thoughts, ". . . his prayer will not merit acceptance. Therefore, he must feel ashamed and debase himself so as to arouse God's abundant mercy. Then God will save him."[17] The rhythm of prayer cannot be avoided. Concentration demands constant, conscious effort. Moreover, it is not only the interference of un-welcome thoughts that disturbs worshipers. More frequently, they are upset by the failure of their supplications. There is no guaran-tee that the most sincere petition will be answered. What is a per-son to do when God seems to be unresponsive? Basically, an individual can do no more than try again.[18] Arele, of course, as-sumes that no prayer ever goes unanswered. However, in the com-plicated economy of the cosmos, the time might not yet be suitable for a positive response to a particular need or want. One can only act in accord with the oft-quoted plea of the Psalmist, "Hope in the Lord / Be strong and take courage / Yea, continue to hope in the Lord" (Ps. 27:14). Such hope is predicated upon faith in God's eternal presence and confidence in his never-end-ing and always effective power of salvation. Arele's intricate meth-ods function within a simple and rather naive theology.

Nonetheless, the most simpleminded theology can be accom-panied by a realistic and hardheaded insight into the human con-dition. For instance, Arele asserted that one of the functions of prayer should be to overcome human self-centeredness. We should not expect that because we want something or are con-vinced that our want is a genuine need, therefore God in His own good time will grant our wish. On the contrary, ". . . a man should not ask God to do this or that for him, because he does not know what is good for him. Rather should he ask that the Holy One Blessed Be He be kind to him. . . ."[19] That sentiment should be reflected in the phrasing of a prayer. Suppliants should word their petition, if such a prayer it be, in such a way as to make clear that they accept God's answer as always being ultimately for their good.

Another important insight of Arele is found in his breadth of understanding concerning the occasions for worship. Actually, while we generally think of "worship" and "prayer" as identical in meaning, they are related to one another as genus and species or general and particular. Worship is the collection of acts of ado-ration of God, of which prayer is the most well-known and com-mon form. Prayer can be both socially dictated or spontaneous, but it always involves some form of verbalization. Here again, Arele is striking in his insight. He writes: ". . . when a man walks along a road and cannot pray or study as he ordinarily would, then he should worship God in any manner possible, at times in one way and at times in another."[20] Even in conversation one has an opportunity to worship, simply by seeing to it that the conversation is not idle talk but is devoted to spiritual concern and search.

The full use of the body, the dancing, and the ecstatic *niggunim* (melodies, often without words) are all elements in the Hasidic style of worship, in which cognitive meaning has little or no salience. Western-trained minds will find it difficult to absorb much of Arele's system, but they will find it difficult to brush it aside as irrelevant to the emptiness and lack of compelling emotion in the "modern" form of "esthetic" worship. Arele led his disciples to new horizons of worship, within the traditional form of the synagogue service. He wanted to rescue prayer from the serious danger of fossilization. Arele strove to overcome the torpor surrounding mechanical recital of the liturgy with what he considered to be stimulating and effective acts of worship.

I should illustrate the previous statement by asserting that Arele, like all halakhists, tries to preserve the traditional liturgy by his *kavvanot,* to which I referred above. He hoped that by treating each word as signifying some larger theological or moral belief, he would thereby infuse vitality into the moribund prayers. What actually happens, however, is that the prayers are deprived of their context and are preserved only because they provide the verbal symbols that are necessary to arouse each worshiper to draw near to some aspect of God's functioning. For God acts in the physical universe, in the Jewish people, and in the individual Jewish soul. The prayer is contained more in the meditative capacity of the worshiper than it is in the printed text. The meaning of each prayer is to be sought not in its overall content and intent but in the symbolism of each of its words. The Arele-inspired form of worship loses this symphonic grandeur of the traditional flow of the service; instead, we have a work that can be interrupted at any moment. Arele's worshipers can find fulfillment at whatever stage of the service they have arrived, without feeling that they have failed to reach the climax toward which the composers of the liturgy are trying to lead them.

Wherever one turns in Arele's writing, one is confronted with the basic challenge and reward of all worship. Our duty and the objective for which we live is the surrender to God's sovereignty, which combines faith in His reality and trust that He will reward the righteous and punish the wicked. Prayer is thus both the means and the end. It stirs humans to faith and rewards them with confidence that their efforts are meaningful and ultimately worthwhile. At the same time, prayer has to be founded on and is, indeed, a form of *teshuvah.* Only those who are conscious of their sinfulness or have determined to dredge it up to their consciousness can truly pray. Taken together, all these elements in prayer constitute a secure, closed system, a cocoon, if you will, in which one is safe from the ravages of the outside world. Arele's form of prayer is an apt expression of the closed community that he created and that his followers have preserved for several decades. Yet Arele would be the last person to argue that he wanted to live in isolation. He hoped that his message would transform the entire Jewish community and the rest of humankind. His perception of prayer was part of his kabbalistic outlook, in which the function of the Jewish people and of each Jew is to repair the world and ensure the advent of the Messiah.

However, as if to anticipate and to criticize the frenetic pursuit of the "Messiah Now" of the Lubavitcher Hasidim, Arele preaches a sober form of messianism. Yes, we must do all we can to ensure the coming and the redemption, but, says Arele, "Do not try to disclose the time [for the coming of the Messiah], which is unknown to all living creatures. Our Judaism is not dependent at all on whether or not the Messiah comes soon or is delayed continuously, God forbid. For sacred Israel has always sacrificed the body and soul in the service of His blessed Name."[21] Arele more than hints at the idea that the real salvation of the Jew is to keep the mitzvot and to be God-intoxicated. Here, he is in the company of a long line of Jews who, whatever they may have thought about the afterlife, never lost sight of the potentiality for fulfillment in this world. The Bible, let us remember, is oriented to the human being's duties as a living creature. Prayers for the coming of the Messiah, therefore, seem to be taken in Arele's vision with a light skepticism. The Messiah will come, but meanwhile Jews can have a rich existence. They should not spend their time in idle speculation about an ideal future.

In essence, however, Arele retreated as far as possible from the hustle and bustle of a full life. As a halakhic Jew, of course, he could not conduct himself in a monk-like routine. He had to maintain a family. But even in this regard, he was spared by the standards of the Fundamentalist communities from most of the duties that might have constricted his life of study and prayer. For all his radicalism, Arele was a typical member of the segment of Jewry that eschews participation in the furtherance of Jewish national life. Having to wrestle with the problems of a productive economy, with the responsibilities of autonomy and sovereignty, and with the need to preserve and enhance Jewish culture under freedom were seen by Arele as eventuating inevitably in error and sin. Presumably, only the life of contemplation and prayer can ensure the moral and spiritual purity of its practitioners. However, avoidance of the responsibilities of the full life is itself sinful. And the prayer of those who avert their eyes from the reality that holds out its arms to them is inevitably lacking much of the real pathos and glory of man's essential nature.

NOTES

1. The frontispiece of *Shomer Emunim* presents Rote's name in the Hebrew characters *resh alef tet ayin,* which can be transcribed in English either as Roth or Rote. The *Encyclopedia Judaica* lists the name as Roth, but in that case, it should have been better recorded in Arele's book as *resh vav tav.*

2. Aaron Rote, *Shomer Emunim* (Jerusalem: Yeshivat Toledoth Aharon, 1964), vol. 1, p. 129a. Cf. vol. 2, p. 294a.

3. Ibid., vol. 2, p. 294a.

4. Ibid., vol. 1, p. 187b.

5. Ibid., vol. 1, p. 37b.

6. Ibid., vol. 2, p. 402b.

7. Ibid.

8. Ibid., vol. 1, p. 97b.

9. Ibid., vol. 2, p. 352a.

10. Ibid., vol. 2, p. 255b.

11. Ibid., vol. 2, p. 268b.

12. Ibid., vol. 2, p. 252b.

13. Ibid., vol. 2, p. 268b ff.

14. Ibid., vol. 1, p. 35b. See also the reference in vol. 1, p. 40b to *Ahavat Yisrael.*

15. Ibid., vol. 1, pp. 35b–36a. In a note, we are told about an occasion when R. Arele extended his recital of the *Minhah* (afternoon) prayer well into the time for *Maariv* (the evening service).

16. Ibid., vol. 1, p. 38a.

17. Ibid., vol. 1., p. 193b.

18. Ibid., vol. 1, pp. 199a–b.

19. Ibid., vol. 1, p. 208b.

20. Ibid., vol. 1, p. 208a.

21. Ibid., vol. 2, 342b. Arele spells this thought out pointedly in the following remark: "We have explained that we must not limit the times of redemption, because God might desire to continue the process of eliminating wars and increasing peace in the world and of extending our stay in *galut*, God forfend. [Despite all this], we, the children of the living God, will certainly continue to worship Him. We will not leave or abandon Him in any way or for any reason, God forbid. For our faith is independent of whether redemption is delayed or comes quickly" (vol. 2, p. 343a).

6

Elie Munk

ELIE MUNK (1900–1981) was a scion of a long and distinguished line of German rabbis and scholars, who spent many years of his career serving the Orthodox community of Paris. His major work, *Die Welt der Gebete,* was first published in 1933, in two volumes, and later translated into English and republished in the United States.[1]

Munk was no less pious and bound by the constraints of Halakhah than Reb Arele, but whereas the latter was a strict traditionalist, Munk was an Orthodox thinker who felt that he had to respond to the rationalist and modernist challenges that affected the attitude of twentieth-century Jews toward prayer. As a result, there is a distinctly apologetic tone in much of his treatment of the daily, Sabbath, and holiday prayerbooks and the holiday *mahzorim.*

Munk begins his exploration of the liturgy by acknowledging the extent to which prayer has become irrelevant to hosts of human beings. He writes: "Modern man has lost the capacity to pray. Rare, indeed, are the individuals, who can free their souls from the paralysing apathy of our days, from the heavy burden of our daily sorrow, from the disastrous spell of Rationalism and materialistic thought, to pray with deep devotion for the realisation of the ultimate purpose in life."[2] In this sentence, Munk outlines the aim and scheme of his study. He wants, above all, to enable his readers to cope, through recourse to the traditional prayers, with the emotional strain of our changing world. However, to accomplish this purpose, he realizes that he must establish the intellectual credibility of the liturgy. His world, for all his rootage in the soil that nourished Arele, is thus far different from the emotional one of the Hasidic thinker. Whereas the latter appeals to the natural piety of the worshiper, Munk tries both to strengthen the intellectual conviction of his fellow worshipers as to the worth of the traditional prayers and to convince recalcitrant Jews that they are missing an important dimension in their lives. He hopes to achieve his end not by philosophizing about prayer, but by detailed examination of the entire range of the traditional liturgy.

Munk states his position thus: "Vague philosophising about the nature and idea, origin and form of expression of the prayers is of little help. . . . Whoever has succeeded in penetrating the external shell of the formal prayer to its innermost core, will comprehend the world of thought and feeling hidden deep in its central sphere. In this manner only, which the authors of the prayers outlined with their clear prophetic vision, will a man be able to find his G-d. For even the still, mystical absorption in prayer which seeks the blissful experience of Union with G-d, cannot neglect the need of searching into the ultimate meaning and content of that prayer in order to be filled and pervaded by it deeply and so totally that the soul, surrounded in longing love of G-d, finds again its Creator."[3] In keeping with his halakhic commitment, Munk believes that philosophical understanding of God, humankind, and the universe is achieved by uncovering the deep meaning of each prayer and by probing for the plain sense and esoteric intention of every word. That method in itself constitutes a philosophical orientation, for the liturgy is thereby assumed to embrace the values, purposes, and perceptions that befit the spiritual career of humankind. Whatever our experience points to as spiritually and morally desirable is embedded in the liturgy. Whatever surfaces as a result of our careful recitation of the prescribed prayers must be absorbed into our character structure and our conception of reality.

The theology underlying Munk's explanation of the efficacy of prayer can be summarized in the lesson that he draws from the benediction that concludes the section of the prayer book known as the *Pesukei D'zimra* (Verses of Song). That blessing ends with the description of God as *Hai Haolamim*, "Life of the Ages," or perhaps "Eternal Life." Munk interprets this phrasing as a contrast to the idea of God as a creative First Cause who acted only once in the distant past. Such a Deism, Munk seems to suggest, would have been implied had the wording been *Tzur Haolamim*, "Eternal Rock." That is to say, once having created the cosmos, God set it on a permanent, unchanging course to a final destination. However, as Life, God is ". . . the constant living source of all activity, the eternal perpetual Power dispensing life to all the world."[4]

This vision is further explicated in the first of two benedictions that precede the *Shema Yisrael*. There God is spoken of as renewing the work of Creation every day. However, such a view raises a difficulty, in that nothing seems to be left for humans to do except to act as automatons. Like the rest of nature, they are said to depend for their daily existence on the arbitrary decision of God to fashion them anew and to define the manner of their functioning. Munk deals with this issue by asserting that the ceaseless divine creativity is executed according to an orderly rhythm, manifested in the laws of nature, in the employment of which humans become a limited partner in managing the ongoing process of cosmic evolution. We must assume such a blueprint for our place in the universe because ". . . no work could ever be planned in advance, no achievement ever attained without this regularity of the phenomena of nature."[5] Munk, like all supernaturalists, sees no difficulty in accepting the simultaneous autonomy of nature and its heteronomous dependence on God's decrees. Nature can be overthrown or reconstructed by God's arbitrary, mysterious will. Thus, prayer can simultaneously be a means of focusing our attention on the wondrous natural order and of causing us to turn to God in humble surrender to the divine will. Munk's theology insists that regardless of the apparent operation of permanent laws of nature, prayer enables humans, against all odds, to appeal for God's miraculous, saving grace. Munk is not bothered by the contradiction.

Naturalists like myself are often prone to dismiss such thinking out of hand. But soberness and probity should give us pause. The choice between naturalistic and supernaturalistic conceptions of reality might, as we believe, be weighted by the evidence in favor of one of the former. However, unresolved questions remain. How are matter and spirit related? How is it that ideas seem to spring out of nowhere? Despite human effort to generate thought, the mystery of its emergence still overwhelms us. Or, to cite another example, even if we are convinced of the autonomy of nature, we must still reckon with the fact of transcendence. We can posit the interdependence of all things, but what is the nature of their unity? We might not agree with Munk's response to these and similar problems, but we must at least think along with him in his effort to find answers to these questions in the liturgy of the synagogue.

The prayer book for Munk is a rich source of knowledge about the operation of the universe. The worshiper learns that ". . . the universe is not a rigid, determined and immutable mass, but an army of stupendous forces, subject at all times to G-d's command."[6] It is in nature that humans discover the evidence of God, the Creator. Munk regards the *Ofanim,* celestial beings, as ". . . the naked forces of nature which form the very foundations of the universe. As the tumultous roar of nature, the thunder, lightning and quaking of the earth, heralded the coming of the Almighty, Master of Nature at Sinai, so in the same way the message of the prime forces of Heaven were revealed to the prophet amidst a mighty uproar in proclaiming G-d as the Creator of the Universe."[7] As far as naturalists are concerned, Kant tolled the death knell for this cosmological "proof" of the existence of a Creator. However, the finality of the Kantian achievement depends on the ability of a person to dispense with or to bracket the question of Creation itself. Many humans are by temperament unable or unwilling to rest satisfied with the idea that the question is likely to remain eternally unanswered. The solution of traditional prayer might not satisfy the rigorous standards of evidence demanded by the scientific mind, but it does, at least, provide a poetic and emotionally satisfying solution for the type of mind exemplified by Munk.

After one has affirmed the position that the material universe is the creation of a living God, the problem persists as to the relationship between the two. God, by definition, is in this vision spiritual. How does He relate to substance and, most particularly, to humans? On the one hand, Munk argues that Judaism ". . . rejects any assumption of a mediator between God and man."[8] Munk has in mind the Christian doctrine of the Trinity. But he cannot escape unscathed. He has to find a way of bringing spirit and matter together. What he has ushered out the back door, he now welcomes through the front entrance. Interpreting liturgical passages that refer to angels, Munk writes that "they form the link between the incorporeal purely spiritual Divine Being and the world of material phenomena. Pantheism which lets G-d dissolve in nature may do without such an assumption."[9] Munk overstates his criticism of a naturalistic theology when he identifies it with a crass pantheism. He ignores the fact that transcendence, as I have indicated before, necessitates reading reality as being an order that can never be exhausted solely by the observation of nature.

In prayer, humans hope to find a way of coping with the cruelties of earthly existence. The problem of evil is particularly acute in the context of a supernaturalistic theology. How can a good God create or countenance evil, whether natural or moral? Munk confronts the problem head-on. He asserts that ". . . evil is not an autonomous power. It is created by G-d, and is used when it is needed for the ultimate benefit of the creation."[10] He thereby expresses his approval of the circumlocution employed by the Sages in order to soften for the unsophisticated worshiper Isaiah's startling reference to God as the "Maker of peace and the Creator of evil" (Isa. 45:7). Once again, Munk begs the question. Who is to say that a catastrophe like a devastating earthquake serves a constructive purpose? Munk recognizes the difficulty but can only fall back upon a pious faith. He states: "God's trustworthiness has to be affirmed because reward is not always meted out in this world. It is often safeguarded for full and certain payment in the world to come."[11] Many of us will reject Munk's solution to the problems of evil and reward and punishment, but he should be credited with perceiving Jewish liturgy as raising these issues as inescapable items for the spiritual agenda of both pious and secular Jews.

The world of prayer for Munk is, like that of the other philosophers in this study, inhabited by individuals who happen to belong to a specific group, in this instance, the Jewish people. He believes that no other text gives expression to the social basis of prayer to the degree that the siddur does. But since Munk claims that the message of the Jewish prayer book needs no alteration and remains the same throughout eternity,[12] his description of the nature and destiny of the Jewish people is colored by the apologetics that I mentioned at the beginning of this chapter.

The comparative mood is brought to the attention of the traditional Jewish worshiper early in every morning service. In the benedictions recited at the outset of the prayers, the traditionally observant Jew thanks God for not having created him as a gentile.

This prompts Munk to reflect that "the knowledge that he is nearer to God than the gentile who scorns and abuses him has made the Jew strong enough to bear his fate."[13] Munk, realizing that his statement might seem to be arrogant, tries to correct this impression. He continues: "However, the Bracha [benediction] by no means assigns a lesser worth to the gentile. This is amply proved by the fact that a great many of the greatest halachic authorities sanction the positive *she-asani yisrael* [who has made me an Israelite]."[14] Jews are happy in their Judaism; other peoples can be equally satisfied in their cultures.

The need to compensate the non-Jew stems from the premise, common to virtually all supporters of the Chosen People doctrine, to the effect that the belief is essential to the effective implementation of the spiritual mission of the Jewish people. Munk states it this way: "This belief in the election of Israel is as indispensable for the fulfilment of its mission, as is a man's belief in himself for the success of any educational endeavors he may undertake."[15] Presumably, Jews who utter the prayers referring to the election of Israel require such reinforcement of their status in order to remain loyal to their people and to sense its worth as a nation. This spur to morale is seen to be doubly necessary when one takes into account the fact that one of the main interpretations of the election is that it is not a reward for any special virtues of the Jewish people. From the Bible on, Jewish sages have sought to prevent the sense of chosenness from becoming, in the mind of Jews, an indication that they belong to a people inherently superior in character to other groups. Munk writes: "Our privileged position as recipients of the Torah was not conferred on us by virtue of our possessing special social characteristics or on account of common national or historical experiences. Israel is the people of religion, and the Torah alone is its constitution."[16] Munk does not realize that the very possession of God's Torah is a mark of special privilege.

Undoubtedly, Jewish prayer must relate to Jewish identity and the vocation that Jewry ought to adopt for itself among the nations. Munk chooses to meet the challenge by extrapolating from the prayer book the complete set of qualities that inhere in our historical self-perception and that are, in his opinion, adequate guideposts to what ought to be the role of the Jewish people in advancing human civilization. The case for Munk's position must, therefore, depend on his ability to extract from the liturgy the values and qualities of individual and group character that merit universal approbation. Such a venture can only be partially successful, for the traditional siddur, being the product of two millenia of spiritual search, is bound to contain both the positive and the negative in the Jews' effort to find their niche in the universe. One has to be prepared, as Munk is not, to sift out the chaff.

An interesting instance of the questionable social understanding of the tradition is to be found in Munk's discussion of rights and duties. Munk argues that the survival of the Jewish people must be attributed to its vocation of mitzvot, of carrying out duties rather than defining and guaranteeing rights. The basic explanation for the riddle of Jewish survival, he says, ". . . is to be found in the Jewish concept of 'right' which is diametrically opposed to that of other nations."[17] Munk argues that to the rest of humankind, the concept of inherent rights is the means of guaranteeing that men and women will live ethically. Moral conduct is preserved by guaranteeing to all their God-given rights. In Judaism, however, it is not rights or areas of power that are assigned to humans, individually or collectively. Rather are they allotted appropriate spheres of positive duties.

Prayer based on Munk's analysis seems to me to be deficient in several ways. In the first place, how can there be duties in any social context without corresponding attention to those who are inevitably affected by the behavior of the other? For example, although the Halakhah requires a husband to satisfy the sexual needs of his wife, the Halakhah is guilty of violating her dignity in other respects—such as her low economic status or her inferior role in the synagogue. A social duty presupposes a right that has to be proclaimed and protected. Secondly, Munk falls into the trap of comparison. His sharp distinction between the duty orientation of the Jewish people as opposed to the assignment of areas of power to the individual is so far from the facts of history and so skewed in its claims as hardly to require retort. Nevertheless, one observation should be made. Even if we accept the centrality of duty, modern liberal society has so expanded the horizons of both duties and rights as to render the traditional liturgical treatment of them painfully inadequate. The twentieth-century discovery of the deprivation of rights, from which women have suffered throughout the ages, is alone sufficient reason to reject Munk's argument. But of course, this is only a single example of the vast rift between traditional and modern conceptions of duties and rights. The obligations imposed in Jewish tradition on males run parallel to the denial to women of the privileges that inhere in these duties.

One more illustration will have to suffice for our purposes. Observance of the Sabbath is a prime duty of every Jew, but can it any longer be legitimate to limit such observance to the regimen of halakhic Judaism? What happens to the right of the individual to choose his way of worshiping God or of expressing his opinion concerning the spiritual intent of the Sabbath?

As I have already commented, Munk strains hard to overcome the impression that Jewish nationalism is deficient in its universalism. I concur with his reading of Jewish particularism as not precluding the dedication of the Jewish people to the salvation of all humankind. My criticism of the doctrine of election and of the comparative mood is intended to free Munk and others who hold tenaciously to Israel's chosenness from the apologetics that its defense entails. For the fact is that Jewish universalism shines forth more brightly when it is presented forthrightly without the scaffolding of God's special relationship with Israel. A perfect example of this universalism is the midrashic interpretation of the significance of Shemini Atzeret. The Bible does not attribute any special purpose to this appendage to Sukkot. So the Rabbis declare that during the Feast of Tabernacles, Israel offers sacrifices for the redemption of the seventy nations of the world. Only on the one day of Shemini Atzeret does God tell Israel to look to its own salvation, by means of its offerings (*Tanhuma ha-Kadum, Pinhas*). This concern for the rest of humanity suffices to prove that particularism need not contradict universalism. But in the context of election, it is hidden behind the cloud of paternalism. Thus, a prayer like the *Alenu*, which pleads for universal acceptance of divine sovereignty, loses some of its spiritual flavor when it includes the clause that God has made us unlike the other peoples of the earth, who worship vain gods.

In sum, it can be reasonably argued that the vocation that Israel ought to adopt should be the direct opposite of what Munk maintains when he writes that ". . . whoever believes that he may water down or reject the idea of the election of the Jewish people, undermines one of the fundamentals of Judaism and denies the mission of our people."[18] Whether the reader follows Munk or finds merit in my departure from the traditional view, it is nonetheless evident that both Munk and I agree that one of the functions of Jewish prayer is to challenge worshipers to clarify for themselves the substance of their membership in the Jewish people. Prayer must inspire Jews to seek a satisfactory response to their desire that their loyalty to the Jewish people confer upon them a commendable moral and spiritual stature.

Munk's point of departure in historical revelation complicates for him other crucial theological questions. In trying to circumvent what he terms the trial and error mistake of philosophy, he avers that ". . . only G-d's revealed law, *Torat Ha-Shem,* gives man the guidance which is suited to his innate urges and desires, and which leads him to develop in accordance with the divine plan."[19] However, the same charge can be leveled against the claims of revealed traditions. They, too, convince only those who are predisposed to be so influenced. The prayer book properly raises the question of truth, but it can, like all other sources and methods of inquiry, provide only proximate answers. The siddur is an invaluable resource in the search for God's plan, but the recital of its affirmations must not lull worshipers into believing that in all instances they have come face to face with divine revelation.

One illustration of Munk's attempt to simplify complicated psycho-theological problems is his handling of the perplexing matter of free will. He hopes to resolve the issue with the following declaration: "The belief in the creation of the world by a free Divine act is the logical basis for the doctrine of the free will of man. Without the acceptance of this doctrine, the revelation of G-d's will to man would be meaningless."[20] One would think that the opposite would hold just as well—or just as poorly. Creation by an act of God's will would seem to place all human efforts under divine scrutiny and conditioning. Creatures can perform only those acts for which their composition equips them. The human mind is thus limited both by its physical formation and by the circumstances that condition its choice of options. This is not to say that humans are not free. It is to state that freedom itself is not an absolute state. Prayer can call men and women to cherish freedom and to pursue it, but its role is only one phase of the human effort to approach rationality, truth, and goodness.

As a matter of fact, Munk himself has to wrestle with the cause-and-effect relationship between God and humans. It is not so much God's self-revelation to humans that enables them to find their way in the universe as it is the reverse. "The certainty of the Divine must grow out of the reality of life, from the historical experience."[21] Or, as the Psalmist suggests, "Truth springs out of the earth, / And righteousness looks down from heaven" (Ps. 85:12). Our experience has taught us that there is sufficient order in the universe to enable us to fashion a meaningful and worth-while human career on earth—not with certainty, but with enough regularity to make the game of life attractive. Among the insights that Munk elicits from the *Amidah,* the Eighteen Benedictions, is the following: "As the interaction of the streams of power flowing from all four directions produces an equilibrium in nature, so in the affairs of men, the proper cooperation of all forces of the good society has its basis in the meaningful and harmonious Divinely established order."[22] It might be that the intuition of God spurs humans to search out the connectedness of phenomena and the proper relationship between each individual and his or her fellows, but it is equally true that experience draws all humans to the awareness of an established order. Whatever be the sequence of cause and effect, it is clear that the attainment of a just society can come only from the harmonization of human efforts with the workings of a divine—meaning orderly—reality. Apparently, Munk perceives divinity not merely in the reign of natural law but in a certain design for the future of humankind. While he speaks here and there of the world-to-come and of man's reward there for his good deeds on earth, his vision of salvation is loaded with a goodly measure of this-worldliness. The destiny of humankind is to create a decent society on earth.

The proper vocation of human beings is symbolized in the Sabbath, to whose importance Munk constantly draws our attention. "Without the Sabbath the world would run the danger of being burned alive through the folly and sin of man, the very being to whom G-d had originally entrusted the world so that he might manage it sanely and wisely."[23] Munk implies that the Sabbath is

God's strategic weapon against human sinfulness. The weekdays are aspects of the natural order and bear the thrust of our creative activity. Of course, the laws of nature and the behavioral endowments of human beings are divinely ordained, but they are both free to engage in deviant activities—nature, in its mutations and destructive acts, and humans, in their moral departures. God prepared the Sabbath, even before the rest of Creation, in order to forestall the complete chaos that might eventuate were humans to lack restraint. The Sabbath motif that runs through the entire liturgy is expected to educate Jews to responsible behavior and to convince them that natural order is not autonomous. All is ultimately under divine scrutiny and control. Therefore, humans must learn to deepen their humility and recognize the limits of their ability to subjugate nature. Sabbath rest is a purposeful backing off from the exploitation of the physical universe. For the Jew, the Sabbath is a guide to the awareness of God's sovereignty and of the duty of human beings to recognize that their role in Creation is only that of a junior partner.

In Munk's view, the Sabbath is a reversal of nature, a step back toward the original act of Creation. He elicits this lesson from the *Amidah* prayer in the *Musaf* (additional) service of the Sabbath in which the hope for the reestablishment of the Temple and its sacrificial system is articulated. The prayer, beginning with the words *Tikkanta Shabbat Ratzita Korbanoteha* (You have ordained the Sabbath and desired its sacrifices), is cast in the form of a reverse acrostic, in which each verse begins with a letter from *tav* to *alef.* Since the prayer deals with the divine institution of the Sabbath, Munk looks upon the day as a symbol of the ultimate restoration of Creation to its pristine, perfect state and of the duty of all persons to assist that process.[24]

One might draw the conclusion from all that has been said above that Munk conceives prayer as having little or no bearing on the individual and his yearnings. However, Munk is vociferous in according to worship a key role in the satisfaction of legitimate human wants. He examines the process of time, for example, in terms of its bearing on the human psyche. He contrasts the psychological reactions of human beings to day and night. Contrasting Judaism to paganism, he says that "the day, in pagan concept, is a battle of man against the power of the gods. The Jew's day is accomplishment in the service and to the satisfaction of his Creator."[25] The mundane activities of the day are hereby considered as potential acts of holiness. The secular world has an important role to play in the fulfillment of all humans. No one should derogate as unworthy or as lacking in spiritual significance what humans do in responding to their biological and social needs. The activities of the day can be rich in spiritual accomplishment.

With the conclusion of long hours of exertion and the fall of darkness, people's mood changes. In the prayer to be uttered before retirement, Munk locates the effort ". . . to elevate the worshiper to a mood of serene faith in G-d, of a purified activity of the mind and of peace of soul."[26] Prayer is not only a duty, obedience to halakhic requirements. It is also an instrument for imbuing human beings with happiness and a sense of self-worth and accomplishment.

Munk does not disappoint us with his attitude toward *kavvanah.* His approach to the siddur would require the worshiper to concentrate on understanding the meaning of every word in the liturgy. But no philosophy of prayer can succeed without the conscious cooperation of the individual in transforming theory into practice. As Munk proclaims, "Everyone is bidden to let his prayer flow out of the spontaneous urge of his heart, and not to let it degenerate into the mechanical recital of a text."[27] Munk's exhortation should earn a positive response from Jews who wish to restore synagogue worship to its former status. The Jewish liturgy is rich with the insights of many generations of spiritual giants. It cannot be taken for granted. Nor can its many messages be understood without knowledge of its background. However, having come to this point of agreement with Munk, I must nevertheless express my conviction that the kind of heartfelt prayer that Munk would like to see is inconsistent with his unyielding determination to breathe life into every word and phrase of the traditional liturgical texts. His hopes are bound to be dashed upon the rocks of our radically changing universe of discourse. Munk has not resolved the conflict between the demands of tradition and the yearnings of the heart, but he has made the study of the traditional literature of prayer a rewarding task for any Jew.

NOTES

1. Elie Munk, *The World of Prayer* (New York: Philipp Feldheim), vol. 1 (1961), vol. 2 (1963).

2. Ibid., vol. 1, p. 1.

3. Ibid., vol. 1, pp. 1–2. In quoting Munk, I follow his practice, common to Orthodox Jews, of writing the word "God" as "G-d." This custom is based on an ancient ban on pronouncing the Tetragrammaton (YHWH), except by the High Priest in the Holy of Holies, on Yom Kippur. Carrying the ban over to English usage is thus without rational foundation but has nonetheless become deeply rooted among many traditionalists and even some liberals, who want to preserve the awe of God's Name.

4. Ibid., vol. 1, p. 87.

5. Ibid., vol. 1, p. 98.

6. Ibid., vol. 1, p. 101.

7. Ibid., vol. 1, pp. 103–104.

8. Ibid., vol. 1, p. 98.

9. Ibid.

10. Ibid., vol. 1, p. 92.

11. Ibid., vol. 1, pp. 62–63.

12. Ibid., vol. 2, p. VII.

13. Ibid., vol. 1, p. 26.

14. Ibid.

15. Ibid.

16. Ibid., vol. 1, p. 48.

17. Ibid., vol. 1, p. 29.

18. Ibid., vol. 1, p. 27.

19. Ibid., vol. 1, p. 108.

20. Ibid., vol. 1, p. 107.

21. Ibid., vol. 1, p. 119.

22. Ibid., vol. 1, p. 124.

23. Ibid., vol. 2, p. 36.

24. Ibid., vol. 2, p. 54.

25. Ibid., vol. 1, p. 308.

26. Ibid., vol. 1, p. 228. See also Munk's remarks about day and night, on p. 203.

27. Ibid., vol. 1, p. 159.

7

Abraham J. Heschel

OF ALL THE THINKERS considered in these essays, Abraham J. Heschel (1905–1972) is probably the most difficult for me to treat. Let me try to explain.

Heschel was an unusual combination of academic, researcher, theoretician, teacher, and social activist. His activism stemmed as much from his warm character as it did from his philosophy, which is not noted for the kind of depth analysis of political, economic, and social issues that one might expect from someone who took courageous stands on matters like racial inequality and the war in Vietnam. Heschel did contribute significantly to the ethicization of theology. He wrote and spoke magnificently about the need to judge theological positions by the degree to which they stir humans to act morally. For him, a theology that posits God as an abstraction is barren. Heschel reinforces for us the principle that a Jewish theology must eventuate in *maasim tovim,* in good deeds. A theology without prophetic passion is humanly as useless as a car without fuel.

One can thus turn to Heschel as an example of how a theology can inspire courageous moral action. However, we do not derive from him any special insight into the social problems that he decided to confront. This is not meant to be a criticism of Heschel. A theologian is not required to be a social scientist. But, on the other hand, we do have to ask ourselves whether Heschel should be included among the thinkers to whom one should turn in order to expose better the roots of the various turmoils of the modern world. To make my point clear, I suggest that in contrast to Heschel's activism, that of Reinhold Niebuhr was founded on a profound effort to probe the forces of conflict in both local and international society. Niebuhr was certainly no less a theologian than Heschel, but he built a unique social theory in which he integrated his neo-Orthodox Christianity with a careful study of the economic and political realities of his day. One does not have to agree with Niebuhr either as a theologian or as a social critic in order to recognize that one has to take seriously what he had to say in both of these capacities. I do not find this to be the case with Heschel. Yet he continues to be recognized in certain Jewish religious circles as an inspiring exemplar of enlightened social theory.

When I turn to Heschel the theologian, I have no less difficulty in determining how to relate to him. On the one hand, he is an acute witness to the shallowness of much theological discourse, in its misreading of human nature and in its often arrogant approach to God as a servant of misguided human ends. On the other hand, Heschel's writings are replete with assertions that we must see ourselves through God's eyes—surely another, disguised version of anthropocentrism. What, really, is Heschel after in this dialectic? Is human hubris overcome when we criticize humans for seeing God in terms of their interests, while at the same time, we presume to lay claim to knowing what it is that God demands of us? How can both ends of the cosmic equation be so grasped and formulated as to preserve the modesty of our claims and maximize their questionable approximation of truth? Heschel's elegant exposition, for me at least, raises more questions than it answers.

If my difficulty stems from Heschel's thinking and not from my own lack of acuity, then an examination of his views on prayer should reveal some of the source of my perplexity.

Heschel wants us, at one and the same time, to recognize how ignorant we humans are and must continue to be and how nonetheless we must cope with that which is ineffable. In a typical passage, he writes: "Intimidated by the vigor of agnosticism that proclaims ignorance about the ultimate as the only honest attitude, modern man shies away from metaphysics and is inclined to suppress his innate sense, to crush his mind-transcending questions and to seek refuge within the confines of his finite self."[1] In other words, humans are expected to ask the "ultimate" questions, which by definition cannot be answered by human reason. Humans must rise above themselves and arrive at a metaphysical answer to the wondrous, ineffable cosmos and their own, equally mysterious self. The puzzle becomes more complex when Heschel asserts that "the ineffable in us communes with the ineffable beyond us."[2]

However paradoxical the foregoing might be—or, less kindly, obtuse—we must credit Heschel with an honest attempt to understand the human predicament. He seems to be saying the following: There is a tendency among modern intellectuals to be overconfident about the percentage of the unknowable they can appropriate, as compared to the vast but accessible unknown. By applying reason, such intellectuals believe, we humans should be able in the course of time to drive back the borders of the unknown almost to the point of inconsequentiality. Meanwhile, we lose our sense of wonder. The world is no longer mysterious. Hence humans have less and less need of God and of prayer. But, Heschel argues, this entire perception is skewed. Its anthropocentrism is transparent. As soon as the universe is perceived and conceived from the human perspective, it is bound to produce a false picture. Instead, we should take account of the two directions in which existence moves. The first is best described in one of Heschel's picturesque descriptions of prayer. He tells us that ". . . to pray is to become a ladder on which thoughts mount to God to join the movement toward Him which surges unnoticed throughout the entire universe."[3] The very force of life, whether in the conscious intellection of humans or in the unconscious evolution of the physical universe, heads toward God. Put differently, reality proceeds or is drawn toward the fulfillment of the transcendent plan that gradually unfolds itself.

On the other end of the cosmic stage stands God, who needs humans. In this perspective, prayer thus expresses our endeavor to become the object of God's thought and yearning, rather than the subject in pursuit of Him. Heschel repeats this emotionally charged view many times, but we have to struggle to grasp what he is getting at. Several possibilities come to mind. In the first place, the term "God" can be considered a correlate of "man," similar to parent-child, teacher-pupil, king-subject, and so on. In every one of these pairs, each term has no meaning without the other. A childless parent is an oxymoron. The same is true of all correlative concepts. This interpretation is further explicated when Heschel declares that "God is in need of man. The ultimate is not a law but a Judge, not a power but a Father."[4] However, human need and divine need are incomparable. Analogies such as those I have cited break down when applied to Deity. God as Judge or Father is totally unlike human counterparts. As a matter of fact, such appellations raise oft-repeated, uncomfortable questions concerning God's justice and "fatherly" love of human beings. A just Judge would not grant humans the latitude that would enable them to slaughter one another. A good and omnipotent Father would not sentence any of His creatures to a life of torture.

Heschel might be referring to the Rabbinic conception of humans as the partners of God in the work of Creation. Whatever God's purposes might be for human fulfillment, they cannot be attained without human involvement. Hence God the Father finds His completion in the accomplishments of His children; God the Judge requires the *teshuvah* and the moral regeneration of humans in order to rid His world of sin. This revision of the traditional theology implies that God, too, is part of a process in which He is limited by the capacities and behavior of His creatures; whether by His own design or by the nature of things is immaterial. The thrust of the image is that God is limited. Again, this cannot be Heschel's argument. He would reject an idea of God that would constrict divine power.

It would seem, therefore, that we might best locate Heschel's concern in the general direction of his thought and in his temperament. Heschel's roots in Hasidism, his charisma, and his poetic nature seem to have generated an emotional predisposition to approach God in personal, rather than in abstract terms. He could not conceive of a God whose relationship to humans could be other than in some way reciprocal to the love of God on the part of the pious person. It seems plausible, therefore, that Heschel, in the passage under discussion, was trying to resolve the sensitive theological issue of whether God should be conceived as a Person or impersonally, as a Process. As he phrased the matter, "Is God a mere word to us, a possibility, a hypothesis, or is He a living presence?"[5] For the purposes of this analysis, it is reasonable to assume that Heschel based his philosophy of prayer on the assumption that God literally hears prayer and responds to it in any way He chooses. Prayer has to be a dialogue with a listening God, in which the aim is for humans to fathom God's need of them and to respond appropriately to this amazing "fact."

Against this background, let us spell out Heschel's views on prayer.

In contemplating God, man has to integrate three methods: worship, gaining the knowledge that inheres in sacred texts, and action. "The first is the way of sensing the presence of God in the world, in things; the second is the way of sensing His presence in the Bible; the third is the way of sensing His presence in sacred deeds."[6] Heschel declares that experiencing God involves the total human person. As Maimonides had taught, in observing the wonders of nature, humans learn to love and revere God and to become aware both of their own minuteness in Creation and of the vast resources of divine grace that are at their disposal. To worship God, to praise Him, and to accept His sovereignty follow inevitably from the realization of the overwhelming miracle of existence. Still, it is not enough for humans to acknowledge God's power. God wants not only humans' submission. God wants and needs their understanding of His blueprint for human destiny. This plan is revealed in the Bible and in the subsequent expansion of Torah in the halakhic tradition. The study of the sacred writings, when its objective is to enhance the student's grasp of God's will, is itself a form of worship, Furthermore, Heschel informs us, a life of mitzvot and good deeds is both a suitable response to the demands of Torah and another section of the trail that has to be traversed on the way to God.

Yet prayer cannot be dismissed as just part of an organic whole. It has its own methods, forms, and content. In Heschel's vision, prayer is a particular way of looking at the world. It is nothing less than seeing the universe from the point of view of God. In prayer, humans rise to a higher level of being.[7] The worshipers forget themselves and are absorbed into the wonder and mystery of the outmost regions of existence. This idealized description of prayer is not as far-fetched as it might seem at first reading. Nonetheless, it is a questionable conception. In support of Heschel's view of prayer as entailing self-abandonment, one might refer once more to the experience of hearing a piece of music and becoming so thoroughly absorbed in it as to lose touch with one's self and one's surroundings. The self and the music become one. However, how does this square with the idea that prayer is designed to enable humans to see themselves and the rest of reality from the standpoint of God? If this conception has any meaning, does it not imply that humans must be keenly aware of themselves and the God from whose transcendent height they now observe the cosmos? It would seem to me that, in contrast to an esthetic experience, in which the listener or viewer hopes to achieve the ecstasy of enjoyment, prayer should foster our ability to apprehend ourselves more clearly in reference to God's transcendence. The objective of prayer is not to forget or repress the self but to improve its quality.

I said above that prayer is a dialogue with God, but Heschel would not accept this idea without qualification. According to him, rather than conversing with God, the worshiper should be attempting to become the object of God's thoughts. Once again, I am perplexed about Heschel's message. Is he arguing for one of the major strands in traditional Jewish religious thought, namely, that God's Providence is eternally present and that it is up to humans to earn the rewards that God's grace can confer upon them? If so, we are told nothing new and are thrust into the maelstrom of the old problem of theodicy. This is hardly what Heschel would aim to achieve. If, however, we take account of the rationalistic streak in Heschel's system, it might be that seeing humanity as an object of God's thoughts is another way of calling upon us to rise above the atmosphere of our own interests and environment into the stratosphere of transcendence. Even as scientists were enabled to look at our earth from beyond its reaches, so Heschel might be suggesting that we humans can and should acquire an ability for self-transcendence that would grant us a wiser perspective on the human condition. But this interpretation, too, is doubtful. Heschel would not want to be known as an outright naturalist. He cautiously avoids assigning so central a role to humans. Prayer cannot be solely a conversation between the "is" and the "ought" or "might be" of human consciousness.

Perhaps this aura of uncertainty is precisely what Heschel wishes to encourage. He might be telling us that when we pray, we should be fully alert to our creatureliness in order not to exaggerate the accuracy of our insight into God's wishes for us. Whatever be the proper interpretation of Heschel's urging us to see ourselves through the eyes of God, he is clearly saying that there is more to the human enterprise than can be contained in our short lives or in the entire history of the human race. This is, indeed, a mysterious, wonderful universe. Through prayer, humans repeatedly remind themselves of this fact. Natural piety alone, Heschel would remark—and we must agree with him—will not ensure our spiritual probity and requisite humility.

Prayer is the medium—or one of the media—by means of which men and women deepen their sense of the ineffable and adapt their minds to the world. This is in contrast to reason, through which, according to Heschel, we adapt the world to our concepts.[8] Here again, we come upon an inevitable semantic problem that inheres in Heschel's intellectual bias. He would have us assume that reason, relying on concepts as its means of communication, is uninterested in or incapable of balancing their subjective and objective foundations. But is it true that reason is prone to impose its mental creations on reality? Many of us, on the contrary, consider such employment of reason as the very antithesis of its proper functioning. Reason, we are inclined to say, prevents any attempt to re-create the world in our own image. Those of us who think in this fashion would look to prayer to ensure that we never obliterate this eternal need to harmonize the tension between our subjective and objective apprehensions of reality. We can thus credit Heschel's constant recourse to the ineffable as a necessary word of caution, even while we might reject his sharp division between the presumed hubris of reason and the humble sense of the ineffable.

It should be evident, if our analysis is correct, that Heschel looked beyond traditional prayer. He sought to rescue prayer from the habitual discipline it has become and to enable it once again to become a vibrant, spiritual experience.[9] Philosophically, Heschel wanted to remove artificial interferences that might stand between worshipers and their experience of God. Nonetheless, Heschel understood that this longed-for moment of discovery or revelation could be reached only along a cultural road that had been prepared by generations of creative ancestors. Prayer is as culture-conditioned as every other aspect of human creativity. However one defines revelation, it is necessarily refracted through the prism of a person's inherited tradition. Therefore, the question arises for Heschel and for his disciples and fellow travelers in other religions as to how the spontaneity of prayer can be preserved while it is conducted within the liturgical tradition of one's ecclesia or one's people. This, of course, is a problem for all who are attached to a tradition they love.

Heschel's Hasidism helps him and us to appreciate life's sublimity. Every life experience can be transformed by the individual into a moment of holiness, provided that he or she can equip himself or herself emotionally and intellectually to grasp its larger dimensions. Tradition can open new vistas for the operation of the imagination. It can be a source of revelation and not only a carrier of an inspiring moment of the past. This is what the Jew seeks in the repetition of sacred liturgy and in the reading and re-reading of the Torah. And this is what Heschel has in mind when he writes: "A scientific theory, once it is announced and accepted, does not have to be repeated twice a day. The insights of wonder must be constantly kept alive. Since there is a need for daily wonder, there is a need for daily worship."[10]

Prayer, as one of life's major functions, endeavors to induce God to reveal more and more of His message or, stated differently, to enable the worshiper to enter more intelligently and emotionally into that which has already been revealed. Each successful act of worship contains an element of discovery or prophecy. And that which is revealed is more than a state of mind. Heschel declares: "If revelation were *only* a psycho-physical act, then it would be little more than a human experience, an event in the life of man. Yet just as a work of sculpture is more than the stone in which it is carved, so is revelation more than a human experience. True, a revelation that did not become known by experience would be like a figure carved in the air. Still its being a human experience is but a part of what really happened in revelation, and we must, therefore, not equate the event of revelation with man's experience of revelation."[11]

Heschel is disarming. He sets up what purport to be mutually exclusive alternatives; he simplifies experiences that are more complex than his designation of them and then builds on this foundation his case for mystery and ineffability. Suppose, he challenges, revelation were *only* (italics Heschel's) a psycho-physical act! It would then be ". . . little more than a human experience." Heschel would have us first accede to the opinion that a psycho-physical experience is of very inferior worth as compared to a divine revelation, because it is *merely* human. Revelation, on the other hand, raises humans above the human level and exposes them to a dimension of existence unavailable to the normal functioning of the mind. Given Heschel's conception, we can now understand why he would have worshipers lose themselves. For through prayer, they must transcend the *merely* human.

However, let us ask ourselves what is really contained in a psycho-physical act and whether or not there is any other non-human or extra-human experience by means of which man can attain insight into the more-than-human. A mental experience is a bringing to consciousness of a person's perception of the phenomena, both physical and conceptual, with which he interacts at a given moment. A mental state of this kind is not a still portrait of reality. It is rather a complex of movements that have their own projection but that can be sent off in a number of possible directions, depending on the aims and abilities of the person. A human experience is a congeries of interaction between a person's immanent involvements and his imaginative flights into the transcendent. The reach of the mind is almost boundless, but it often eventuates in nothing more than that—imaginative constructions that have no basis in reality. Hence, this *merely* human experience turns out to be a temptation to read the world only through the often myopic vision of one's own eyes. The claim of revelation has no more validity than can be gleaned from the ordinary, natural methods of proof. This is why prayer, too, is a hazardous enterprise. How are persons to know when they have succeeded in envisaging life from the vantage point of God? How can they know that God has answered their plea for enlightenment and inspiration, that He has, in truth, revealed Himself?

Heschel skirts these issues by concentrating on the way of thinking, rather than depicting and substantiating its content. He claims that ". . . the source of truth is found not in a 'process forever unfolded in the heart of man' but in unique events that happened in unique moments in history. There are no substitutes for revelation, for prophetic events. . . . At Sinai we have learned that spiritual values are not only aspirations in us but a response to a transcendent appeal addressed to us."[12] Instead of viewing immanence and transcendence as two connected poles of the natural functioning of the mind, Heschel, like other revelationists, would have us believe that there are two distinct sources of knowledge. One, in which the mind is the active and efficient force, is *only* human; the other is a result of a stimulus and an emanation that descend upon our consciousness as a result of the willed action of a transcendent Being. But, as we have previously maintained, the active and passive functioning of the mind, notwithstanding its mysterious quality, is all part of one system. Immanence and transcendence are two poles of a continuum. Revelation and discovery are the sublime outcome of thinking that harmonizes immanence and transcendence. Moreover, this same sublimity and mystery are characteristic of the mistakes and the horrors that often stem from this same natural operation of mind. Why are these aberrations not attributed to the revelatory acts of God?

In brief, Heschel's effort to find a more authoritative and secure base for the improvement of humans than that of normal intellection fails, or at least does not succeed, in the view of this observer. Nonetheless, there are other facets to Heschel's conception of prayer that merit our sympathetic attention, if not our complete approval.

The reader might conclude that Heschel's appeal to and for revelation is whistling in the dark and that prayer is a waste of time. This would be a hasty judgment. The long career of worship in its various forms should point to a fact of human nature that we should do well to continue to explore. Above all, we humans seem to have the need to project for ourselves standards of value and behavior that we believe are more than subjective impositions of our own ego on the cosmic process. Heschel writes: "The fact that man with undaunted sincerity pours into prayer the best of his soul springs from the conviction that there is a realm in which the acts of faith are puissant and potent, that there is an order in which things of spirit can be of momentous consequence."[13] This conviction, it seems to me, is common to all those who seek to extract meaning out of the rugged terrain of our uncertain universe. And for such men and women, prayer is a stimulus to faith and to its strengthening. Heschel makes a valiant effort to contribute to the revival of prayer as an important option for sincere seekers of life's potential for meaning and personal growth and fulfillment.

In tracing Heschel's philosophy of prayer, we come frequently upon important questions, cogently posed, and answers that are beclouded with haziness. Heschel is not to be blamed for his inability to provide satisfactory solutions to some of these problems, inasmuch as theologians and philosophers have records of constant disagreements among themselves. My difficulty with Heschel is rather his habit of hedging his bets. Consider the following: "The essence of Judaism is the awareness of the *reciprocity* of God and man, of man's *togetherness* with Him who abides in eternal otherness. For the task of living is His and ours, and so is the responsibility. We have rights, not only obligations; our ultimate commitment is our ultimate privilege."[14] In this passage, Heschel addresses himself to a number of perplexing issues. Does God's otherness mean that He is completely separate from humans, as would seem to be implicit in Heschel's references to reciprocity— apparently between two distinct persons—and togetherness, also between two independent partners in the cosmic enterprise? Since the reciprocal relationship of God and humans is not between equals, how are we to determine the rights and responsibilities of each party? What is the meaning of an ultimate commitment? Are the terms determined by humans or God or by contractual agreement between them?

Heschel's rhetoric is deceptive. On the one hand, he wants us to eliminate all doubt about God's absolute sovereignty. But equally, he wants us to respect the independence of human creatures and the power of their mind. The dilemma is unavoidable once one takes the position that God not only is separate from the cosmos and His creatures, but is capable, if He so wills it, of determining or intervening in the order of nature and human affairs. When humans address God in prayer, are they engaged in dialogue with a separate Being or Person, or are they trying to tap spiritual resources in themselves that have lain dormant and await their self-confrontation as worshipers? If the former, what does Heschel mean by reciprocity? On the basis of what criteria does such a God answer prayer? Is He subject to arbitrariness? If so, divine-human reciprocity is asymmetrical. If there are procedural rules to the dialogue of prayer, what are they, and how can humans know them? Heschel, to say the least, is unclear.

Nor is Heschel definitive in exploring the alternative of a reciprocal God-man relationship based on a naturalistic vision. In order for humans to be responsible, they have to be free and capable of defining the parameters of conduct appropriate to that station. In this search, God as subject would not be willful. His behavior would be authoritative, in that humans would have to abide by the transcendent rules of the divine nature. But God, too, would behave in ways that would be susceptible, in theory at least, to rational understanding. What else could be inferred from the numerous biblical references to the commandment to know God's Name—meaning something about God's essence or will? Prayer would thus place heavy emphasis on human self-exploration and self-transcendence. Response would come in the form of enlightenment and strengthened will. While such prayer would be personal, it would be addressed to a Reality in which humans are a participant but that is beyond their ability ever to exhaust.

Heschel straddles these alternatives, hoping that the dialectic will bring together all sections of the theological spectrum. Our commitment to God is an act of faith that we humans are not pursuing a chimera when we pray for guidance or when we act out our convictions. However, we must also know that while our quest for God always falls short of perfection, we must continue toward our goal. For the delight that Heschel would have us experience lies in the very effort of playing the game itself, rather than in its successful outcome.

Heschel's parallel between the respective tasks of God and humans also leads us to confusion. The life of humans is one of unconscious and conscious growth, of experiencing and learning, of stimulus and response, of pain and enjoyment, of problems and solutions, of vitality and death. All of these have no bearing on the "living" God. God's life, whatever else it might be, can only be inferred by humans from their limited knowledge and perspective. So while it is legitimate to speak of humans as God's partner in Creation, that is so in the sense that we can create only within the confines of the physical and spiritual domain into which we are born. Prayer can do no more than help orient us to this reality. God's life is the soil in which mortal beings grow and die—a sober thought, which focuses our attention on what we really are or should and can become.

Heschel properly views prayer as an endeavor to make changes in human character. His approach is helpful to all who seek to refine human nature. Like other serious theologians, Heschel regards a religious service as intended to identify and clarify for the worshipers the ideals worthy of their devotion and to generate the moral courage and energy that will enable them to act out their convictions.

However, Heschel glosses over the issue as to how those changes are to be accomplished. He underplays the psychological operation that takes place within the person between what he or she is now and the person that he or she might become. Prayer or meditation can assist worshipers to strengthen their attachment to ideals that have been sanctified by the collective conscience of inspired and saintly souls of every age. Such a view of prayer is consistent with human psychology. But Heschel is dissatisfied with this orientation. Instead, possibly in deference to generally accepted norms in the organized religious community, he avoids any intimation that the God of prayer might be conceived in a way other than that of a listening Being. As I indicated above, Heschel does not bother to explain what the God who needs humans—and therefore attends to their calls for attention—actually does in response to their appeals. All that Heschel can tell us is that the universe was not made to please the human ego.[15]

In the light of the foregoing, the God of Heschel's prayer is the subject and not the object of our attention.[16] Therefore, the burden of prayer is to create the mood that is conducive to minimizing one's wants and greeds and to open oneself to God's love and plan for His creatures. Heschel realizes that humans cannot remain completely in this passive mood. They can and should love God, but that love is tested by the evils caused by natural disturbances. Humans should sense that there is an order in the universe. But where is it all heading? So Heschel tackles the agonizing problem of evil.

Heschel combats the thought that the presence of evil is an indication of the injustice of existence. On the contrary, he writes sensitively: " 'There is no justice in heaven' is a cry in the name of justice, a justice that cannot have come out of us and still be missing in the source of ourselves."[17] After stating the problem forthrightly, Heschel answers with equal candor. He cites the famous story recorded in the talmudic tractate Menahot 27b, which tells of the challenge hurled at God by Moses to explain why the great Sage, R. Akiva, was tortured to death by the Romans. Is this the reward for a life devoted to the study of God's Torah and obedience to His moral standards? The answer that the Talmud puts into the mouth of God is: "Be silent, for such is My decree."[18] Heschel accepts this answer, inferring that this is an appropriate response for reasonable men. In prayer, then, unfortunate men and women should strive to overcome their bitterness at their lot and, like Job, accept the fact that they are incapable of probing God's ways. In Heschel's opinion, Judaism, echoing Job, deals with the reality of evil by proclaiming the wonder of existence and heralding the ability of human beings to do the will of God.[19] Here, at least, Heschel is clear. He advances a theology that posits a God who is "wholly other" and absolutely sovereign and who is pitted against mortal human beings, who rarely understand even their own soul. In this unbalanced confrontation, our only hope for enlightenment is God's willingness to reveal something of His essence and His expectations about human conduct. Heschel relates to this challenge, as well.

Heschel focuses his and our attention on the role of humankind in bringing about evil. From ancient times to our own day, our wickedness has caused one tragedy after another. Heschel hammers away at humanity's increased insensitivity to the monstrous horrors that we ourselves create. In this way, Heschel dulls our minds to the real problem of evil, which is natural evil and not the moral crimes of which we humans are guilty. The latter problem is not only created by humans; it is soluble by them. Natural evil, however, is built into the structure of the universe. Humans are victims. We can, of course, improve our natural environment by utilizing its laws intelligently; and we can increase its destructiveness by misusing natural resources. But, as far as can be deduced from the facts, we humans will continue to suffer death and the pangs of misfortune not stemming from our behavior.

Insofar as natural evil is concerned, prayer to a God who is capable of hiding Himself is a problem. In Heschel's system, it would seem that this question must either be underplayed or that the worshiper must surrender in the end to God's inscrutability. From a human perspective, the death of an innocent child as a result of disease is evil, but prayer must enable the grieving parents to suppress their outrage and continue to love God.

The affirmation and love of God are worthy goals. But cannot this state of mind be induced without a theology in which God is conceived as a Judge meting out sentences to innocent beings? Cannot prayer be developed to enable men and women to seek God in the struggle against both moral and natural evil, a struggle in which God is as much a victim of reality as humans? This possibility is dismissed too readily by Heschel. He is bound to the biblical insistence on the inseparable unity of nature and the moral realm. The Psalmist, for instance, concludes his masterful hymn to the God of nature with the following words: "Let sinners cease out of the earth, / And let the wicked be no more. / Bless the Lord, O my soul. / Halleluyah" (Ps. 104:35). Prayer, in the last analysis—or so it seems from what Heschel implies—is surrender to a theology that exalts God's power and mistrusts the ability of mortal human beings to make moral judgments about the order of things. God's omnipotence and goodness must remain unchallenged. Therefore, although nothing can prevent persons from expressing their pain in prayer, their real piety demands silence.

Nevertheless, the silence need not be a silence of consent. Even God cannot uproot from humans the doubts that erupt into their consciousness and plague their sense of justice. Humans will recite the words that articulate their feelings. At this point, Heschel, as a traditionalist, asks properly about the role of history-laden liturgy. He has no trouble in answering his own question. It is the fixed prayer that facilitates our worship, making it possible for us ". . . to affiliate our minds with the pattern of fixed texts, to unlock our hearts to the words, and to surrender to their meanings. The words stand before us as living entities full of spiritual power, of a power which often surpasses the grasp of our minds. The words are often the givers and we the recipients. They inspire our minds and awaken our hearts."[20] This is so because traditional prayer expresses the collective mind and heart of the Jewish people and brings to our attention thoughts that we should ponder but often do not. We humans forget; we are unstable, and we frequently lack the requisite imagination that would stir us to the core of our being.

Heschel has hit upon a basic justification for our trying to preserve the institution of public worship. He perceives that secularization has made inroads into all the religions. Sacred tradition alone is inadequate as a means for restoring the vitality of group prayer. Heschel understands the need for liturgical revision, but he is wise enough to assert that "to abridge the service without deepening the concentration would be meaningless."[21] One of the conventional steps in the effort to cultivate *kavvanah* is to conceive prayer as a halakhic requirement. For the act of worship then becomes a collective duty, and individual Jews rise above themselves in the realization that they are participating in carrying out a sacred covenant between their people and God. That awareness converts their supplication into a moment of sacred history. Heschel adds that this is true whether the individuals are or are not aware of their membership in this transgenerational order. However, this reservation compromises Heschel's insistence on the need for concentration. How can Jews comply with Heschel's plea for *kavvanah* unless they are *conscious* of being a cell in the living body of the Jewish people?

Moreover, on what are the worshipers supposed to concentrate? Obviously, in keeping with Rabbinic concepts, they must address their prayer to the God in heaven, the living God of Israel and of all humankind. But after having told us that prayer is intended to stir our minds, Heschel proposes the following outcome: "To strengthen our alertness, to refine our appreciation of the mystery is the meaning of worship and observance. . . . We must continue to pray, continue to obey to be able to believe and to remain attached to His presence."[22] Heschel would have us open our minds to the living God, but he cannot tell us what that means, other than that we must await a revelation. True, the mind should reach out, but Heschel offers no guidelines as to what to seek and when to know that the quest has been rewarded by some insight into truth. Can those guidelines be more trustworthy than is our faith in the potential capacity of human reason?

Heschel leads us to a form of worship that appeals to the soul of poetic and sensitive men and women. He is powerful in his criticism of the cynicism, the apathy, and egocentrism that pervade our modern society, and he is correct in his call for a better realization of the wonders of our universe. But in the end, his criticism, if acted upon, would sacrifice human intelligence to a pious surrender to mystery.

I should not want to end these reflections on Heschel's philosophy of prayer by leaving the reader with the feeling that I lack respect for his effort. It should be evident by this time that none of the thinkers encountered in these pages succeeds in convincing more than a handful of disciples that he has discovered the single formula for effective and inspiring prayer. Along with the proposals of all the others, however, Heschel's appeal for humility, for resuscitating piety and the sense of sublimity should be taken seriously. Heschel himself states honestly that the entire enterprise of prayer is a risk and an uncertainty. As he writes, "It is within man's power to seek Him; it is not within his power to find Him."[23] All that we mortals have, says Heschel, is openness to God's willingness to reveal Himself to us. We can debate with Heschel as to what revelation is all about. But the most naturalistically inclined among us cannot deny that we know little, if anything, about how we come suddenly upon a fruitful idea, hit upon a melody that we have never heard before, or find the key to the solution of a problem on which we have long worked without success.

Heschel is sometimes dismissed by his critics as being a poet who dabbled in theology and hid his confusions in beautiful rhetoric. I believe this type of criticism is unfair. Heschel struggled with an intractable problem, and he has helped us realize that although we shall probably not find a universally acceptable and accepted answer, we must continue to seek it. That is no mean adventure.

NOTES

1. Abraham Joshua Heschel, *Man Is Not Alone* (Philadelphia: Jewish Publication Society, 1951), p. 44.

2. Ibid., p. 131.

3. Abraham Joshua Heschel, *Man's Quest for God* (New York: Scribner's, 1954), p. 7.

4. Abraham Joshua Heschel, *God in Search of Man* (New York: Farrar, Straus and Cudahy, 1955), p. 68.

5. Ibid., p. 9.

6. Ibid., p. 31.

7. *Man's Quest for God,* p. xii.

8. *Man Is Not Alone,* p. 11.

9. *God in Search of Man,* p. 3.

10. Ibid., p. 49.

11. Ibid., p. 184.

12. Ibid., p. 197.

13. *Man Is Not Alone,* p. 239.

14. Ibid., p. 242. See also pp.101–102.

15. Abraham Joshua Heschel, *Who Is Man?* (Stanford, Calif.: Stanford University Press, 1965), p. 84.

16. *Man Is Not Alone,* p. 128.

17. Ibid., p. 132.

18. *God in Search of Man,* pp. 69–70.

19. Ibid., p. 378.

20. *Man's Quest for God,* p. 32.

21. Ibid., p. 35.

22. *God in Search of Man,* p. 137.

23. Ibid., p. 147.

8

Jakob J. Petuchowski

JAKOB PETUCHOWSKI (1925–1991) was distinguished by his effort to explore the traditional liturgy for the full measure of its spiritual treasures. As a member of the faculty of the Hebrew Union College, he might have been expected to be more inclined toward so-called "creative prayer" than he was. But Petuchowski was a leading figure among liberal intellectuals who believed that the potential of the classic liturgy had not yet been thoroughly tapped. The Reform movement as a whole has come a long way in reexamining traditional ideas and practices that had been discarded by earlier generations of the movement. Petuchowski contributed significantly to this trend.

In his short but closely reasoned treatment of Jewish worship, *Understanding Jewish Prayer,* Petuchowski sets himself the goals of clarifying the function of prayer, in general, and of elucidating the historical and theological development of Jewish prayer, in particular. His objective is both academic and practical. His study of the traditional liturgy and the ways in which it came to expression in the synagogue is motivated by his desire to revive the ability of Jews to pray sincerely and with passion.

Petuchowski comes right to the point. He raises the crucial question as to what is meant by *kavvanah* and how it is to be acquired. *Kavvanah* is clearly more than can be achieved by concentrating on the prayer book and endeavoring to address God sincerely and honestly through imaginative interpretation of its contents. Of course, that manner of worship is fundamental to the conduct of synagogue prayer, but it has to be acknowledged that it is only a late stage in the history of Jewish spirituality. *Kavvanah* begins and has its most effective form of expression in the spontaneous, unstructured experience of each individual. *Kavvanah*, devotion, attention, inwardness—these and other characteristics of sincere prayer are natural responses of men and women to the exigencies of their lives.[1] Prayer is first and foremost the immediate and instinctive reaction of the individual person to situations that demand his or her gratitude, concern, fear, wonder, or any other basic emotion. In all of these instances, the person is often unaware that he is engaged in prayer. A sigh of relief, for example, should be seen as an abbreviated way of recognizing the tenuousness of existence and expressing one's gratitude for one's good fortune. Petuchowski seems to exaggerate in his evaluation of the implication of certain types of spontaneity, but he is undoubtedly correct in locating the roots of prayer in commonplace human experience.

Were humans to rest satisfied with responding to their unreflective concerns and instincts, there would be no occasion for formal worship. However, men and women are thinking beings, and they cannot help but reflect on the experiences that cut to the roots of their being. They try to place what happens to them in a large perspective. They want to understand the significance and the implications of events that affect them. And they need to sense that what has occurred or what they would like to have occur has cosmic meaning. As Petuchowski phrases it, "Prayer, we might say, presupposes that finite, mortal, limited man can address himself to eternal and infinite God, that human heart and divine mind can be attuned to each other."[2] According to Petuchowski, prayer is inaugurated in human emotion but aspires to reach the heights of understanding that can only be scaled by the mind. Petuchowski designates this characteristic of prayer as hutzpah (insolence). For how can we humans expect to penetrate the mystery of existence and call out to God to satisfy our wishes, many of which are misguided? Yet without the hope that our supplications are attuned to the divine will or capable of being so adjusted, we mortals could hardly make sense of our lives.

We Jews are aided in our address to God by the fact that we are the heirs of many generations of our people who preceded us in an ongoing, collective conversation with God. Petuchowski bases his philosophy of Jewish prayer on the assumption that every group of worshipers starts with an apperceptive mass. Its members are heirs to an accumulation of knowledge and assumptions that have been distilled out of the collective wisdom of the best minds of the people. It is appropriate, then, that each generation should employ its patrimony in order to cope with its own spiritual turmoils. Thus, isolated, individual worshipers are rarely that. They are a link in a chain of culture-bound generations that include their own. Their prayer is conditioned and supported both by their historical ancestry and by their contemporaries. Whatever might have been the genesis of prayer, its spontaneity cannot be extricated from its cultural matrix. The prayer of a Jew must inevitably be expressed in terms that are uniquely Jewish.

Petuchowski has thus identified two types of worship—the occasional outpourings of the individual soul, which need no social appurtenances, and the structured, slowly evolving forms of prayer of organized religions. It is the latter, of course, that is the main focus of Petuchowski and the other thinkers we consider in this work; for it is here that the crisis of prayer is manifest.

From one point of view, there is no crisis. Group worship today is not a new enterprise. All of the historical religions are continuations of traditions that were fashioned by a continuous stream of men and women who, although invisible today, inspire present-day worshipers to come together regularly in fellowship. No other aspect of group culture seems to generate the power that prayer possesses in binding a society across the spans of time and space. In what sense, then, is there a crisis?

In the first place, despite what I have just written, the cement seems to be losing its adhesiveness. Barring a few notable exceptions, attendance has fallen off drastically in synagogues, churches, and even in mosques in some parts of the Moslem world. Just as serious is the fact that regular worshipers are drawn together less by their common search for God than by their cultural and social ties. Understandably, Petuchowski sees this historical bond in positive terms. For Jews, it is precisely the continuity of tradition, tying each generation to its total ancestry, that lays the groundwork for Jewish communal prayer. There could be no Jewish group prayer ". . . if today's worship were to be something totally and entirely different from yesterday's worship service, or last year's, or that of a hundred years or two thousand years ago".[3] Unfortunately, Petuchowski's apologetic for the preservation of traditional liturgy—which, incidentally, seems to attract a large number of intellectuals who have surrendered the cognitive aspects of prayer in favor of an unreflective emotionalism— succeeds only in doing justice to the need for continuity. It fails to help the modern Jew to adjust to the need for change and growth.

It is not that Petuchowski overlooks the problem. On the contrary, one of the important features of his approach is his acknowledgment of the dilemma faced by the modern worshiper. He, no less than the talmudic Sages who prepared much of the text of the traditional siddur, cautions that we must not fall into the trap of *keva*, of reciting prayers without any of the immediacy that characterizes personal, spontaneous prayer. Petuchowski remarks that "if Progressive Judaism is to remain faithful to its own inner dynamics, there will never be an end to the process of prayerbook revision."[4] How, then, can *keva* be avoided while basing group worship on maximum adherence to the classic liturgy? Petuchowski finds an outlet in Heschel's interpretation of the language of prayer. Words are held by Heschel to be external to the person who utters them. Even those words that are conjured up by ourselves have a life of their own. It might be, Heschel suggests, that the words written by the Sages of old express more adeqately than our own the thoughts that we wish to express to God. The fact that Jews have done this for two millenia lends credence to Heschel's defense of the traditional text of the prayer book. Nonetheless, it is a weak reed on which to rely. The "old time religion" is attractive, but in the last analysis, it must pass the tests of cogency, relevance, and plain honesty of discourse. Petuchowski perceives this tension and underscores the need to avoid extremes in either direction. "The dialectics of *qebha'* [*keva*] and *kawwanah* are an on-going process. What is required, at any given time, is the striking of a balance between the two, rather than an over-emphasis on one or the other."[5]

I do not argue with Heschel, Petuchowski, and others in their effort to preserve as much of traditional prayer as possible. I take exception to their implicit assumption that because the words of prayer are loaded with poetic overtones, they can be given almost limitless meanings. The idea that words are so pliable has a long history; countless generations have attributed to the same vocabulary connotations that are often quite remote from and even contradictory to their origins. It seems to me, however, that the combination of intellectual laziness and looseness in reading meanings into terms not coined for those purposes has reached its limits. The endeavor to find *kavvanah* in *keva* must at times founder on the rocks of casuistry and the boring pace and repetitiveness of communal prayer.

Another item in the defense of the classic liturgy is the fact that the composers of the siddur did attend to the need to find room for personal expression. Petuchowski recalls that the Talmud records the private prayers of a number of Rabbis, which were recited at the conclusion of the Eighteen Benedictions.[6] It was at this point in the service that worshipers were encouraged to offer up their own supplications. These prayers, which were meant to mitigate the pressure of *keva*, could nominally still be appended to the *Amidah*, but in practice they have been replaced by a fixed meditation. Almost all participants today read the additional prayer and eschew their own meditation. With the best of intentions, the introduction of personal prayer into public worship is an awkward effort. Such prayer can succeed, if at all, only to the extent that individuals can remove themselves from the service and retire into their private world. But this is not what Petuchowski wants. His purpose is to enable the worshiper to find spiritual satisfaction in the group liturgy.

Yet Petuchowski refuses to identify *kavvanah* with *keva*. He understands that innovation is essential if devotion is to be pursued. Again, he has recourse to the history of the liturgy. He proves that the tendency to "reform" the prayers never ceased, although in the past such reform always took the form of adding to the service. Nothing was excised. Nonetheless, argues Petuchowski, ". . . adding to the inherited liturgy is as much a 'reform' as omitting from it. Both the adding and the omitting are ways of indicating that the tradition, in its crystallized form, no longer meets the religious needs of a new generation."[7]

It appears that the tension between *kavvanah* and *keva* is unavoidable, with the balance in one direction or the other depending, among other things, on the relative conservatism or liberalism of the worshipers. Although supporting the release of spiritual creativity, Petuchowski seems to weight the scales in favor of *keva* and the retention of the liturgical heritage as the only legitimate framework for Jewish community worship. Such adherence to age-old prayers gives each Jew ". . . the ability to pray as a Jew, the opportunity of experiencing a dimension of prayer which is accessible only to the faith community of Israel standing together before the God of Israel, and the proud awareness that one is personally involved in the task of weaving the perennial tapestry of Jewish prayer out of the strands of spontaneity and tradition."[8] The fact that a liberal should direct our attention to the need to plumb the depths of the prayer book that was normative among Jews for almost two thousand years should be viewed not as a reversal of history and a return to ancient ways. It should be regarded as an effort to recapture insights that might inadvertently have been overlooked by modernists in their necessary but sometimes hasty and shallow pursuit of relevancy.[9]

The problem of *keva* is closely tied to the question as to whether or not prayer is a mitzvah, in the sense that it is not only a meritorious act but one that the individual is obligated to perform. As an obligation, prayer is not a matter of choice. As Yeshaiah Leibowitz never tired of repeating, prayer is incumbent on Jews even when they are least disposed to engage in it. According to Leibowitz, the late maverick Israeli philosopher, there is no relationship between a person's mood or need and the call to prayer. The latter has nothing whatsoever to do with helping mourners in their sorrow or ill persons in their pain. Prayer is a duty that Jews must obey because they are Jews. Petuchowski, however, first instructs us that it is only the recital of the paragraphs of the *Shema Yisrael* (Hear, O Israel, the Lord our God, the Lord is One) and the praying of the Eighteen Benedictions (the *Shemoneh Esray* or *Amidah*) that are obligatory. The rest of the liturgy belongs historically to the free determination of the worshiper. Petuchowski points out that it is questionable whether or not the *Shema* should be viewed as prayer at all. The biblical command to recite these paragraphs is directed to having the Jew rehearse its wording and reflect on its message. On the other hand, Petuchowski affirms that the obligation to repeat the benedictions of the *Amidah* is an order to pray, pure and simple. But for the most part, Petuchowski insists, Jewish prayer remains in the category of *reshut*, voluntarism. There is no basis for Leibowitz's depriving prayer of the designation "offerings of the heart."

Nevertheless, Petuchowski readily admits that the sparse attendance at so many synagogue services in our day would seem to indicate that the concept of prayer as an obligation has largely lost its hold upon the modern Jew. What, then, does one do with the element of obligation, without which fewer worshipers would make their way to public services?

Petuchowski's answer is socio-psychological. He writes that ". . . time-honored and universal Jewish practice is itself a source of obligation—even in instances where the purely human origin of a given practice is clearly recognized and admitted and where no claim of a direct divine revelation is being made."[10] Loyalty to the Jewish tradition, Petuchowski says, is a value in itself and a spur to the continuation of practices and contents even when we are not convinced of their cogency. By praying from a liturgy with some of which we might be uncomfortable but that possesses the sanctity of the ages, we thereby contribute to Jewish survival. Petuchowski hesitates to give a forthright answer to the question as to whether the Jewish prayer tradition can be preserved in the long run by means of a hands-off policy. Prayer is not an heirloom or artifact to be placed on a shelf, to be taken down occasionally for dusting off and polishing. Rather it is a living expression of a people with feelings and aspirations. True, every generation must come to terms with its ancestry, for the latter has conditioned its character and provided it with the impulse to dream its own dreams. But is it the respectful thing to do to leave the heritage fallow, unplowed and unseeded? Should not the sense of obligation also be accompanied by respect for our own convictions in addition to a pious gratitude for our creative ancestors? We, like them, must build on the foundations raised by those who have preceded us, but we, like them, must replace the bricks that we know are no longer serviceable. Petuchowski sometimes gives the impression of believing that the discipline of common prayer can be maintained indefinitely without giving major consideration to the conscious needs and the conscience of the contemporary, critical worshiper. It may be that there are and always will be Jews whose devotion to ancestors outweighs their own moral and intellectual integrity. But as long as this spirit characterizes many worshipers, mature and open-minded Jews will continue to absent themselves from public worship. They will find little incentive to join the congregation of worshipers.

There is another perspective in which the obligation to pray must be seen. Petuchowski is on solid ground when he claims that prayer cannot be spontaneous alone. It requires practice. The occasional stimulus to prayer can easily lead to frustration if the person has had no experience in translating sudden need into prayerful expression. Like any other skill, prayer requires training. "The ability to pray with which we have been endowed is an ability which we can develop further by actually engaging in the act of praying regularly. But it is also an ability which may atrophy because we do not sufficiently make use of it. In this respect, it is like most other abilities."[11] The habit of prayer has to transcend all considerations of content. Whether the liturgy be completely traditional or riddled with changes and additions, worshipers cannot afford to wait for the moment when they "feel like praying."

By absenting themselves from community worship, Jews lose out on several preconditions of effective prayer. They lose touch with their fellows who look to them for support in their hour of pain, grief, or happiness, just as they would miss the presence of others were they to fail them under similar circumstances. The absentee from regular prayer loses the inspiration, however rare, that springs out of the prayer book, when the ancient words suddenly reveal unsuspected meaning. Missed also is the rich vocabulary that binds together all generations of the Jewish people, that creates a mood appropriate to the human search for God and for self, and that makes available the mental tools to be employed in that quest. Without the routine of prayer, precious moments of spiritual enthusiasm are lost. The average person does not know what to do with such moments, let alone find ways of expressing what is in his or her heart. All this, inherent in Petuchowski's message, should be borne in mind by those who believe that nothing is to be gained by trying to become part of the praying community.

However, Petuchowski does not deal with the obverse side of the coin. Do not worshipers who are impelled by a feeling of obligation also suffer by acceding to a routine that often stifles their search for meaning? Are they not deprived of time that they could spend in expanding their knowledge or animating their soul by delving into spiritually elevating texts or engaging in worthwhile conversation with family and friends? Do they not play the role of hypocrites by lending their strength to an institution about whose future they have serious doubts? Why should they not seek some other outlet for their spirituality? The answer is that only a few scattered persons really care enough to look for a replacement for synagogue worship. Hence, in practice, the choice for the person who attends synagogue out of a sense of obligation has to be between complete passivity and the endeavor to uncover whatever riches lie buried in the recital in community of the ancient words of address to God.

Let us remind ourselves of the fact that prayer is only one phase—although the crucial one—in the worship of God. Every prayer service is composed of other forms of expression that are directed to animating and interesting the congregants. Petuchowski calls these aspects of the service entertainment, and he traces their employment back to biblical times. For instance, no one can doubt that music is indispensable in community worship. However, as Petuchowski rightly remarks, it ". . . is there for the entertainment of the worshiper rather than as a requirement of the Deity."[12] Although the music of prayer in the traditional synagogue has been restricted for two millenia to vocal (male) renditions, it was developed on a grand scale in the First and Second Temples. Instrumental music and mixed choruses are described in biblical passages and elaborated in the Talmud. Following the destruction of the Second Temple in 70 C.E., the use of musical instruments was discontinued in worship services, and under the restraints of the puritanical attitude that the Sages developed toward women, female voices were excluded from the evolving synagogue service. This ban, however, should be construed as an attempt to safeguard the people from the licentiousness that characterized other groups in ancient times. It was not a rebellion against the esthetic element in life, in general, and in prayer, in particular. As Petuchowski emphasizes, "Voice, ear, nose, eye, palate and hand, all of them, in one way or another, are involved in the performance of the religious rites of Judaism."[13]

Our tastes may differ from those of our ancestors, but we cannot deny that prayer for them was adorned with many ornaments that engaged all the senses and were intended to honor God with beauty. Equally, though, they were intended to delight the worshipers. *Hiddur mitzvah,* the esthetic embellishment of a ritual, is one of the unique perceptions of the halakhic tradition. It takes into account the need to attend to the side benefits that may accompany the performance of a meritorious or necessary ritual act. For instance, we humans differ from other creatures in converting the biological act of eating into a spiritual and esthetic experience. Although they are irrelevant to the biological need of ingestion, the preparation of palatable foods, the decorative setting of the table, the recital of grace, and the observance of rules of politeness—all these add flavor to the fulfillment of a physiological need.

Petuchowski entitles this propensity for esthetic embellishment of worship "entertainment," because its purpose is to titillate the worshipers during their prayers. Jewish liturgy even contains a strain of play. Petuchowski cites some of the medieval *piyyutim*, religious poems, that were composed not only as prayers but as riddles and intellectual exercises that were meant to arouse the interest of the congregants. Undoubtedly, entertainment and play become the attractions for many a synagogue Jew. Petuchowski, however, cautions against misplaced emphasis on these features of community worship that are extraneous to the main function of prayer. He indicates that just as there are rules to every game, so must the entertainment and play that we append to public prayer be circumscribed by appropriate modes of guidance.

Petuchowski bases his approach to the rules of Jewish prayer on the assumption that it is a stage in a process dating back to the sacrificial cult. While the form of sacrifice has been outgrown, the idea behind the Temple cult still suffuses the prayer service. Petuchowski states his position, as follows: "The modern synagogue stands in succession to the ancient Temple. That is why, in addition to all of its other functions, the synagogue must aim to provide the modern Jew with the kind of spiritual and religious outlet which his ancestors found in the Jerusalem shrine. And that includes, in addition to legitimate 'entertainment' and social 'relevance,' a service 'to be performed in faith and obedience,' an opportunity of performing the *mitzvah* of prayer, and a liturgical framework which possesses something of the permanence of the old continual burnt-offerings."[14] The idea, then, is that Jewish worship, embodied in a long-evolving liturgy, is a special kind of game that ". . . has its rules—rules which 'are absolutely binding and allow no doubt.' "[15]

In recounting another person's philosophy, we must try to think along with him or her. Only then may we criticize. So we have to ask ourselves why Petuchowski, who was clearly not an Orthodox Jew, was so concerned with the rules of the game and their permanence. The answer, I believe, is not hard to find. We have already noted that Petuchowski wanted to preserve as much as possible of the traditional liturgy. He was motivated by several considerations. One was the inherent quality of classical Jewish prayer, which deserves our respect. Another was his feeling that there is much spiritual richness in this liturgy that has yet to be extrapolated. A third consideration was Petuchowski's recognition that the sanctity and depth of modern creative prayers cannot match—or at least, have not yet equaled—those of the age-old liturgy. Yet Petuchowski himself, by indicating the importance of play, entertainment, relevance, and the like, shows that the prayer service needs revitalization—something that can only be accomplished by according change its proper place.

In stating the case as he does, Petuchowski puts us into a mental straitjacket. True, we should all play by the rules of the game. But why must the game remain always in the form to which we have become accustomed? The rules of public prayer are human conventions. As a game, prayer is no less a human creation than the sacrificial cult. We have to ask ourselves today whether or not prayer has to be conceived anew, and if so, what changes have to be made in the established rules. Petuchowski asks, how can we vitalize the tradition? But to complete the picture, he would also have had to attend more avidly than he did to revaluating the ancient liturgy. I suspect that like many other thinkers, particularly in the latter half of the twentieth century, Petuchowski was reluctant to press too hard on the literal meaning of the liturgy. Insisting on intellectual exactitude in the interpretation of the words of the siddur would necessitate not only altering the content of a significant number of prayers; it would also call into question some of the theological foundations of prayer, in general. Then, too, Petuchowski was reluctant to lose the emotional flavor of tradition and apparently thought that much of that quality would be lost by too much intellectualization. As we have

noted, he was prepared to license considerable poetic interpretation of the liturgical language.

Admittedly, Petuchowski argues well for the almost complete
retention of the ancient prayer book. Its faults and limitations can
be overcome, Petuchowski implies, by reading our ideas and ideals into the undisturbed text and by utilizing various play techniques to compensate for any doubts we might have. As against
this approach, I suggest that the problem cannot be solved this
easily. Petuchowski slides too facilely over the significance of the
absence from the synagogue of most Jews. Many of them are spiritually alert and prefer not to compromise their convictions for
the sake of what to them is a spurious group unity. Their concerns
have to be addressed, too. Many of these Jews, particularly in Israel, are conversant with the meaning and rules of the prayers but
are unprepared to recite them while overlooking their intent. At
best, the solution of Petuchowski can appeal to the minority of
Jews who constitute the mostly sparse congregations of contemporary Jewry. I do not claim that radical alterations of synagogue
worship will attract hordes to community prayer. But neither is
marking time a helpful stategy in confronting the crisis.

I hope I shall not be accused of equivocating if at this point I
declare that many of the knowledgeable abstainers from worship
in the synagogue are sometimes guilty of underestimating the
theological depth of the authors of the siddur. In spite of my
opinion that the nomenclature of prayer should be consonant
with the beliefs of the worshipers, I accept what inheres in Petuchowski's approach—namely, that before discarding or revising
the content or wording of the traditional liturgy, every effort
should be exerted to extract the last ounce of plausible meaning
and inspiration from the long-accepted prayers. A good example
of too hasty propensity to dismiss traditional concepts is the rejection of petitionary prayer. We can readily understand the reasoning of those who scoff at such supplications. The whole temper of
our modern, scientific age is to deny that there is a listening ear
or that a divine response could alter anything that would interfere
with the inherent order of the universe. However, does this critique of petitionary prayer exhaust its essence?

Petuchowski's answer is that "petitionary prayer does not convey any information to God, which He previously lacked, but it

affords you the relief of verbalizing, in His presence, whatever it is that you are striving for."[16] In other words, petition is observed to be one type of introspection, in which worshipers acknowledge that they must rely on a power beyond themselves in order to satisfy both their needs and their wants. Furthermore, when our petitions can find roots in what is sanctioned by tradition, our faith in the propriety of our purposes is strengthened, and we feel attuned to the demands of God or the cosmic order. In some instances, when we turn to the prescribed supplications of tradition, we find there horizons that we have not imagined in our own limited vision.

Private petitions tend to be egocentric. But those recited communally in a hallowed liturgy impel sincere worshipers to consider the needs and concerns of their fellows. At times, they are struck by the narrowness of their ego, and they are ashamed. Or, as they become aware of the broad experience of their ancestors, they realize that their dreams and aspirations are swept along in the steady stream of their people's view of reality. They are encouraged to reject those of their wants that bespeak a mean, unworthy perspective on the human condition. At the same time, they are buoyed up by the knowledge that many of their lacks are identical with those of the masses of their people and that they need not be reticent about proclaiming their deprivation. A prayer of petition is a way of raising to consciousness a person's resentments and purposes. By frank articulation, worshipers are then challenged to examine their values and the quality of their concerns and style of life.

These extrapolations of the implications of petitionary prayer are convincing, however, largely as a critique of naive supernaturalism. If one believes literally in a listening God who responds to the appeals of men and women, then the emphasis is placed not on the nature of one's needs but on the theological conundrums of divine response. Is it not silly for humans to alert God to human deficiencies that are surely known to Him? Is it not the height of arrogance to ask the all-powerful and omniscient Deity to revise His cosmic blueprint in order to satisfy a person's idiosyncratic wants? Petuchowski reminds us that these and similar reservations about prayers of petition disturbed the Sages. He cites examples that clearly indicate how the Rabbis perceived and responded to the danger of egocentrism. As an illustration, he quotes the following prayer of Rabbi Eliezer: "Do Thy will in heaven above, and grant equanimity to those who fear Thee below and do that which is good in Thine eyes. Blessed art Thou, O Lord, who hearest prayer."[17] No less than we, the ancients understood how ridiculous it is for anyone to place himself at the center of the universe. Therefore, in sober moments, they would recognize that they had to be subservient to God and not expect Him to change His mind at the behest of any mortal.

Petuchowski subtly shifts our focus from the God who answers prayer to man who becomes aware of having to expand his spiritual horizons. However, since humans individually are self-centered and collectively self-interested, Petuchowski argues for the retention of the fixed set of wide-ranging petitionary prayers. Since these requests often conflict with each other—one family wants a sunny day for its picnic, while the farmer pleads for rain to water his fields—God's answer cannot be the kind of "yes" or "no" that anti-religionists frequently ridicule. Petuchowski maintains that ". . . my very ability to pray shows me that I am 'in tune' with the divine will, that I am assured of divine help in my striving for the realization of the goals formulated in my prayers."[18] Petuchowski engages in a sleight of hand. He ignores the possibility that some of the traditional petitions are really not in tune with divine ordinance but instead are misguided wants of imperfect men. The prayer for triumph over enemies might conceal a chauvinistic streak in one's people that can be uprooted only in defeat. The wish for the restoration of the Davidic dynasty, even when taken as an appeal for sovereignty but not for the return to monarchy, might mark a rejection of the ethnic pluralism that should characterize a liberal, democratic state. Where does God stand in political matters of the type just mentioned? Surely it is a dangerous bit of theologizing to view the uncritical recital of traditional petitions as putting the congregation into harmony with God's will. Traditional petitionary prayer is not the simplistic request to God uttered by egotists, but neither can its approximation of God's will be ascertained merely by stating it is so. My ability to recite the prescribed petitions might be indicative of my desire to be at one with my fellow worshipers, but it is no proof of my being in tune with the will of God.

To pray for knowlege would seem to be not only a human disposition but an expression of the power humans need in order to
perceive and obey God's will. Such a prayer is the first petition in
the Eighteen Benedictions and concludes with praise of God as
the Giver of knowledge. Petuchowski interprets this apposition of
petition and praise as an indication that prayer is answered not
by what happens to the solitary individual but by the grace that is
bestowed upon the whole of society as a result of the granting of
wisdom and cognitive power to favored individuals. While it is
theologically understandable to credit God with apportioning to
humans distinctive skills, one is dubious about the cogency of a
theology that must then also attribute to God the deprivation suffered by many humans who are denied the simplest power of autonomy and self-maintenance. We may praise God as the
Dispenser of knowledge, but is there any point to praying to a
supernatural God to distribute the divine largesse more equitably
or, better, more humanely?

Petuchowski's hymn to the great insights of the traditional liturgy deserves our attention and commendation, but not without
serious reservations regarding his theology. He is too much of a
modernist to ignore the doubts that are raised today about the
efficacy of prayer. But he is too enamored of the tradition to treat
it with the "radical criticism" it needs if the canons of intellectual
honesty are to be respected in the synagogue. One is likely to
be suborned into acquiescence to partial truth when one accepts
without second thought what Petuchowski has to say, for example,
about the dual role of praise and supplication in the petitionary
prayers in the middle section of the Eighteen Benedictions. Petuchowski writes that these prayers ". . . praise God for what He has
done, for what He can do, and for what He will do. And the recipients of God's 'answer' are mentioned in the plural, not in the
singular. The individual thus learns to look upon himself as a part
of the whole faith-community of Israel. The concerns and the
woes of his people become his own woes and concerns, even as
the hopes and aspirations of the group become those of the individual. In the process, the individual Jew begins to see his own
needs from a larger perspective—a perspective which enables
him, even in moments of personal distress, to praise God as well
as to petition Him, to thank as well as to plead."[19] This is all well

and good as long as one is prepared to ignore or to twist the meaning of the plea to destroy the heretics or the request for the restoration of the Davidic dynasty. Do petitions such as these express the "hopes and aspirations" of the Jewish people? Are those Jews who take exception to such expressions less pious or dedicated to the pursuit of truth than those who read what they wish into the words? Prayer becomes trivialized if it fails to address itself forthrightly to the questions that disturb worshipers and help them express honestly their profoundest beliefs.

Much traditional prayer lacks meaning for average worshipers. Then too, the liturgy often requires them to suspend their desire to be honest. They recite notions about which they have doubts or with which they disagree. Yet they persist in repeating the formulas. Why? Probably because of what Petuchowski perceives as their loyalty to the Jewish people or because it is the emotion generated by prayer that is the key factor in communal worship. This is most evident in the case of Jews in the Diaspora, who, by and large, do not understand the Hebrew text. But even Israel Jews often lack the background to appreciate the structure of the siddur or the meaning below the surface of the words.

In the Diaspora, prayer in the vernacular is necessary in order to introduce as much meaning as possible into the service. Nevertheless, as Petuchowski observes, most interpolations into and translations of the liturgy lack the emotional force of traditional prayers in Hebrew, whose meaning the congregants rarely comprehend. How to navigate between the cognitive and emotional aspects of prayer is nothing new. The Sages, mystics, and philosophical rationalists all wanted worshipers to understand what they say to God, and many of them preferred prayer in the vernacular to the meaningless gibberish of the Jew who might be able to read the Hebrew letters but has not the slightest inkling of their meaning. Admittedly, however, Petuchowski sees the other side of the coin. For the learned Jew, there is everything to gain and little to lose in praying in Hebrew. Probably the only advantages of the vernacular for the scholar in the Diaspora would be to enable him or her to keep in touch with the less erudite congregants and here and there to gain added insight into the Hebrew original. In congregations accustomed to supplementing the service with additional readings, many of which are composed in the vernacular, there, too, the scholar might find inspiration that would be lacking in a Hebrew translation of the same text.

For the non-Hebraist who is nonetheless a devoted Jew, Hebrew prayer, Petuchowski declares, offers ". . . a very 'special' kind of communication. It carries the overtones of eternity, the intimations of a transcendent reality—just because its sounds do not translate themselves, for him, into any objective references to mundane existence."[20] Undoubtedly, Petuchowski has hit upon an element in the worship experience without which even the most value-laden and profoundly meaningful words cannot stir the heart. Indeed, words can sometimes interfere between worshipers and their apprehension of the transcendent reality of God that stimulates them to prayer and that is, at the same time, the outcome they desire. Obviously, we need both cognitive and emotional experiences in group worship, but one cannot be purchased at the expense of the other.

Finally, Petuchowski asks the crucial question, "Can modern man pray?" His answer, for the Jew, is concentrated in four sentences. "For prayer is not the shutting of one's eyes to reality. It is the glimmer, the intimation, the daring which leads to the transcending of reality. Not all men, ancient or modern, have had the courage and the vision to do so. But those who established and carried on the classical tradition of Jewish prayer always did."[21] Like any other faculty of humans, prayer, while natural, has to be cultivated. For some persons, it is easy and necessary to pray; others seem not to require the practice. They might even view it as a kind of spiritual appendix best left untouched.

The determination to pray or not is dependent upon one's theology. Supernaturalists, confronted by the problem of theodicy, either lose their faith and the ability to pray, or they join wholeheartedly in the Jewish tradition of demanding an answer from God as to why there is evil. The naturalist, too, can either conclude that prayer is a farce or that it is a method of gaining a wiser perspective on the human condition than is available to the nonworshiper. In any case, Petuchowski points out, the argument for prayer is profound. Briefly, he cites the following: (1) Since the synagogue service is a poetic creation, it has to be studied. It should not be expected that it will always be appreciated. But the potential is always there. (2) It should not be expected that every prayer will appeal to individuals or to their fellows in the same way or with the same force at all times. (3) The power of God and the ability of humans to contribute to the quality of life are two sides of the same coin. Self-praise of humankind is idolatry when taken in isolation from the ultimate sovereignty of God. (4) In prayer, humans acknowledge that evil is in some way a part of God's working in the world. It is shallow and ignorant for humans to reject God because they cannot solve the riddle of evil. Prayer enables them to remain positive toward life despite their doubts.

I shall return to some of Petuchowski's questions in the final chapter, but I shall end this summary of his penetrating analysis of the subject with his statement that "the reach of prayer may and should outdistance the grasp of our philosophical and theological definitions. God, to be God, must be greater than our concepts of Him. But true prayer cannot very well voice strivings and aspirations which run counter to the very nature of God as we conceive of Him. This seems to be the profound truth behind the Rabbinic requirement that the creedal element of the Jewish worship service, i.e., the recitation of the *Shema* and its Benedictions precede the prayer of petition."[22]

Whether or not one agrees with Petuchowski's analysis or with some of his affirmations, one has to appreciate his achievement in outlining the problem of prayer in an essay covering only sixty-three pages.

NOTES

1. Jakob J. Petuchowski, *Understanding Jewish Prayer* (New York: Ktav, 1972), p. 3.

2. Ibid., p. 5.

3. Ibid., p. 6.

4. Jakob J. Petuchowski, *Prayerbook Reform in Europe* (New York: World Union for Progressive Judaism, 1968), p. xii.

5. Ibid., p. 351.

6. *Understanding Jewish Prayer*, pp. 11–12.

7. Ibid., p. 14.

8. Ibid., p. 15.

9. Petuchowski criticizes the extremes to which some of the nineteenth-century Reformers went in their zeal to modernize the prayer

book. He describes the siddur as combining ". . . past, present, and future, accompanying the Jew on his strange and lonely path through history—always, and under all circumstances, having something appropriate to say to him. The Reformers of the nineteenth century frequently failed to see that dimension of the *siddur,* and, failing to see it, they deprived themselves and their children of some of the inner strength which comes from an awareness of historical continuity" (*Prayerbook Reform in Europe,* p. 351).

10. *Understanding Jewish Prayer,* p. 22.
11. Ibid., p. 23.
12. Ibid., p. 27.
13. Ibid., p. 28.
14. Ibid., p. 33.
15. Ibid., p. 34.
16. Ibid., p. 37.
17 Ibid., p. 36.
18. Ibid., p. 40.
19. Ibid., p. 42.
20. Ibid., p. 48.
21. Ibid., p. 56.
22. Ibid., pp. 65–66.

9

Eugene B. Borowitz

THE SIDDUR has always been subject to change, albeit mostly in the form of additions. It is a living classic, not only by virtue of its uninterrupted use but because it breathes the vitality of the Jewish people. If, then, we are to address ourselves to the current crisis in prayer, we cannot rest with the foregoing chapters, all of which deal with thinkers who are no longer with us. There are many living persons who have important observations to make about the state of Jewish prayer, but I limit myself to two men *(yibadlu l'hayyim arukim)* whose thought on worship I consider to be most suggestive. In addition to them, I must also examine some of the questions and responses of feminist theologians and liturgists who have undoubtedly opened a new era in the history of worship and prayer.

This chapter will be devoted to Eugene B. Borowitz (b. 1924), who has taught theology and Jewish thought for many years at Hebrew Union College–Jewish Institute of Religion, in New York City, and has to his credit a long list of publications covering a wide range of subjects. His formal reflections on prayer are mostly connected with his membership on or chairmanship of ideological committees of the Central Conference of American Rabbis, for whom he was asked to prepare commentary. In addition, however, Borowitz scatters many important comments on prayer throughout his many works. I take Borowitz seriously, because his theological statement focuses our attention on the nature and relevance of the entire enterprise of worship.

Borowitz knows that "... one may not expect to find in Judaism one systematically integrated idea of God."[1] At the same time, "An idea of God that will not let men speak to him or let him be of help ... in meeting the varied experiences of life is not an idea for Jews."[2] Thus, the criterion for an acceptable Jewish idea of God "... cannot be intellectual, for in Judaism thought, as aggadah, is essentially free. The standards must come instead from the primary realm, that of action or life. It must, because of the centrality of Torah, be a functional criterion, not an intellectual one."[3] It is to determining the nature of this functional relationship between man and God, between the Jewish individual and God, and between the Jewish people and God that Borowitz has devoted much of his serious theologizing.

Borowitz designates his position as "Covenant theology." While he believes that the Covenant between God and Israel is unique, he regards the dialogue between humans and God as a universal phenomenon, to which he applies the term "covenant," in lowercase. He tries to preserve the traditional Jewish claim to a special association with God, while endeavoring simultaneously to avoid denying other religions their claims to authentic experiences of God. What, then, is Covenant theology?

Throughout his unending search, Borowitz formulates and reformulates his meaning. A few examples will illustrate both his certainty that he has hit upon a satisfactory theological foundation for prayer and for other facets of the Jewish religious outlook. It is pertinent to add that Borowitz is careful to acknowledge the tenuousness of all theologizing, including his own.

In one of his earliest works, Borowitz writes: "Whatever the Jew understands by God, it must make some kind of Covenant between God and Israel possible; it must make Israel's continuing dedication to him reasonably significant; it must explain Israel's suffering and make it possible for the individual Jew to intertwine his destiny and that of his people."[4] Further on in the same volume, Borowitz adds the note that the Covenant confers a special mission on Israel. "Its purpose was to remind all mankind of him until they came to know him too, to acknowledge him as their God and to live by his law."[5] As we shall see, Borowitz has great difficulty reconciling this divinely ordained mission with his rejection of Israel's election as a sign of superior cosmic status. Surely, moral and spiritual responsibility falls upon all peoples, for the universal divine-human covenant presupposes the equality of humankind. All are commanded to overcome their creaturely weaknesses and fulfill their assigned human obligation. That duty is always to act in partnership with God, in accordance with His will. God and all humans must act together in order to transform and repair the world.[6] What, then, is the difference between covenant and Covenant?

Nevertheless, Borowitz surmises that Israel's Covenant has to be both historically and theologically unique. The former prerequisite is easily handled, inasmuch as no one can deny that the history of every nation is idiosyncratic. But if Israel is assigned a special role by God, then that uniqueness is converted into a privilege. In one way or another, the Covenant has to be dated back to the Sinaitic theophany. Borowitz acknowledges that ". . . if nothing really happened at Sinai, if nothing could have happened at Sinai, then for all its intellectual utility, the Covenant theory is meaningless."[7] Borowitz's answer to his own question is misleading. It dismisses the possibility that what did take place was the attribution to God's revelation of a system of values and a humanly enacted body of law that had gained divine authority among the Israelites. At Sinai, if indeed there was such a historical moment, it is altogether possible that a great leader like Moses could have convinced his people that their tradition, together with his own additions, came from on high. This naturalistic explanation seems to me more reasonable than the selection of Israel as God's instrument. However, it does not, in and of itself, lessen the authority of the Torah. That authority, even in Borowitz's development of the Covenant, must rest on whether or not the supposed content of revelation really represents God's will for Israel and the rest of humanity. In the same way, all the nations must prove the divinity of their covenants, not by mere assertion but by substantiating rationally and experientially their moral and spiritual claims. The appeal to Sinai turns out to be a question and not an answer.

Questioning, however, is of enormous importance in theology, as it is in all mental disciplines. Borowitz faults theological liberals for underestimating the reality of God and letting the pendulum swing too far in the direction of faith in man. How can we humans, with all our failings, remain faithful to God's will unless we are partners with a transcendent God. "Being God's partners, we have great power and we should exercise it. Yet we live not as isolated selves or merely as a special sort of animal, but as people linked to God, thereby having personal access to the final standard for all human action."[8] Borowitz poses the right questions.

He is worried about two aspects of the divine-human relationship. He fears human pride, and at the same time, he realizes that religious history is replete with mistaken notions about God's commands. He also recognizes the need for continuity of and loyalty to law, but he refuses to relinquish human autonomy in judging facts and in making value judgments.

Borowitz finds the most satisfactory, but not complete basis for his response to these questions in the thinking of Martin Buber and Franz Rosenzweig. Each of these men regard Torah as created by people, ". . . but only in response to a real God who stands over against them."[9] But while Buber knows that Torah, or God's will, is a communal as well as individual responsibility, he fails to integrate our individual love of God and the historical experience of God of the Jewish people. In the opinion of Borowitz, Buber places too much emphasis on the individual's sense of rightness. This accounts for the tendency toward antinomianism, of which Buber has been accused by so many critics and which Borowitz, too, finds unsatisfactory. Borowitz looks for a solution that is ". . . more than ethics and less than Orthodox Halachah."[10]

Borowitz has wrestled with this problem throughout his career. In 1977, he formulated his answer, as follows: "My own solution comes . . . in ending the split between one's self and one's Jewishness. When one is no longer a person who also is a member of the people of Israel but is, at the core of one's being an integrated Jew-human, then the gap between 'what I personally must do' and 'what the Jews need to do' falls away. That is not the same as saying that God gives us a law that all of us can know objectively. I do not believe God gives or has given such a Torah. . . . I believe Torah arises from the relationship between God and the Jewish people, the Covenant, and that I and other Jews are the living bearers of the relationship."[11]

I sympathize with Borowitz, as he tries to sail through these murky theological waters, but I am disturbed by his inability to clarify the meaning of the God-human relationship. He alludes to this relationship as one of love. Love certainly entails the mutual acceptance of obligations on the part of both partners, but in a human love affair the lover and the beloved address each other and learn to agree on their respective duties. In the course of a human love relationship, novelty of expression often occurs, but its appropriateness is subject to the reaction of the other. This confrontation of lover and beloved is far different in the case of God's love of humankind and human love of God. Undoubtedly, the relationship is impossible without the ability of human beings to transcend themselves and to develop guiding standards of thinking and conduct. However, those standards are no less humanly invented, even if we declare them to be an outgrowth of our relationship with God.

Borowitz tries to solve part of the problem by asserting that the Covenant is between God and an entire people, thereby eliminating some of the mistakes that characterize individual or single generational claims to experiencing God or appropriating His will. Borowitz defends his position on the role of peoplehood in the Covenant by attacking Mordecai Kaplan for what he claims is the latter's exaltation of ethnicity almost to the point of idolatry. Even if the charge were true—which it is not in view of Kaplan's repeated declarations that God is transcendent and that both the individual and the group must beware of playing the god— Borowitz does not help us to explain how we know when God has spoken. Kaplan can at least appeal to rational criteria that he knows are never absolute and always subject to refinement and correction.

Still bothered by the problem of apprehending God, Borowitz tries another formulation of how the Covenant comes about. In 1990, he writes: "I conceptualize the Covenant in relational and personalistic terms rather than the more familiar contractual, ethnic or (neo-Kantian) ethical ones. I place a heavy emphasis on the human role in the Covenant without thereby, I devoutly hope, demeaning the active involvement of an independent, other God, the senior partner in our intimate association."[12] From this statement, we infer that Borowitz locates the Covenant in the mind—or perhaps more clearly—in the feeling of the individual that he or she has somehow received a message from God. Earlier descriptions by Borowitz of the important role played by Jewish national tradition in the genesis and evolution of the Covenant seem here to become less pertinent. Instead, Buber's relationism and personalism seem to supercede Borowitz's prior assertion that Jews must see their individuality and their Jewishness as identical or at least as inseparable.

Futhermore, it is difficult to understand what Borowitz has gained by his rejection of the familiar contractual, ethnic, or ethical conception of Covenant in favor of his relational or personalistic one. By declaring God to be other, Borowitz has introduced a senior partner, but he has given us no hint as to how individual Jews are supposed to perceive their role in the partnership. By underplaying the contractual, ethnic, and ethical approaches, he has left himself and us with the grave problem of how to escape a complete subjectivism. It will not do for Borowitz to beguile us by asserting that the Covenant should be conceived as ". . . less a contract spelled out from on high than a loving effort to live in reciprocal respect."[13] For in order to live in mutual respect, it is essential that both parties have adequate access to one another. God, however, seems reluctant to share divine prerogatives with us humans. So, since Borowitz has found rational methods of locating God to be weak reeds, he is forced to turn to a defense of revelation, albeit with careful dialectical affirmation of the human role. "By turning God's revelation into mere human growth and self-determination, it [liberal religion] helped destroy our faith in stable human values and made us prey to moral anarchy."[14] At the same time, Borowitz cautions against returning uncritically to old paradigms of revealed religion with their apodictic but frequently false or immoral (to a modernist's way of thinking) rules for human behavior.

Borowitz's caveat is insufficient to conceal his rather cavalier handling of faith in human growth. By his insertion of "mere," he wants to leave the impression that the advances produced by the human mind are not as substantial as those resulting from revelation. But there is the rub. Human growth is self-corrective in a way inapplicable to divine revelation, unless, of course, the truth of supposed revelation is subject to the judgment that we associate with genuine human growth. For is not the essence of that growth the ability to approximate truth more accurately and to discover mistakes and sins with greater perceptiveness and sensitivity? Human advance is not unilinear, and anyone who thinks otherwise has no understanding of the dynamics of existence. Human growth is an enormous achievement and not a "mere" indication of how wrong the wisest of men or women can be. We return, then, to square one. Before Covenant can become a useful basis for the satisfying theology that Borowitz seeks with his consummate honesty, he will have to find a way to overcome the human proneness to err, whether the point of departure be the claim to have received a revelation or the articulation of some human reading of reality.

I venture to suggest one line of thinking that might be fruitful for Borowitz to follow. It is based on his remark that ". . . when we seek God as a partner in every significant act we invest our deciding and doing with direction, worth, hope, and, in failure, the possibility of hope."[15] Here, it seems to me, Borowitz has stated the issue clearly. If I understand him aright, he is saying that humble humans, in their perception of reality, must always attend to their limited reach. There is, on the one hand, a realm of transcendence on which humans are ultimately dependent but that they can only partially and uncertainly penetrate. Nevertheless, humans have good reason to hope that their efforts to transcend their state of ignorance and to correct their current mistakes have every chance of success. This kind of relationship with transcendence, I maintain, is appropriate to what humans know about themselves and the possibility of their limited fulfillment. If humans are willing to be satisfied with the modest salvation that seems to be achievable by mortal beings, then covenant, as the human endeavor at self-transcendence, has a chance.

In 1980, Borowitz defines the core of Jewish religion. He declares: "The axis, the pivot of Jewish religion is not the idea of God but the life of Torah. The root religious experience of Judaism is not escape from sin or suffering. It is the positive sense of hearing God's commandment to the people of Israel and its single selves."[16] Action, not abstract thought or theory, is the Jewish way. Borowitz thus reverses the direction that Reform Judaism had taken, away from the halakhic mood. He concedes that traditionalists also agree that Jewish law is not only inspired by God but also contains a large measure of human input and convention. But whereas the traditionalists attribute greater weight to divine inspiration, ". . . liberals see Jewish law . . . as an exercise in human spirituality."[17] Liberalism ". . . places far more trust in human power than does Orthodoxy but gives far more place to God than did classic religious liberalism."[18] In other words, Borowitz, like many of his Reform colleagues, now probes the Halakhah for its divine inspiration concerning what the Jewish people *knows* [Borowitz's term][19] God wants of it. However, both Borowitz's liberals and the Orthodox are caught up in the same difficulty of having to substantiate their claim to know God's will. The Covenant liberals are no better off theologically than the traditional halakhists if they believe that God has somehow revealed Himself fully to humankind. They can only claim a greater modesty, in that they grant other peoples their covenants and acknowledge more willingly that human perceptions of God's revelation are sometimes mistaken.[20] But the basic problem remains as to how the divine partner is recognizable when it is human consciousness and reflection that are at the root of all explanations.

Before turning directly to Borowitz's reflections on prayer, it will be helpful to quote one more statement, which is a fairly complete summary of major aspects of his Covenant proposal: "For liberalism, the law is created by the people of Israel as a result of standing in Covenant with God. For them, the Jewish tradition is essentially a human invention. This is saved from simple humanism because the tradition arises not out of the people's sense of self but from its recognition that it is bound to God. It seeks to be true to itself by doing God's will as best the people of Israel can understand it. In this construction of chosenness, then, people play a self-determining, autonomous role; they are their own lawmakers. They are also God's partners as part of the Household of Israel's historic devotion to the Covenant. Hence their freedom is conditioned by God's reality and Jewish community and tradition, a situation which makes spiritual anarchy hardly conceivable and an eccentric Jewish practice unlikely."[21] Enough has been said by me in regard to most of the points in this summary to make superfluous further comment on the Covenant. It is time to present Borowitz's contribution to divine-human relationship in prayer.

Borowitz has not yet written systematically about prayer, but there are enough passages on the theme scattered throughout his corpus to enable us to piece together his overall philosophy of worship, including that branch we know as prayer. Moreover, as I have indicated, Borowitz's theology of Covenant virtually implies that men and women are constantly in quest of genuinely prayerful dialogues with God. Covenant (whether in lower- or upper-case), causes humans to pray or acts as a prerequisite of their ability to establish contact with God.

Life with God, or covenant relationship with Him, means, according to Borowitz, ". . . a life of prayer, one in which we can speak of God out of the fullness of what we are and long for, expecting to be inspired by God's own strength and trusting that, if not now, we shall soon know God's answering concern."[22] Note that Borowitz refers to speaking *of* God, not *to* Him, Her, or any more sexually neutral object of worship. I do not wish to press the point too vociferously, because Borowitz has said enough to indicate that his relational theology implies the possibility of experiencing God. Men and women, Borowitz would say, are not limited to talking *about* God. Nonetheless, the wording here indicates that being aware of God and claiming a personal relationship with the Deity are not the same as declaring that God is to be conceived as being, in some manner, a Person who can be addressed in terms analogous to those of human dialogue. Prayer cannot be considered to be a form of verbalization, at least from the divine side. "God speaks" in ways other than those of human language.

I believe that Borowitz is correct when he surmises that each human being chooses his or her philosophical stance—pragmatist, phenomenological, idealist, or whatever—on a prerational level. That is to say, those of us who prefer to be rationalists do so, at least initially, not because we have come to this conclusion after a careful analysis of the intellectual options, but because of some compelling intuition or temperamental bent. This prerationalism, however, cannot be permitted to run riot, and each person is called upon repeatedly to justify the method and content of his or her thinking. Borowitz, indeed, tries to do just that. In true academic fashion, he first dismisses Hermann Cohen's idealistic ethics and Mordecai Kaplan's "humanocentrism." One cannot pray to an idea; nor does communion with one's better—or best—self seem to offer inspiring or very profound approaches to prayer. Instead, Borowitz associates himself ". . . with the many who believe our moral gropings testify to a reality that so transcends us in stature and quality that it rightly sets an independent standard for our behavior."[23] Once again, we come upon the muddle of transcendence. I shall not repeat here my assessment of the way in which Cohen and Kaplan regarded transcendence, but I shall try to be as respectful of Borowitz's view on the subject as he is of these two diverse thinkers.

Borowitz is right in searching for as objective a standard of human behavior as he can find. Cohen and Kaplan played the same game, as must every hunter of truth and goodness. Furthermore, an objective standard must, in some way, be both transcendent and other. If human judgment were totally independent and autonomous, how could we possibly differentiate between subjectivity and objectivity? Indeed, how could one escape from solipsism? Borowitz is dissatisfied with theologies that he claims project God as if Deity were an emanation from humans. However, who, except for that rare absolute philosophical idealist, would maintain that reality is identical with or a simple extension of a subjective state? Cohen might be faulted for exaggerating the extent to which reality is idea; Kaplan can be caught up when he occasionally permits his moral passion to outrun the actual pace of human progress. But neither of these men should be misunderstood as believing that truth or goodness can be apprehended as solely immanent categories. What humans define as true or good is refracted through the prism of their minds and is given currency in human discourse. But the ultimate referent of this discourse is not a human creation. All that we humans can do is continue to search for the truth and goodness that seem always to escape our full and accurate comprehension. Hence, covenant theology can no more provide humans with communion with God or apprehension of divine will than any other form of worshipful appeal. All men and women stand in judgment before the bar of transcendent reality.

Borowitz, however, wants the comforting warmth of the prayer to which there is a personal response, the surety that God can and will bring about the Messianic Day—in short, all the benefits that the "old-time religion" promises to the true believer. Borowitz, neverthless, remains a liberal. The promises will not be translated into reality without the heavy input of rational men and women for whom tradition is not absolutely binding. Prayer, too, cannot be merely a repetition of inherited liturgy. It has to be part of the flux of the nonrational encounter of humans with God. Yet

Borowitz eschews spiritual anarchism or antinomianism. Traditional norms cannot be dismissed or superseded whenever a person or a group experiences uncritically some moment of "enlightenment."

All the thinkers we examine in this book are at one in their realization that the synagogue is far from being the focal point of Jewish spirituality. "The synagogue," Borowitz writes, "instead of sensitizing persons, emphasizes decorum; instead of creating community, it builds institution; instead of changing society, it serves itself."[24] Yet the synagogue and its liturgy must continue to play their role as the fountainhead of Jewish worship. However, in order for that function to be performed effectively, the synagogue will have to recapture its former spontaneity, something that requires a fresh theology. That theology will have to heighten trust in the direct experience of God, much like the love relationship between human beings who accept one another unquestioningly. Love loses its spark when either the lover or the beloved takes to rationalizing his or her feelings. In a similar way, argues Borowitz, there is and has to be a nonrational side to worship that renders theologizing *about* God an unwarranted disturbance in the worship act.

Thus, the scheme that Borowitz sketches for us is based on skepticism about reason. Indeed, he says: "As we have learned to trust reason less, we have become more available to the direct experience of the holy."[25] Given Borowitz's commitment to liberal canons of human autonomy and respect for the ability of the mind to perceive error and to expand the horizons of knowledge, it is difficult to understand the antirationalism inherent in his approach to the holy. The explanation seems to be one of temperament. Apparently, the ordinary and the accessible have less appeal to him than the ineffable and the mysterious. It is not that Borowitz turns his back on the workings of reason; he is just dissatisfied with its accomplishments and wary of its pretensions.

Since the experience of love is so patently a nonrational phenomenon, why cannot access to the sacred be similarly elusive to reasoned analysis? The door is thus opened to the unmediated experience of God. I continue to have difficulty with this claim, because of its too facile analogy between human love and communion between humans and God. If, for example, prayer is at its

profoundest when mind and reason are bracketed and pure experience of God takes over, the rationalist has a right to question
the nature of that experience. He will not deny that worshipers
feel whatever they say they feel, but careful thinkers will want to
have more than mere assertion before they can be convinced that
communion with God has occurred. The nonrationalist comparison between the dynamics of human love and those of men and
women engaged in worship or supposedly encountering God
does not hold water. In human love, we reiterate, the two persons
are physically present to one another, a fact that enables them
to meet without rational purpose or the need of justification or
explanation. Not so when anyone maintains that he or she has
had a God-experience. Religion might be a love affair with God,
but just as parents would like to see their beloved son or daughter,
so do those of us who aspire to experience God want to hear more
than a declaration of success on the part of those who assert they
have met the divine Beloved.

There is another good reason, it seems to me, why Borowitz's
truncated form of rationalism should be questioned. Examine,
for instance, his remark that " . . . if Israel does not have some
special link with God, then Jews might just as well celebrate their
individual belief all by themselves. Private celebration will be not
only more convenient but less fraught with the risks of boredom
and personal irritation which are the steady threat of public worship."[26] Borowitz would have these two sentences constitute a syllogism—if . . . then. But his syllogism is faulty. In the first place,
every people has a special or unique relationship with God by
virtue of its special history and spiritual growth. The "if" is a
redundancy. But more significant is the implication that the need
for group worship is a function of the specialness. Nothing of the
sort. Prayer in a minyan or congregation of worship is meant to
fulfill needs that cannot be satisfied in solo worship. I repeat: only
in public worship can humans experience their equality before
God, an awareness that escapes them in the hurly-burly of everyday existence. It is only together with other members of their
people that individuals can sense what they share in common with
their fellows. Only in such a setting can the members of a group
rededicate themselves to the furtherance of their shared ideals.
Group prayer enables the worshipers to comfort one another in

their respective sorrows and to spread individual joy to the rest of the congregation. Personal and group prayers serve different, legitimate purposes. There is, indeed, a time to be alone and a time to be in company, in prayer as in other moments in life.

In interpreting the joy of the Shavuot festival, with its commemoration of the theophany at Mount Sinai, Borowitz remarks: "We rejoice not simply with one another but with him, for what we celebrate is that we know him and continue to serve him, and that of all human communities ours has been permitted to have had this intimate and continuing experience of him."[27] Jewish prayer, in other words, is distinguished by its articulation of the messages of Jewish history. It is by recalling and rehearsing the evocative events of the Jewish epic that Jews learn to know God. But this is not the same as saying that were it not for the privileged history of the Jewish people, individual Jews would have no reason to join the congregation of Israel at prayer. Borowitz disapproves of the theology of election, but he cannot divest himself of its mood of comparison and mission.

The fact is that Jewish prayer has always made room for both personal, solo expression and the more widely practiced recital of the group liturgy. The Psalms, the personal prayers of the *Tannaim* and *Amoraim,* the poetic expressions of medieval and modern piety and spirituality, the petitions and protests of sensitive souls have all articulated individual experiences. Many of them have captured the hearts of large numbers of Jews, and some have entered the pages of the siddur. "The man who prays in the synagogue prays as a participant in a Jewish history that continues into the living present, and his prayers, therefore, express the needs of the community in which he stands. . . . The individual Jew should seek to pray with a congregation. But if he cannot . . . then he may pray alone. Even alone, he should pray the congregational service . . . preferably at the time the congregation is praying."[28] Here we note another example of Borowitz's dialectical approach. He accepts the centrality of group prayer, but he also refuses to dispense with personal outpouring. He abhors the boredom of repetitive recital of liturgy, but he acknowledges the importance of keeping alive the age-old form and content of the prayer book.

These pendulum swings should not be construed as hesitation

or confusion. The ambivalence we have been describing is not Borowitz's alone. It is the problem faced by everyone who wishes to preserve the synagogoue and its contributions to worship and to the moral and spiritual sensitization of all Jews. It characterizes those who are also conscious that novelty is essential to *kavvanah*, to honesty, sincerity, and vital human growth.

As far as I can see, Borowitz has hardly attempted, as yet, to state a position on several issues that are entailed in trying to revitalize prayer—as, for instance, has been done by Lawrence A. Hoffman, the subject of our next chapter. But Borowitz has posed several of the central theological difficulties.

How are we to balance adhering to the Jewish liturgical tradition while also encouraging articulation of modern views of God, the cosmos, and humans? How are we to give voice to our criticism of traditional theodicy without undermining the faith of the average worshiper? How can we introduce variety and novelty into the synagogue service without trivializing the content of the prayers? Borowitz is biting in his criticism of some of the exaggerations of the urge for relevancy. He mocks those who think it possible—perhaps with the help of computers—to structure the service so as to take account of all the different emotions and intellects that worshipers bring with them to the synagogue. He and other liberal theologians do whatever they can to breathe life into the ancient text of the traditional prayer book. However, Borowitz has expressed himself most cogently in this area largely as chairman of a committee of the Central Conference of American Rabbis mandated to interpret and assess its important declaration—*Reform Judaism: A Centenary Perspective* (1976). I have already considered some of his observations about the *Centenary Perspective*. I add just a few more.

The semantics of prayer is a never-ending problem for liturgical authorities and laity alike. The traditional prayer book provides numerous terms for addressing God—YHWH, *Yah,* Our Father, Our King, *Makom, Adonai, Elohim, Kadosh,* and many others. Each name fits the mood of the particular prayer. Borowitz understands that the prayer book must speak in the idiom of the day, in the language that modern men and women understand and in which they most comfortably express their aspirations, hopes, and commitments. But he is critical about the tendency to overlook the emotional power of the traditional liturgy. He maintains that ". . . we are more likely to recognize God as a Process than as a Shepherd. Yet there is something in that ancient way of depicting God that still moves us, and it is not clear how many of our modern terms for God will survive for centuries, not to ask about millenia."[29] This problem, I believe, is not subject to a final solution. How could it be otherwise, seeing that every person reacts differently to key words on the basis of his or her education and unique experience? Moreover, one cannot expect a prosaic word, used in common parlance to communicate new information about reality—Process, Force, Power, Source of Energy, and the like—to compete with the hallowed language of the ages. Nonetheless, the traditional language also has its difficulties. How can one speak of God the Shepherd, after the Holocaust? How can one describe God as stretching the earth over the waters, when we moderns picture our globe differently and when we stand in awe of our vast, expanding universe? We need new, poetic ways to articulate our emotions. Borowitz is correct in stating the problem and indicating that we can only try to avoid shallowness.

He is correct, too, in explaining that worship cannot always be crystal clear to the worshiper. Prayer and other forms of worship are not acts of intellect alone. We cannot attend to every word in the liturgy, and we are carried along by the melodies of the service and by the cadence of the language. For Jews in the Diaspora, therefore, Borowitz pleads for as much Hebrew as possible, even if most Diaspora Jews are Hebraically illiterate and are unlikely to master enough of the language to understand more than scattered words. He comments: "Prayer should be heartfelt, but Jewish prayer includes joining one's heart with the hearts of one's people, and, through their words, to the hearts of those Jews who by their faithful continuity made possible one's own Jewish life."[30]

The semantic issue has become further complicated by the disclosure of the sexist composition of most traditional prayers. As the years go by, Borowitz attends increasingly to this challenge, which is simply one area of the total revolution in lifestyle occurring before our eyes. In his later writing, he strives to use gender-neutral terms, but he admits that convention is sometimes easier to follow. Nonetheless, the real problem is how to speak of and to God in non-anthropomorphic terms. All we can do, and here again Borowitz is frank, is to await the advent of poetic geniuses who will endow us or our offspring with greater insight into Deity and an ability to enter into more stirring communion with the Holy.

Universal covenant and Covenant for the Jews are the means by which all humans are said by Borowitz to confront and be confronted by God. I have accompanied Borowitz and indicated where I find it difficult to think as he does. There is, however, another strand in Borowitz's philosophy that offers, at least to me, a more congenial approach to prayer. He suggests: "If we have even a dim, troubled, barely verbalizable acknowledgment of an unshakable demand for value at the heart of the universe, one that we must, to remain human, answer and exemplify, then we have found our personal way to what our tradition in various ways called God."[31] Admittedly, my rationalist bias comes to the fore in arguing that Borowitz has touched on another way to regard prayer, a way that may not be suitable for all temperaments but will appeal to tough-minded men and women.

Borowitz notes that prayer begins with an inchoate feeling, amounting to an ineffable conviction, that we are commanded to adhere to a set of values. The source of these values is as mysterious as thought itself. They do not belong in the category of reason, although they have to be confirmed by rational experience. If we can somehow be convinced that our values are rooted in the moral structure of the universe, we have approximated what tradition calls belief in God. "God" and its synonyms are thus the terms that express our faith that our views of physical order and moral responsibility are no illusions, although they are only proximate and in need of constant correction. In the context of such an experiential theology, prayer revolves around two foci. The first is intellectual preparation. Before coming to worship, men and women must acquire a sense of reality. Each person, in accordance with his or her ability, must strive to divest himself or herself of false ideas about physical and human nature. To bring illusion and error into the synagogue is to risk the danger of silliness, or worse, idolatry. The second focus is the steps that can be taken, through the togetherness of congregational worship, to strengthen faith in the worthwhileness of continued striving for rationality and adherence to accepted and acceptable values and purposes. I believe that such an approach is implicit in much that Borowitz has written, but it is not spelled out. Instead, Borowitz gets tangled in Covenant theology, whose pitfalls I have sought to analyze. He wants to preserve the emotional warmth and confidence of traditional prayer without retreating from the advances of modern freedom, autonomy, and experience. He is suggestive and probably helpful to a lot of Jews, but the questions I have posed remain in force.

NOTES

1. Eugene B. Borowitz, *How Can a Jew Speak of Faith Today?* (Philadelphia: Westminster, 1969), p. 19.

2. Ibid., p. 21.

3. Ibid.

4. Ibid., p. 23.

5. Ibid., p. 83.

6. Eugene B. Borowitz, *Exploring Jewish Ethics* (Detroit: Wayne State University Press, 1990), pp. 150–151.

7. *How Can a Jew Speak of Faith Today?*, p. 71.

8. Eugene B. Borowitz, *Reform Judaism Today,* bk. 3 (New York: Behrman, 1983), pp. 166–167.

9. Ibid., bk 2, p. 130.

10. Ibid., p. 131.

11. Ibid., pp. 131–132.

12. *Exploring Jewish Ethics*, p. 478.

13. Eugene B. Borowitz, *Renewing the Covenant* (Philadelphia: Jewish Publication Society, 1991), p. 223.

14. Ibid., p. 238.

15. Ibid., p. 169.

16. *How Can a Jew Speak of Faith Today?*, p. 17.

17. Eugene B. Borowitz, *The Masks Jews Wear* (New York: Simon and Schuster, 1980), p. 232.

18. Ibid., p. 233.

19. Ibid., p. 232.

20. The liberals are no innovators in their reservations about the divine origin of certain biblical verses. The traditional commentators and theologians frequently departed from the literal text (e.g., "An eye for an eye" meant monetary compensation). The Kabbalah distinguished between the chaff of the text and the fine flour of its secret, real mean-

ing. Abarbanel often denies that the literal text expresses God's will. His criticism stems from his sense of history, his logic, and his moral and literary taste. Skepticism about what God said is to be found throughout Jewish tradition. The problem today is that the legitimacy of belief in revelation is itself cast into doubt.

21. Ibid., pp. 233–234.
22. *Renewing the Covenant,* p. 60.
23. Ibid., p. 124.
23. *The Masks Jews Wear,* p. 176.
24. *Reform Judaism Today,* bk. 3, p. 33.
25. *How Can a Jew Speak of Faith Today?,* p. 66.
26. Ibid., p. 68.
27. Ibid., pp. 122–123.
28. *Reform Judaism Today,* bk. 2, p. 23.
29. Ibid., bk. 2, p. 82.
30. *Renewing the Covenant,* p. 43.

10

Lawrence A. Hoffman

LAWRENCE A. HOFFMAN (b. 1942) identifies himself as a liturgist, rather than a philosopher or theologian. A colleague of Eugene B. Borowitz at the New York branch of the Hebrew Union College, Hoffman has delved into every facet of the history, theory, and practice of prayer. He ranges over the psychology, sociology, structure, content, language, and esthetics of group worship. Hoffman's approach to liturgy is so holistic, all-inclusive, and meticulously thought through that, despite his disclaimer, he belongs also under the rubrics of philosopher and theologian. His breadth of interest is itself a philosophical statement. The reader will already have discerned that I look upon philosophy as basically disciplined thinking, and in this respect Hoffman certainly excels.

After producing a solid piece of scholarship outlining the development of the siddur, particularly during the geonic period,[1] Hoffman turned his attention to a wide range of problems in present-day worship. He began with a gloomy assessment of the situation, declaring that ". . . most religious ritual in modern-day America is banal, poorly conceived, barely understood (even by those who direct it), and bordering on irrelevancy."[2] Hoffman does not presume to speak of the synagogue service beyond the borders of North America and particularly the United States. His caution is meritorious, and I shall try to emulate him.

Much of what Hoffman has to say is inapplicable to the Orthodox and *haredi* synagogue practices in Israel. It can be safely said that few, if any, of the shortcomings of ritual in the American Jewish home and synagogue are of concern to Fundamentalist or Orthodox Jews in Israel. Nor, in Israel, do the slowly growing number of liberal congregations have to face some of the problems of ritual and worship that plague Diaspora Jewry, at least not to the same degree. Israelis, for example, do not have to deal with translation, although many of them are ignorant of much of the historical background and theological foundations of the liturgy. Knowledge of Hebrew is no guarantee of meaningful prayer. For traditional Jews, relevancy is itself irrelevant, inasmuch as daily, rote recital of the liturgy is part of their normal way of life. Nor do such Jews have to be concerned about the qualifications of the prayer-director, since many worshipers in their synagogues are capable of leading the service. There is literally nothing to direct, except in a few "cathedral" synagogues in which professional *hazzanim* are challenged to use their vocal talents not as *performers* but as heighteners of the *kavvanah* of the worshipers.

Hoffman's studies relate to the vast majority of Jews who do not participate in traditional worship because of their strong antipathy to its form and content. He wants to help improve the quality of praying of the small percentage of Jews who do frequent the synagogue in varying degrees of regularity. To the extent possible, he wishes to help such Jews gain a greater appreciation of the worth and relevancy of the prayer experience. His main appeal is to Jews who have been touched by secular influences. If, in recent days, a sizable number of modern-educated Jews have gravitated to traditional forms of religious expression, it is clear that there is a hunger for spirituality on the part of seemingly estranged Jews. Some of them are desperate enough to look for the certainty and self-confidence they have failed to achieve in their life of Jewish illiteracy. And having lost their trust or confidence in rational canons of judgment—it is questionable whether they ever activated them in regard to their Judaism—they fall prey to the warmth, the rich regimen of practice, and the dogmatism of the extreme traditionalists. Some of the "new religionists" are more cautious and pause in the outer chambers occupied by the liberal Orthodox. The latter manage to convince the newcomers of the desirability of having a compartmentalized mind, half of which is committed to the world of scientific understanding of the universe, while the other half is devoted to the uncomplicated regularity of a hallowed tradition. These Jews cannot be dismissed, but they are not subjects to whom the kind of thinking that Hoffman represents will appeal. Nonetheless, the things that attract the old and new traditionalists must be understood and respectfully considered. Hoffman tries to take account of this important group of Jewish worshipers.

Which comes first, theory or practice, has been a continuous question from Rabbinic times to the present. Hoffman states his position forthrightly, when he writes, ". . . I believe that theology arises out of successful prayer and does not precede it."[3] The statement, it seems to me, oversimplifies a complex situation. Every prayer, after all, presupposes the theology of its drafter. The theological ideas underlying the words of worship do not spring up spontaneously. Of course, there can also be a kind of spiritual behaviorism that enables a person to utter prayers without any cognitive expression and nevertheless to derive some kind of religious inspiration or satisfaction from the act. Hoffman, I take it, wants to sacrifice neither intellect nor emotion. Hence, he looks to the words of prayer and the manner in which they are uttered to evoke the theology. This works if one confines prayer to the recitation of the traditional liturgy and endeavors to uncover its rich, often untapped spiritual treasures. However, this is not the case when men and women strive to find fitting expression for their thoughts about God, the universe, and humankind. The tradition cannot always provide the right words or meaning. In such an instance, theology gives rise to new prayers and new forms of expression.

What is important is not which comes first, theology or prayer, but the relationship between the two. Are they coherent and consonant with each other? Does the theology impel men and women to pray? Is the prayer an honest expression of the theology it purports to concretize? Do the various parts of the theology—its conceptions of God, humankind, and the cosmos—fit together harmoniously? Hoffman argues vociferously that successful prayer requires not only a consistent relation between theology and liturgy but a similar harmony between all segments of what he calls the prayer system. It is here that Hoffman makes a major contribution to an understanding of the crisis in prayer and to efforts at overcoming it.

Life is made up of interlocking systems and subsystems—the family, the neighborhood, the city, the state, regions, humankind as a whole, and countless others. The quality of life depends on the degree to which these systems manage to complement one another. Wherever conflict occurs in one system, it affects the relationship with other systems. A breakdown between husband

and wife or between parents and children, for example, causes tension in the family's relations with relatives, friends, and neighbors. The ripple effect might have even more far-reaching consequences in the functioning of the various members of the family in their work and activities outside the home.

In brief, Hoffman views prayer as one element in an organic whole made up of theological, social, psychological, emotional, organizational, esthetic, and other factors. A misplayed instrument in a large orchestra distorts the music. Similarly, group prayer cannot succeed unless all aspects of its system perform efficiently. The talmudic Sages knew, for instance, that without a unified congregation, prayer cannot be acceptable to God. They felt, too, that a single Jew who refused to join his fellows at prayer would thereby render the group worship ineffective. Hoffman carries the spirit of the Rabbis further, into areas seldom considered by philosophers of prayer or by those empowered to lead group services.

Theologically, Hoffman fits into the mood of those who seek God-experiences rather than definitions of God. He declares that ". . . images of God as 1) a Person-like partner in dialogue whom we meet in community and 2) an internal Presence within each person are but two positions on a spectrum paralleling the older conceptions of God as 1) a Person who is distant from us and 2) an utterly transcendent Being beyond our knowledge at all."[4] Hoffman thus tries to mediate between the ancient conception of God as some kind of Being and the nonrational but not irrational attempt to find God in a relational experience. He continues: "Probably the most satisfying master image is somewhere between absolute transcendence and complete immanence in the philosophic sense of the word: not God as an impersonal force far beyond us, nor God as the inner voice of conscience, but God as friend and comforter, who meets us in the human encounters that matter. When our worship develops a spiritualized display of those human moments on which we base all hope of meaning, we will have discovered worship that works."[5]

Much of our criticism of Borowitz's Covenant theology applies here. The proposal that we find God as friend and comforter whenever we have soul-warming encounters with our fellow humans fudges the issue. Human friendship is a wonderful and uplifting experience that strengthens our hope for a better human race. But all this is human cogitation, and the idea that God "meets" us, that is, sets out purposively to initiate or to respond to our quest, leaves us with painful questions: When one's encounters end in despair or disappointment, does this mean that God is absent or that God discriminates against us? Or perhaps we are incapable of understanding? But if the latter, what makes us so sure that we have encountered God when fortune favors us?

Hoffman himself asks these questions. He assumes that most people identify God's presence with peak experiences, such as seeing glorious sunsets, observing the sublimity of nature's vastness from a mountaintop, or fearing for one's life in a foxhole. But he realizes that there are other, ugly, sad, devastating experiences that cannot be easily associated with a good God. Therefore, Hoffman seeks a way of conceptualizing Deity so as ". . . not to confuse God's presence in general with any particular cultural manifestation thereof; then freed from the need to look for God in situations that have been satisfactory examples in one era but may not be so any longer, we can look afresh at our time and see where God is most likely to be found for us."[6]

If I understand Hoffman's meaning, the implication is that humans must define for themselves the experiences in life in which they wish to find God's presence. He cites as one instance the common view that God is felt in the love of two people for one another, a fact that should promote mixed, rather than separate seating in the synagogue. If we follow this line of thinking, however, identifying God's presence is a human perception or interpretation, based upon a personal or group set of values. But this is precisely the problem in every attempt to conceptualize God in a neutral or objective way. Suppose one argues that the love relationship between two people refracts not the presence of God but the egocentric passions of the two parties. Given such a comparison, mixed seating can be regarded as an interference with the worshipers' efforts to commune with God. This is the argument of the traditionalists, and if one accepts the premise, it makes sense. To escape this dilemma, it is necessary to come to some consensus as to the facts of human nature on which we ought to base our values and purposes. Such objectivity is no guarantee that we can achieve universal agreement on how we ought to pray or, for that matter, conduct any of the other affairs of life. Free choice is certain to result in disagreement. However, the attempt to escape rational judgment inevitably fails, even though rationality itself can easily be mistaken or traduced. The need for humility and caution applies to all the ways in which human beings apply their consciousness to the perception and understanding of the universe and themselves.

The theology of relationism, as delineated in similar ways by Borowitz and Hoffman, fails, in the last analysis, to hide its subjectivism. The following sentence by Hoffman is a clear illustration of this point: "If we learn to see the liturgy transcending words, even great words, we inherit a window on the past and present alike, in which the image on the other side of the glass may look remarkably like ourselves."[7] In other words, the God who addresses us in relational theology is in a real sense a projection of the self. There is nothing necessarily wrong in designating the object of such self-transcendence as God. But then, one has to abandon all ontological claims concerning a separate and independent Other.

However, since Hoffman maintains that theology is drawn from prayer, and not vice versa, let us follow him in his treatment of worship.

Philosophies of public worship must deal with the dynamic roles played by the individual, the group, the tradition, and the cultural environment. Hoffman is eminently comprehensive in calling our attention to the total system in which verbal worship or prayer takes place. He writes, for example, that, ". . . worship . . . does more than evoke the presence of God. It provides religious identification, declares what is right and what is wrong, and explains why being a Christian or a Jew is ultimately valuable. Worship defines a world of values that group members share; it both mirrors and directs the social order in which the group lives."[8] The implications of this broad scope are far-reaching, too much so for this brief consideration of Hoffman's contribution to the study of prayer; but I shall touch on some of the more significant points.

As a social institution, a prayer service can be successful only if it is adjusted to the wide variations of background and interests of the participating worshipers. Hoffman states the matter very effectively: "Successful worship demands that the interface be-tween subsystems not be in conflict. In essence that means that all present must constitute a group, able to send and to receive messages appropriate to the worship ritual. The props must be mutually significant to all. Individuals must not feel out of place. Everyone must belong. If the Worship Moment is the successful communication to each individual that this group is ultimately significant, there must be such a group present, and its members must be able to identify with its significance."[9]

The social context is crucial as a prerequisite for engendering a sense of belongingness that the worshiper must feel. It is also central in the manifold problem of communication. Prayer in-volves the ability of the members of the congregation to share a common vocabulary and cultural medium as well as a vocabulary for addressing God and receiving some form of response.

The interplay of the sociocultural and the theological is spelled out by Hoffman. He writes that ". . . from the celebration of ritual-ized patterns that cohere endlessly and that are repeated regu-larly, we internalize expectations that even the chaos of life is only a small part of a larger pattern, if we only look hard enough to find it. Thus we learn to have the faith that prohibits our giving up on life in the middle of its inconsistencies."[10] What makes this socialized ritual effective as a prayer experience? It is not the repe-tition, although without such regularity, group worship would lose its power. The ability of prayer to make it possible for the participants in worship to feel God's presence has to be found in the content of the liturgy. "How are we aware of God in prayer? Through the synecdochal vocabulary of our time that best sug-gests the reality of a master image that itself best reflects the cul-tural background in which we stand."[11] Thus, a congregation is bound together by an evocative vocabulary that enables everyone to understand not only the words of the liturgy but also to be joined in the larger meanings they suggest. It is then that God's presence becomes manifest.

Hoffman's use of the poetic figure of synecdoche is novel and suggestive, but it cannot resolve the inherent difficulty that colors all attempts to become "aware of God." Can the leap or the pro-gression from the part to the whole be said to be more than a culture-bound construct of a supposed transcendent reality? I do not question the necessity for belief in such a reality. Without a larger perspective than what we experience at any moment, we could hardly make much sense out of the discontinuities of life. Nevertheless, Hoffman obviously means more than the idea that prayer is an exercise of inference about transcendent divinity. Prayer is more than intellect; the synagogue is not an experimental laboratory or a classroom for speculation. Granted. But what can awareness of God be, if it is not substantiated by some grounding in worldly experience? And here, too, Hoffman runs into the difficulty of those who are dissatisfied with rationalism as a means of escaping from the confines of their cultural sources. Awareness of God is, inescapably, a reflection of historical circumstances. In worship, one wants to rise above such a confine. I have no difficulty with this aim, as long as we recognize that our vision of the larger perspective must always be subject to constant supervision and intelligent correction based on disciplined verification.

Now rational experience cannot and should not be limited to what is current or immediate. The stream of rationality follows the waters that flow before it as much as it makes way for those that pursue it. Without tradition, which, let us remember, has rendered possible our present state of knowledge, no form of rationalism could live up to its name. The question of tradition is always: wherein does it commend itself to the critical mind of today, and wherein has it performed a service that is no longer applicable?

The tradition is represented in prayer mainly by the liturgy. Whether they adhere to its halakhic form or are drawn to one of the various revisions of latter-day liberal liturgists, the worshipers in the synagogue are always interpreting or selecting elements of the tradition and seeing the past through the lenses of their respective outlooks on life. Hoffman attributes overriding importance to the input of the individual worshiper. He says: "Nothing happens in the service which the man who has come to pray does not himself bring about. The fixed order of the prayers, the leadership of respected figures, the communion with neighbors, the special room devoted to the worship of God—all these may help. They may be valuable to the individual, even indispensable. They remain means, instruments, accessories. They cannot take the place of the individual's own action, his turning to God in attentive respect."[12] In other words, the act of praying is valueless without *kavvanah,* toward which the individual must make the major contribution. There is nothing in the liturgy itself that can generate *kavvanah* unless each congregant wishes it to happen.

What impels an individual to engage in prayer with a group of his or her fellows? The precondition of such worship is the individual's sense of belonging to a community that has set the cultural, spiritual, and psychological Gestalt, the overall mind-set, that he or she imposes on reality. It is in a group culture that the hope arises that God will share in the human effort to change what exists into something better. "Prayer," Hoffman declares, "is a cultural creation, fashioned by people who may have only a dim perception of what they are about as they go about worshiping, but who know nonetheless that their preoccupation with the 'stuff' of prayer is important in their lives. Undergirding the liturgical creativity is the twofold sense that the community that worships is of supreme significance. It asserts beliefs, that others deny, and it posits plans at which others scoff."[13] Thus, the individual comes to prayer inspired and motivated by an attachment to a community that, in prayer, becomes supremely conscious, through its individuals, of its values and purposes. It is only individuals, of course, who are conscious. To speak of group consciousness, therefore, is a conventional way of describing the consensus of the community's members. Consensus, however, is a multigenerational phenomenon, and what is transmitted as group consensus from one generation to another has to pass through the experiential prisms of each stage of the group's life. The power of consensus accounts for the conservative tendency of tradition, and the force of experience suggests how change sometimes sweeps aside previous consensus.

As a liberal, Hoffman naturally puts more emphasis on the role of the worshiper in the development and usage of liturgy than is likely to be the case for traditionalists. Nevertheless, his rule of thumb that nothing happens unless the worshiper wishes it to occur applies equally to all types of suppliants. All have to look to their prayers as gates to God; otherwise, theological sophistication and liturgical majesty cannot produce their desired effects. It is obvious that there is a problem of integration of factors. A person is motivated to worship within a social context of which he is almost completely a product. Very few of us are capable of creating or refashioning entire systems of relationships, but we must all endeavor to piece together all the elements of our culture that bear on an enterprise of interest to us.

Thus, *kavvanah* is an art that requires the ability to see the system of prayer as a whole and to be dedicated completely to making it work. Since it is a rare person who possesses these qualities of mind and heart, it is no wonder that true prayer is achieved by so few. Hoffman clarifies the problem, but even his broad theoretical scope cannot cope with the impact of temperament. Affectual differences seem to play a major role in the worship of free men and women. And temperament is too subjective a matter to be channeled easily toward or away from devotional prayer.

However, once the desire to pray is aroused, there is much room for devising strategies of implementation. Hoffman has given comprehensive thought to the problem of how to make the system and subsystems work smoothly and effectively. He makes us all aware of the inherent limitations of and built-in constraints on all efforts of religious denominations consciously to refashion prayer. "The good thing about open canonical decisions is that they are made beyond the whim of any one person or committee. They take generations to be decided."[14] As I indicated above, the forward thrust of intentional change runs up inevitably against the conserving resistance of the collective wisdom of the ages. This is the nature of the creative tension that guards us from precipitous manipulation of hallowed tradition. Equally, however, we know that we must not permit habit and nostalgia to undermine our conscience and our pursuit of truth.

In the effort to establish contact with God that is at the heart of prayer, it is not abstract truth that is the goal but feeling God's presence. For this to happen, Hoffman argues that we must step beyond reason and a rationalist approach. He maintains that modern worship differs from that of previous ages in which ". . . both the content of what is said in church [and by implication, what is said in the synagogue] and the form in which the content is presented are subservient to the idea of truth."[15] Hoffman points out that although the church certainly attended to the role of art in worship—note, for example, the tremendous impact of Gothic architecture in communicating the transcendent power of the Christian message—its purpose was ". . . the imparting of truth, the spreading of doctrine, the demonstration of correct opinion and knowledge of what the church knew to be the case."[16] Noteworthy is the fact that the message of truth was delivered not by the liturgical word, which in the Catholic ritual had become the private province of the clergy and was not understood by the masses. Instead, the truth was communicated by a combination of the uplifting impression of the vaulted church and the artistry of the ritual and its appeal to all the senses. The truth lay in the emotional and spiritual impact of the total system.

While the synagogue lacked the kind of of visual estheticism that characterized Christian worship, it, too, expected that the beauty of Judaism would be strengthened in the act of prayer. But in contrast to Christianity, the message of truth was learned, at least by Jewish males, in the study hall. Nonetheless, the recital of prayer was expected to comunicate its share of toraitic truth and beauty. In our day, however, says Hoffman, we ". . . should see liturgy as an art form and truth as an artistic construct. What we need now is greater attention to art as a proper, indeed divine, goal of liturgical life."[17]

Hoffman has much to say about the need for liturgical change and particularly about liturgical novelty and creativity, but it is the human and divine relationships in prayer that are his main focus. As he describes his view, ". . . I mean to replace a category of books with a category of human activity: the community at prayer, an activity that I understand as organized around a set of relationships between people and their neighbors, people and their holy texts, people and their God."[18] In other words, prayer is the whole system of relationships that occur when a group of people, united in fellowship and cultural commonality, gather in a space specially designated for the purpose of establishing communion with God. The relationships are both the cause and the outcome of the complex of liturgical words, song, and movement that make up the form and content of every worship service. Hoffman is very convincing in his message that prayer is not only and perhaps not even primarily the recitation of words.

Words, of course, are crucial, but if they were the only factor in public prayer, there would be no need for the elaborate structure of space and practice that characterizes every gathering of worshipers. Prayer, however, is a form of ritual, the elements of which are capable of endless combinations and permutations but are more likely to follow an unchanging or slowly changing pattern. "A ritual," Hoffman writes, "is the way we humans play out a given script of behavior during a specific duration of time. Since the play is repeated regularly, we prepare ourselves for the high and the low points of the script, and could, if need be, graph them. Without ritual there would be no meaningful use of time, except for accidental events that force us to laugh or cry."[18]

What, then, has to be considered in the preparation or conduct of a prayer ritual? In the first place, there is the congregation itself. Hoffman points to the obvious but seldom considered fact that the quality of a worship service is significantly dependent on the ability of the worshipers to communicate with one another. If the members of a congregation are strangers to one another, their prayer is likely to be flat, and the group as a whole is unlikely to appreciate what Hoffman calls the high point of the service. The camaraderie of worshipers is affected, among other factors, by social status, cultural background, psychological readiness, and personal states of mind. The formulators and the leaders of public worship must therefore do whatever they can to raze the walls of social separation. Hoffman covers a variety of possibilities. One such possibility is to arrange synagogue space in such a way as to reduce the distance between clergy and laity and between each worshiper and his or her fellow congregants. On the other hand, Hoffman acknowledges the success—or apparent success—of a large cathedral-type service. The problem is a subtle one, but there is little doubt that the spatial and esthetic framework of a service must be suited to the social background, sense of oneness, and ideological disposition of the congregants.

Hoffman has stated the problem of space and aroused the consciousness of prayer leaders to its parameters. However, I doubt that any solution can be more than proximate. Consider the relatively simple instance of the junior congregation as a means of overcoming the intellectual distance between children and adults. Hoffman has reservations about its advisability. Removing children from the familial and adult environment deprives them of the latter's warmth and the latter of the physical presence of their hopes for the future. How does one assess this loss against what might be gained by enabling children to avoid the boredom of adult services and the opportunity to gain an appreciation of the tradition on their own level? Is it not advisable to experiment with forms of liturgy and worship on the child's level that would be less acceptable in the adult setting? The answer is not at all self-evident and probably depends on each set of circumstances.

Or, to cite another problem that arises now and then, what kind of space can eliminate the gap between two groups of worshipers, natives and new immigrants, who are separated by the barriers of language and culture?

A similar example of the complex interplay between prayer space, social proximity, and interpersonal readiness for group worship is to be found in the strength and weakness of the *havurah* type of service. The rapid development of *havurot* from the 1960s on indicates the hunger of many Jews for a more active, emotionally stirring, and participatory religious service than is available in almost all modern synagogues. Worship in the latter is strait-jacketed by the fixed, formal seating arrangements and the rabbi's orders as to what, when, and how the congregation should pray. It took a generation of young seekers to break away from this formalism and to organize small fellowships of men and women, almost all in the same age range, who were prepared to experiment with the artistic facets of worship. While some experimentation with the verbal content of the liturgy did take place, the stress of this new style of worship was on egalitarianism, participation, informality, spirited singing, and body language. No one should underestimate the importance of the *havurah* message, but neither should it be assumed that the movement has dealt adequately with the problems of age and cultural differences, the theological foundations of prayer, the educational preparation of the next generation of worshipers, and the other aspects of worship under freedom and voluntarism. My reservations should not be interpreted as a rejection of the *havurah* idea. They are intended only to indicate that even Hoffman's insight into the enormous scope of Jewish worship leaves us with many unanswered questions about the theory of worship and unresolved problems of implementation. We can only support his view that there has to be a variety of services to meet different tastes, intellectual preparedness, and social compatibility. As Hoffman comments,

". . . religions are no longer so monolithic that a single prayer service can evoke wholehearted assent from all its members."[20] When worshipers are dissatisfied with a service, they become passive, stop coming, try other synagogues, or, if they are sufficiently motivated, establish a new outlet for their spiritual needs and tastes.

Hoffman's wide-ranging treatment of prayer is the logical outcome of his view on the genesis of belief in God. He states: "It is not the case that I believe in God and therefore worship; rather, I find worship so compelling that I cannot doubt God's reality."[21] This assertion, I believe, as in his claim that prayer precedes theology, and not vice versa, overstates the case. There are many instances of men and women who emerge from a state of nonbelief or unbelief, become theists, and then take the logical step of joining a worship community. Nevertheless, Hoffman has a point. Franz Rosenzweig confesses that it was the inspiration of an Orthodox religious service that convinced him to remain a Jew and that apparently deepened his theistic conviction. If we cannot accept Hoffman's one-directional view about the relationship between belief in God and worship of God, we can agree that effective public prayer can generate new dimensions of faith. That is so because ". . . worship is the means by which we picture the really real, celebrating it as the underlying pattern in creation. . . . It is the artistry by which we paint the canvas of a world shaped not by happenstance but by the way we believe things ultimately cohere."[22]

Like his colleague, Borowitz, Hoffman seeks a new way to harmonize the rational and emotional aspects of religion, in general, and prayer, in particular. But a passage like the one just quoted suggests to me that Hoffman has erected a straw man. What has he said if not that worship consists of a set of acts, verbal and sensual, by means of which we reinforce emotionally and artistically a rationally produced construct of the universe? It is true that such a construct might exercise its hold over a people long after it has been replaced in the minds of advanced thinkers, scientists, and scholars by more informed opinion. This is what happens in the formulation and persistence of myths. Hoffman says, "I wish to . . . indicate that every historical perspective is selective in what it chooses to emphasize or to omit, and that examples of these histories are encoded by religious communities as ritualized reminders for public occasions."[23] We see once more that it is the human intellect that pictures the universe whose management is celebrated in prayer. What happens, however, is that these constructs tend to become incarcerated in their ritualized forms and remain resistant to change. The rituals act as an emotional insulation that protects the pictures or the myths from the ravaging effects of advancing intellect and experience. Even liberals are hard put to adjust the emotionally powerful ritual—in our case, the ritual of prayer—to the fast-changing, rational image of reality. Perhaps that is why Hoffman tries to underplay the element of truth in prayer, in favor of its esthetic and emotional parameters.

Having stated my criticism of Hoffman's position on the rational and emotional components of prayer, I must express my agreement with his profound understanding of the cultural and artistic aspects of group worship. Traditionalists try to defy the cultural matrix of worship, conducting an unceasing battle against *hukkat hagoyim,* imitation of the gentiles. Any alteration in the form or content of the prayers is to be rejected as a surrender to foreign influence, despite the fact that the traditional synagogue service is replete with content and artistic practices that have their origin in non-Jewish sources. One need only cite the many traditional melodies that are copies or adaptations of folk tunes of the many lands in which Jews have resided for the last two millenia. The architecture of synagogues everywhere in the Jewish world is more often than not a carbon copy of foreign concepts of religious space.

Since outside influences are bound to affect Jewish worship, it behooves religious leaders to respond positively to the esthetic standards governing the maturation of Jews and non-Jews alike. The American synagogue should be recognizable to Jews from other continents as authentic houses of Jewish worship, but they will have architectural and cultural features that only an American or other Diaspora Jew is likely to appreciate fully. The music of the American synagogue has many sounds that are unheard in Europe, Israel, or Africa. The translation of traditional prayers and the composition of new prayers in English are strange fruits of the American experience. Even secular Jews in Israel are ill at ease when confronted for the first time by an Americanized service, both liberal and modern Orthodox.

We should expect that Jews in Israel will develop a new esthetic outlook and culture in their religious development. This new estheticism has already begun in the architecture and internal décor of a few synagogues, in the creation of religious articles, and most vividly in the music that has been composed for liturgical use. It must also be expected that Hoffman's recommendations for the arrangement of space and the placing of prayer leaders and congregants will require a different set of concepts in Israel than those he suggests for American synagogues. But this is a matter for far more lengthy and profound consideration than can be dealt with here.

However, let us expand on one point in Hoffman's estheticism: his appreciation of the role of music in prayer. Music, he suggests, ". . . plays many functions in our services. It gathers us together as community, develops emotional moods, provides quiet time for meditation, lets us sing in great elation, interprets sacred texts, and so on."[24] Thus music, the rhythmic partner of speech, functions as a social force, an emotional generator, and an intellectual adjunct. But its effectiveness is dependent on its appeal to the ear of the congregation, and that appeal is culture-dominated. The gap between Sephardic and Ashkenazic sounds is sufficiently forbidding to prevent many members of both ethnic complexes from sharing worship experiences—at least until their ears have adapted to the unaccustomed melodies and rhythms. Sacred music is, therefore, very subjective, depending on what it actually does to the worshiper. Hoffman states simply that ". . . music is considered sacred not on account of what it is, but on account of what it does."[25]

The subject of synagogue music is, in itself, worthy of extensive examination, beyond the interesting comments of Hoffman. For instance, there is a striking difference in the pronunciation of Hebrew between Israel and the countries of the Diaspora. Many of the traditional synagogue melodies do not fit the rhythm of Hebrew as it is spoken in Israel, particularly by sabras (native-born Israelis). In order for Israelis to sing these melodies, they have to distort their usual emphases or alter the tunes to fit the rhythm of their pronunciation and accent. In either case, something rings false. More serious is the fact that much synagogue music is composed more with an ear to popular folk sounds than to the real sense of the prayer. A classic example is the way in which the majestic words of the *Adon Olam* hymn, which lists some of God's attributes and acts, are sometimes chanted to the tune of a German beer song. The melody undoubtedly brings the service to a merry conclusion, but it perverts completely the intent of the hymn. Clearly, the "sacredness" of music that twists the meaning and intent of a profound hymn must be called into question. What applies to music applies equally to all the other esthetic elements of prayer.

Hoffman's rhetoric might mislead a careless reader. I hope that I have not been guilty of so gross an error as to underestimate the profundity of his message. When Hoffman speaks of the performative and theatrical aspects of public worship, one might suspect that his proneness to dramatize the prayer experience diverts him and his readers from the exalted purpose of drawing worshipers to God. Or, when he talks of a prayer service as a system or a field, one might be tempted to classify his approach as too centered in sociology. Such reactions would be unfair to Hoffman's vision of prayer as an immense complex that has to be studied with all the tools at our disposal and that has to be handled with the light touch that befits all great traditions. Hoffman himself should be presented in the perspective of the revolutionary spiritual, social, cultural, intellectual, and political upheavals of our day. His conception of prayer and the way to revitalize it must also be cast against the background of the radical challenges to Jewish creative continuity that arose in the last half of the twentieth century. An analysis of this type is beyond the scope of this introductory essay.

NOTES

1. Lawrence A. Hoffman, *The Canonization of the Prayer Book* (Notre Dame, Ind.: University of Notre Dame Press, 1979).

2. Lawrence A. Hoffman, *The Art of Public Worship* (Washington, D.C.: Westmore Press, 1988), p.ix.

3. Ibid., p. xi.

4. Ibid., p. 177.

5. Ibid.

6. Ibid., pp. 161–162.

7. Lawrence A. Hoffman and Tim Flinders, *Beyond the Text* (Bloomington: Indiana University Press, 1989), p. 3.

8. *The Art of Public Worship*, p. 56.

9. Ibid., p. 80.

10. Ibid., p. 175.

11. Ibid., p. 170.

12. Lawrence A. Hoffman, ed., *Gates of Understanding* (Cincinnati: Central Conference of American Rabbis, 1977), p. 56.

13. *Beyond the Text*, p. 75.

14. Lawrence A. Hoffman, ed. with Janet R. Walton, *Sacred Sound and Social Change* (Notre Dame, Ind.: University of Notre Dame Press, 1992), p. 334.

15. *The Art of Public Worship*, p. 122.

16. Ibid.

17. Ibid., p. 123.

18. *Beyond the Text*, p. 150.

19. *The Art of Public Worship*, p. 5.

20. Ibid., p. 82.

21. Ibid., p. 148.

22. Ibid.

23. *Beyond the Text*, p. 123.

24. *Sacred Sound*, p. 328.

25. *The Art of Public Worship*, p. 251.

11

Feminists

OF ALL THE UPHEAVALS that have rocked the twentieth century, the one that is likely to have the most far-reaching and lasting effects is the feminist revolution. The changed and changing status of women affects not only the feminine half of the human race, but the other fifty percent as well. The revolution has long been in the making. The signs of the eruption have been evident throughout the centuries, but little attention was paid to the power that was slowly gathering force, much like the the failure to note preliminary turmoil before a volcanic eruption. Nor is there yet full realization on the part of either sex of the consequences of the new emerging order. I include myself among innocents who know that nothing can ever remain the same in the relationships between men and women but who can only guess at the directions they will take.

However, in regard to prayer, we can at least review what has happened and is happening before our eyes and evaluate, however hesitatingly and reservedly, the emerging patterns.

First of all, the synagogue is becoming a bisexual institution, in unprecedented ways. The Reform movement pioneered in its egalitarian attitude, but it is only in the past few decades that the training and employment of women rabbis and cantors have significantly reduced the sexist bias of spiritual leadership in Reform synagogues. The same applies to Reconstructionism, whose founder, Mordecai M. Kaplan, provided much of the theoretical inspiration for the thought on the subject among liberal Jews. Although Kaplan's views on religious equality for women were bitterly resisted for decades, they have gradually, although inconsistently, been adopted by a majority of Conservative congregations. Kaplan was able to implement his egalitarian position long before his students and colleagues at the Jewish Theological Seminary surrendered to logic and community pressure. He subordinated what he considered to be anachronistic vestiges in the

Halakhah to the authority of ethical probity and straight thinking. The Conservative advance toward egalitarianism has lagged for decades. That progress has finally accelerated is due to the liberal construction of halakhic conceptions on the part of the majority of Conservative rabbis. Nonetheless, a significant minority within the Conservative ranks refuses to go along with this more elastic halakhic rendition.

Even in Orthodoxy there are signs of ferment, especially among the women. While Orthodox women remain loyal to traditional law and seek to raise their status by means of its canons of development, they are becoming impatient with the slowness of the process and resentful of the benighted attitude of many rabbis. It is unlikely that these modern Orthodox women will remain silent in the face of the kind of male chauvinism described by Susan Weidman Schneider.[1] She tells of the consternation of a devout woman who heard her rabbi declare before the start of the *Neilah* (closing) service of Yom Kippur that those women who wish to leave early in order to prepare the meal should do so quietly ". . . so as not to disturb the worshipers." The congregant felt insulted and degraded. She, too, was a worshiper. But the force that motivates spiritually alert Orthodox women is their sense of deprivation that results from their exclusion from full participation in the prayer service. Their present-day general education, which inspires many of them to university degrees and academic achievements of all kinds, and the broad Jewish education that many of them enjoy have expanded their spiritual vistas. They want to apply what they are learning to the recitation of the prayers and the reading of the Torah. Jewish women want to dance with the Torah scroll on Simhat Torah and to lift their voices in praise of God. They resent being denied those privileges on the supposition that their participation in song and dance alongside the men might stimulate the latter sexually.

In the non-Orthodox denominations, equality has advanced to the level of leadership, both on the lay level and on that of professional responsibilty. The training and employment of women rabbis and cantors are accepted features of the liberal religious landscape. Even in Israel, which usually lags behind religious developments in the American and other Jewish communities in the Diaspora, the Progressive (Reform) and Masorati (Conservative) movements are rapidly adjusting themselves to the new era. Women occupy several pulpits in liberal Israel synagogues, and women lead prayers both as volunteers and professionals. Within halakhic Jewry, the drive for equality under the Halakhah is led by feminist adherents such as Professor Alice Shalvi[2] of the Hebrew University (at this writing, rector of the Schechter Institute of Jewish Studies), Peninah Peli, and many other colleagues. As far as I know, the Orthodox feminists do not yet call for permitting women to serve as rabbis and cantors or Torah-readers in the normal synagogue, but some of them have established separate female minyanim, in which all of these functions are carried out by women.

Separate services for women have been motivated by both negative and positive considerations. The negative reason is obvious. As long as women are excluded from equal participation in public worship, they will seek other outlets for their spiritual yearnings. For long centuries, such a step was never contemplated, because it is only in the recent past, as a result of the impact of expanding freedom, that those yearnings surfaced. Now that many women are no longer prepared to repress their natural desires, they seek outlets wherever they can.

For Orthodox women, the only recourse they have at present for praying in conformity with the Halakhah on a level with men is to conduct all-female services. Even this practice is opposed by some halakhists, but it is unlikely that they will be able to turn back the tide. It will be interesting to watch the development in Orthodox ranks, because the role of women is undoubtedly one of the most crucial challenges to the ability of the Halakhah to maintain any degree of authority over the Jewish mind.

However, more important than the resentment against exclusion is the positive motivation for separate services for women. The momentum of the feminist revolution has outstripped the ability of either men or women to fathom and cope fully with its various dimensions. Most particularly, the search of women for their self-identity has found them ill-equipped. Nor could it be otherwise. Much research is still needed before we shall have a definitive answer to the following question: Aside from the obvious physical differences between males and females, are there any fundamental psychological and spiritual qualities that distinguish

the sexes from one another? The conventional tendency to regard women as more gentle and merciful than men appears to
have little or no basis. Courage is asexual. Ambition and assertiveness are gender-neutral. And so on. If there are distinctive traits
along sexual lines, they have not yet been convincingly discerned.
But women, after being suppressed and repressed throughout history, naturally wonder if at least some of the social evils and disor-
ders that afflict humankind are not the result of male tyranny.
Hence, they ask themselves, perhaps there are special feminine
qualities of mind and heart that should be brought into play for
human benefit. Moreover, the disclosure of these characteristics
is deemed essential by some feminists for the full flowering of the
free woman. This is as true in prayer as in all other walks of life.
Women today are impatient with the sexist biases that dominate
the spirit, structure, content, and semantics of the synagogue.
Nevertheless, when the biases are overcome, will men and women
be seen to be identical in their spiritual needs and psychological
dispositions?

Accompanying the developments sketched above all too super-
ficially, some of the most serious and intense theorizing about
prayer is being done by women. Feminists are still in the stage of
having to demonstrate that women have spiritual needs whose
satisfaction might have to be achieved by new forms of behavior
or in ways that are not essentially different from those employed
by men. What those needs are is a subject of considerable speculation. Until now, it has been assumed in Jewish law that the religious obligations of women are a function of their God-given
duties in relation to parents, husband, children, and the community at large.[3] The attention that has been paid in traditional Judaism to the broad spectrum of needs that women have as human
beings has, with notable exceptions, too often been skewed. One
such exception is the recognition of the sexual drive in women,
which husbands are expected to satisfy. This and the normal biological needs are treated in the Halakhah with humane understanding. But scant heed is paid to the possibility that women
share with men the sense of wonder about reality that leads to
worship, the urge to know, and the will to sense the command
that inheres in the mitzvot. Today, however, women are reaching

out to new spiritual horizons, and they refuse any longer to accept their traditional status as handmaids of men.

Spiritual needs and characteristics require clarification in any discussion of prayer. Are there basic differences between the sexes? Are men, for example, more prone than women to seek God or in greater danger from the temptations of the flesh? Are men more apt to be sexually aroused or spiritually distracted in the presence of women than the latter are when in the company of men? Or, more profoundly, do the biological distinctions of the sexes evoke unique emotions, generate different yearnings, and call for special male- and female-oriented ritual? Susannah Heschel writes that ". . . feminism's central insight contends that . . . our most basic understandings of human nature are drawn primarily from men's experiences."[4] That was the case until now. Henceforth, investigation of human nature cannot be conducted by men alone. Nor can its findings be considered valid unless it gives equal weight to the behavior of women.

As a result of their determination to explore the implications of their own experience, women are supplying new data for a broader understanding of human nature. Thus, there are many women who have been stirred by their monthly period and its suggestiveness of renewal and opportunities for spiritual recleansing. Jewish women have discovered new meaning in the act of ritual immersion in the *mikveh* (ritual bath or pool) and in the blessing of the new moon. These and other manifestations of female sexuality have inspired the composition of prayers and separate services for women alone. Paradoxically, the resentment against separation has eventuated in a modern equivalent of the traditional view that *kavvanah* requires mutual distancing of the sexes. Only this time, the conception and the ritual consequence have been initiated by women. The great majority of women prefer joint services with men. The resort to all-female services seems to apply mostly where women continue to be excluded by the men from full and equal participation in synagogue worship, but also as the result of the failure to include in the liturgy adequate outlets for women's special needs.

The consciousness of biological distinctiveness on the part of women and their attempts to grasp its spiritual meaning are a significant new development in the search for a more accurate

understanding of human nature than we have possessed until
now. However, the verdict is not yet in on whether *physical* distinctiveness of men and women has its parallel in different *spiritual*
characteristics or needs. The menstrual cycle is certainly dramatic
and easily elicits among sensitive women the desire for renewal.
The feeling of purity that ensues from the cleansing process undoubtedly produces spiritual overtones. But while men have not
been endowed with so dramatic a bodily transformation, they too
experience the need for cleanliness of body and mind. Whether
it be by means of the *mikveh* of the traditionalist or the bath or
shower of the modernist, the sense of cleanliness can readily become a spiritual opportunity for men, as much as it is for women.
Nonetheless, feminists have a case when they object to the absence from the prayer ritual of their experience and its associated
vocabulary.

Is there, however, a basis for a distinct, feminist theology? It is
one thing to recover some of the feminist echoes of Jewish mysticism and to utilize them in order to highlight feminine concerns.
It is something quite different to establish the mystical recourse
to so-called female attributes of God as a foundation for a satisfactory theology. Such an effort might help to balance the scales
between rationalist and mystical theologies, but introducing the
feminine theme is no more legitimate in talking about or addressing God than is the long-standing male bias. Feminist efforts to
gain equality in public prayer are a necessary political step, but it
has yet to be proved that they will be helpful in the formulation
of an improved theology of prayer. The fact that women who pray
in all-women *minyanim* are often able to feel greater warmth and
inspiration in their worship than they do in the usual synagogue
service is evidence of their need and right to share in every aspect
of group prayer. However, it is doubtful that this separatism has
any theological justification.

Further, we should not dispute the need to offer women the
chance to express in prayer the powerful emotions that overtake
them when they undergo the special experiences that are peculiar to their sex. Amy Eilberg expresses movingly her feelings following the birth of her daughter and the quality of her praying
on that occasion. She describes how her encounter with the
prayer book ". . . was loving, gentle and deliberate, generated

more by the energy of caring and caregiving than by the need to discharge a legal obligation. My encounter with the *siddur* and with God was suffused with the same spirit that had filled my days since Penina's birth, days in which tasks of caring for a new-born baby felt like acts of exquisite sanctity. The God that I imagined that night had not missed my *davening* those intervening days, understanding that my days had been filled with holiness, while I nursed the baby, rocked her, changed her and loved her. This God understood the intrinsic sanctity of acts of nurturance. This *feminine* [italics mine] God, after all, was the model of all human acts of creativity and caregiving. It was from Her that we had learned to create and nurture new life. Far from judging me in my hiatus in addressing Her, She rejoiced that I had instead found Her, and myself, in the midst of caring for my infant daughter."[5]

Rabbi Eilberg's emotions are pure and her deep piety an enviable response to her sublime experience. Nor need we question the revelation to her of the love and gentleness that reside in the divine quality of the universe. However, on what grounds does Eilberg associate the aforementioned attributes with the feminine side of God? Are not men, in their better selves, gentle and loving? And are not women capable of cruelty and viciousness? We all have to learn to divest ourselves of the many vestiges of our prehuman and subhuman ancestry and to acquire and cultivate those qualities that make us human. In God, they are all one, neither masculine nor feminine. It might have taken the miracle of birth to enable Eilberg to appreciate the vast store of love and gentleness in the cosmos that make life bearable; but a similar state of mind occurs no less among men—undoubtedly including her husband—in moments like those described so beautifully by her. I know that is true in my own case when each of my three children was born. But unlike Eilberg, I had not conceived of or experienced God previously as she did, as ". . . the angry, thundering God" who could disapprove of her failure to daven while she was recovering her strength after giving birth and devoting herself for a period of time to adjusting to her infant and learning to care for her. Why should anyone conceive of such a God and attribute these arbitrary and derogatory qualities to the masculine side of Deity? Evidently, some of the feminists, having plumbed previously untapped depths in their souls, regard them as as peculiarly feminine or possessed by women in greater measure than by men.

The feminist assault on the male-oriented vocabulary of Jewish prayer should be met with understanding and sympathy. But it requires also a sense of balance. This is what Arthur Green supplies when he asks, "Is it really women who alone are in need of feminine imagery? Do images of the divine feminine belong only to women? Might they not belong to, and respond to the needs of, men as well as women? . . . Might one not argue that men need the feminine, as women would need the masculine if religious life involves something like what the depth psychologists call a search for polarities?"[6] Of course, Jewish tradition is replete with references to the feminine side of Godhood, but, as Green so aptly indicates, these are all based on the way Jewish males have perceived femininity. Today, women rightly insist on speaking for themselves. This self-probing is in its early stages, and the outcome cannot now be predicted. However, we can at least see its first effects on feminist efforts to create new liturgy and to amend traditional prayer in the direction of gender-free or bisexual vocabulary.

Feminists are aware of the pitfalls along the road of correcting the gender bias in Jewish prayer. One of them comments: "Some committed Jewish feminists . . . are cautious and even suspicious of newly created liturgy and rituals and prefer to find significance in tradition."[7] In this respect, there is no difference between men and women. Men, too, are divided as to how to go about revitalizing synagogue worship, particularly as regards the liturgy. Some worshipers are convinced that the way to increase and deepen devotion is to uncover the multicolored mosaic that lies beneath the surface of the traditional words of prayer. All we need is a better theology, and the true meaning of the words will be exposed or be made to reflect the intention of the worshiper. Orthodox women are apt to find this to be a congenial method, because it enables them to air their often heterodox sentiments without departing from the halakhically sanctioned liturgy. They are supported by both liberal Orthodox rabbis and a considerable number of non-Orthodox men and women who are also tied to the charm of the traditional liturgy.

Eliezer Diamond, a Conservative scholar, writes thus: "To tamper significantly with the liturgy we have received is to run the risk, it seems to me, of remaking God in our own image. Better to engage the prayers we have received, and, bringing to bear our individual imaginative faculties, encounter the God each is meant to find."[8] Is it better to employ the language that expresses the image of God as it appeared in the minds of less-informed generations—especially when much of the plain meaning of the texts they wrote defies our reason or conscience—than it is to amend it or supplement it with our own terminology? In the latter instance, we at least accept responsibility for what we utter. Should we not say what we mean and mean what we say, instead of trying to twist the intent of our ancestors or reading into them our own ideas?

However, there is a large coterie of feminists who feel impelled to seek new forms of expression that will voice more adequately their self-image, their newly articulated aspirations, and their lately released spiritual passions. They want to dispel what Tikva Frymer-Kensky has called the "subliminal image" of traditional prayer that God is male.[9] Frymer-Kensky echoes the views of most feminists that there is need for female God-language. To the credit of this group, it must be said that they recognize the inherent difficulty in finding the right terminology. Frymer-Kensky, for instance, examines the use of *Shekhinah* (Divine Presence) as a synonym for God. This feminine term has the advantage of being widely employed in tradition. On that ground alone its use needs no justification. Yet even recourse to a traditional liturgy has its drawbacks. First of all, the term *Shekhinah* has a history of its own. It is unclear whether the *Shekhinah* was seen by the Rabbis as indicative of God's immanence.[10] Were scholarly judgment to conclude that *Shekhinah* is cast in feminine form but is deficient in feminine meaning, the word might lose some of its appeal for extreme feminists. Moreover, to the extent that *Shekhinah* evokes a sense of God's Presence and closeness, it tends to underplay the elements of transcendence and awe. Meanwhile, its use by feminists remains popular. However, Frymer-Kensky remarks, it ". . . has become almost the female deity, rather than a female facet of God".[11] She fears that extensive recourse to this synonym might work subliminally to produce a dualistic image of God.

God-language is always problematic, in every religious tradition and in the philosophical and theological spheres as well. No single term can prove adequate to the quest for the answers to the many mysteries of existence and to the determination of the significance of the human episode. From the moment when human beings began to reflect about divinity, they created a rich vocabulary, each word of which related to whatever aspect of existence troubled them. Creator of the Universe; Judge of All the Earth; *Makom* (Space); Our Father, Our King; YHWH; Yah; Merciful God—these and countless other synonyms of God are actually shorthand symbols for the basic experiences of life that continue to arouse curiosity, wonder, fear, awe, gratitude, bitterness, perplexity, and all the other emotions of human consciousness. In entering the field of God-naming, feminists are as hard put as men have always been to find fully satisfying nomenclature.

For several decades, Marcia Falk has been writing prayers in both Hebrew and English and, on her own testimony, has become more and more aware of the need for continuous naming of God, in response to new knowledge, outlooks, and feelings. She has coined many new terms and phrases for God, some of which have been adopted in American synagogues. Falk has concentrated on gender-neutral terms, each of which would enable the worshiper to attend readily to the life experience treated in the particular prayer. This poetess-liturgist has found her most effective outlet in the composition of blessings, which, she says, ". . . could be read as a kind of *midrash* on the tradition."[12] For example, in one of her early blessings, a benediction over wine for the holidays, which she wrote in English and Hebrew, God is addressed as *eyn hahayyim,* wellspring of life.

Frequently, Falk writes her prayers and blessings as meditations, in which God is implicit but unnamed. A good illustration of this important approach is her "Blessing before Going to Sleep":

> Sleep descending,
> on my lids,
> on my limbs,
> I call to mind—
> the gifts of the day
> the gift of this day—
> and give thanks.[13]

Falk's feminism, it seems to me, is notable more for its realization of the manifold varieties of human experience and the need to include as much of them as possible in our prayers than it is for her efforts to balance the scales against the masculine bias in Jewish prayer. Hence, she sees her mission as one of trying to ". . . set in motion a process of ongoing naming which would point toward the diversity of our experiences and reach toward a greater inclusivity within the monotheistic framework".[14]

The meditation upon retiring at night cited above and some of Falk's other blessings raise the interesting question as to how far God-language requires God-naming. That is to say, is it necessary to articulate the Name of God in prayer in order that God be addressed or God's Presence be felt? Falk answers in a significant statement. She asks, where in her prayers is the divine to be found? She declares: "Nowhere in particular—yet, potentially, everywhere that attention is brought to bear. For that reason, I suppose, one could call them 'atheist' or 'pantheist'; yet for me both these epithets miss the point. If the divine is everywhere—as many monotheists believe—or, to put it slightly differently, if everything is capable of being made holy—as rabbinic Judaism seems to teach with its scrupulous attention to the many details of ordinary life—then surely we needn't worry about localizing divinity in a single apt word or phrase. We may find it wherever our hearts and minds, our blood and our bones are stirred."[15]

For all except those who are bound to premodern images of humankind, the feminists have made their point. Traditional Jewish liturgy has to be thoroughly overhauled or, at the very least, reinterpreted and supplemented so as to reflect our up-to-date understanding of the human condition and enterprise. Actually, the Jewish prayer book has always been adjusted to the events of Jewish history and the vicissitudes of the lives of individual Jews. At times, new prayers were added or old ones permitted to pass into disuse; at other times, *piyyutim* or other types of prayer were composed in order to record traumatic events. Mostly, Jewish worshipers followed the practice of reading into the traditional text the meanings that occurred to them or extrapolating from it the ideas or emotions that were germane at the time. Many of these steps were taken as a matter of course, as if this is what tradition is all about. However, today we tend to be more self-conscious about the ways in which we interpret and reinterpret classic tradition or go about trying to enrich it. We assume responsibility for maintaining the integrity of our ancestral heritage. We are reticent, or should be, about putting words into the mouths of our forefathers or distorting their meanings. And even when we have outgrown their vision, we are reluctant, especially in the matter of prayer, to discard their formulations. They have become too precious as a means of connecting us with the hallowed generations of our past. If I judge the efforts of the serious, responsible feminists, they are as divided as men concerning what is and is not legitimate in tampering with the siddur. Their emphasis on ensuring that femininity be accorded its proper due in synagogue worship is long overdue and can no longer be viewed, as it was only a few decades ago, as an oddity of hypersensitive women. Nonetheless, even the down-to-earth feminists and their male defenders seem to be resting their case on questionable assumptions about differences between the sexes and what awareness of those differences does to the psychology of the worshiper.

Let us, by way of illustration, turn again to the essay of Eliezer Diamond. He describes his experience when he puts on tefillin and recites the touching verse of Hosea, "I will betroth you to myself forever; I will betroth you to myself in righteousness and in justice, in kindness and in mercy. I will betroth you to myself in faithfulness; and you shall know the Lord" (Hos. 2:21–22). As Diamond winds the strap around his finger, he imagines ". . . himself as a woman being espoused by a male divine lover/ husband. This imagery suggests the possibility of intimacy with God. It is not enough for me to know that God is present; I wish to experience delight in that presence, and thinking of God as spouse and lover makes that delight possible. . . . I am convinced that biological character differences do exist between men and women, but that both men and women share to some extent both sets of characteristics."[16]

How is one to react to Diamond's confession? I have to take his testimony seriously, but in doing so, I find it difficult to know how to interpret his remark. Since Diamond does not inform us what character differences are biologically induced, I haven't a clue as to what he means. He compounds the difficulty when he tells us in the very next sentence that "I am called upon during most of my waking life to engage in masculine behavior as defined by me and my community."[17] So male/female character differences are subjective or socially, rather than biologically, induced! Then, too, if a woman decides to express the "masculine" side of her character and to pray with tefillin, should she try to experience God by imagining herself as a man in pursuit of or in communion with the elusive, infinitely desirable Goddess? Goethe described Faust's ceaseless quest as "Die ewige Frau zieht uns hinan" (Eternal Woman attracts us). Are we now to look upon women as pursuing "the Eternal Man" or as imagining themselves as being the Man, their latent masculinity? The attractiveness of all this sexual imagery, which has its historical roots in Jewish mysticism and has been revived by the unabashed sexuality of our age, is obvious. It is also a salutary development in having exposed the hypocrisy of some of our traditional mores and the ignorance that underlies them. But it also constitutes a danger to clear thinking about human nature and the tenuousness of all theologizing.

Admittedly, human nature cannot be defined solely by recourse to the behavioral sciences. Psychology, anthropology, sociology, and other human sciences can provide sober and necessary information about humans, but they cannot guide us as we face the questions of life's meaning, the purposes worthy of human devotion, and the standards of moral conduct. The attempt to feel God's presence through sexual imagery borders on the ridiculous. It is, as I have insisted, based on an unfounded perception of human nature. If and when it can be shown what character traits are genetically male or female based, I might have to lend more credence than I now do to Diamond's thesis. Meanwhile, if we follow his trend of thought, we might have to conclude that the person closest to sensing God's presence is the homosexual. But then, this type of sexual separation might lead to a theological dualism; there are two gods, each one of whom is androgynous, but neither of whom is capable of embracing the other in loving union. A theology that denies or ignores the fact that all human affirmations about reality are inferences from experience and are to be judged by their greater or lesser authentication can still appeal to free-flowing imagination. However, it does not deserve the credit accorded to it in many circles of supposedly disciplined scholars.

Let us return to the feminist effort to reformulate the language of prayer. There are basically three ways of handling the problem: reinterpreting existing prayers, most of which are masculine gendered; balancing addresses to God by introducing feminine terms; and writing new prayers with neutral God-language. Of course, these methods need not be mutually exclusive. They can be and are utilized in different combinations. Sylvia Barish Feldman, for one, argues that ". . . utilizing balanced, gender-specific imagery may, in the end, be a more effective, sensitive, and meaningful use of language than eliminating gender altogether."[18]

The real problem, however, is not so much gender as it is theological and psychological. Gender might be more important an issue in Hebrew than it is in English, because each word in Hebrew is gender-laden, but that difficulty can be overcome by concentrating on the poetic intent or overtone of the word, phrase, or entire prayer. In most instances, whatever gender be the reference or the form of address to God, anthropomorphisms are generally assumed in Jewish thought to reflect the limitations of human language rather than to bear the truth of God's nature. Indeed, Feldman properly points out that were we to dispense entirely with gender-laden terminology, we should lose much of the essence of human life. She writes: "Contemporary human beings experience life and God's role in their lives as sons and daughters, as partners in loving sexual relationships, as mothers and fathers. Gender roles have powerful positive meanings."[19] This means, however, that it is crucial to the prayer experience to determine whether or not the liturgy relates honestly to what is known about the spiritual nature of men and women. Prayer, in other words, might be regarded as aspiring to experience what is divine in the human potential.

This conclusion might seem to some to be crass humanism, but it is nothing of the sort. It seems to me that what feminism has accomplished is to strip both men and women of their illusions about their respective natures and to open the way to a better understanding of God's will for the human race. Feminism unintentionally lends credence to theological approaches that take their point of departure from the study of human life and from an evaluation of its possibilities, limitations, and moral and spiritual imperatives. Such study, with its dedication to fact and its openness to spiritual adventure, can succeed only if it accepts the need to harmonize the humanistic and theistic tendencies in all humans.

Inevitably, however, all theological discourse comes up against the inadequacy of language. Rita M. Gross states the problem clearly. She writes: "Before anything else can be properly discussed, one must understand the inevitable limitations of all religious language. *All* expressions used in the religious enterprise are, in the long run, analogous and metaphorical. Every statement contains a bracketed 'as if' or 'as it were.' Statements about God should not be taken literally. They do not exhaust the possibilities at all. Rather, they are the most adequate expressions available within current idioms—linguistic conventions that function as tools, used to point to that which transcends language."[20] Gross then proceeds to recommend a policy of balancing God-language by utilizing feminine imagery. That imagery is to be fashioned in two ways. The first is to mine the many classical texts, particularly those of the Kabbalah, to which, until recently, scant attention had been paid. They contain many allusions of value to a feminist revision of the liturgy. These terms can then be introduced as substitutes here and there for the traditional, masculine usage. The second method is to invent new forms of address.

Gross bases her approach on the assumption that a gender-free vocabulary in prayer is impossible, since worship is founded on a divine-human dialogue. Prayer would be an anomaly were God to be conceived without the possibility of relating to Him/Her as person to Person. A gender-free person is impossible. But heretofore, all references to God as Person have been to God as male. Thus, Gross would have us see God as embracing femininity as essential to the divine, all-embracing nature. The only alternative would be to adopt an outright naturalist theology. Gross refers to this alternative as follows: "Unless Jewish theology *and practice* take a 180-degree turn from the metaphor of relationship with a personal deity to the metaphor of a nonpersonal Ultimate, to which one could scarcely *daven* and which would be unlikely to give *mitzvot*, they too will have to continue to use anthropomorphisms, all of which are always problematic and inaccurate nonliteral manners of speaking."[21]

A choice has to be made between a theology of relationship

between humans and a God upon whom they project their own ill-defined attributes and one in which God is conceived as the transcendent Process that gives unity and meaning to the human experience. For the naturalists, however, God, while not a Person, is nonetheless a Power that does command and deserve the awe and gratitude of all humans. Command follows in the wake of every new disclosure by humans about themselves and their natural environment. They realize that they cannot violate the laws of the physical and moral order. Gratitude, in turn, stems from the recognition that despite all the discontinuities in existence, it is responsive to human purposes that are just and in keeping with progress toward cosmic unity. Although Gross presents the naturalist alternative, she feels that the necessary recourse to anthropomorphic language makes the incorporation of feminist imagery in a relational context a preferable alternative for prayer in the modern synagogue.

A similar tack is taken by Judith Plaskow, who suggests that in order to clear the way for feminine God-language, we must overcome the whole psychology of feminine Otherness that is associated with halakhic mentality and practice. In contradistinction to many of her feminist colleagues in Orthodoxy and, to some extent, in Conservatism, she holds out little or no hope that the metamorphosis in mentality can be brought about by halakhic methods. "For *halakhah* is part of the system that women have not had a hand in creating, neither in its foundations, nor as it was developed and refined. Not only is this absence reflected in the content of *halakhah,* it may also be reflected in its very form. How can we presume that if women add their voices to the tradition, *halakhah* will be our medium of expression and repair? . . . To settle on *halakhah* as the source of justice for women is to foreclose the question of women's experience when it has scarcely begun to be raised."[22]

Plaskow's forthrightness regarding Halakhah is not confined to prayer. I assume that her barbs are directed at the halakhic method and sources of authority and the fact that up to now it has been a totally male province. However, even if women were to succeed in gaining an equal role in halakhic decision-making, Plaskow would still hold her reservations about Jewish law as a means of meeting the need for introducing the feminine reality into prayer. Prayer ought not be a matter of legal determination. Plaskow argues that the Torah, the basis of Halakhah, has to be circumlocuted if the feminine motif is to find its proper place in the liturgy. "Feminism," she says, "demands a new understanding of Torah, God and Israel: an understanding of Torah that begins with acknowledgment of the profound injustice of Torah itself. The assumption of the lesser humanity of women has poisoned the structure and content of the law, undergirding women's legal disabilities and our subordination in the broader tradition."[23]

Plaskow's anti-halakhic thrust is only a prelude to what she thinks is the real business of the feminist. Her program calls for recovering, reexploring, and reintegrating the femaleness of God into the ways in which both men and women theologize and go about reconstructing the language of prayer. Furthermore, Plaskow urges us not to delude ourselves. The synagogue service will not be refashioned unless the Jewish community as a whole emancipates women and permits and encourages them to express their true feelings and ideas. Prayer is a political, as well as spiritual, issue.

This chapter is necessarily even more incomplete than the previous ones that dealt with individual thinkers. Feminism has hardly gotten off the ground. In the coming decades, it is bound to evoke new expressions of opinion. It will inevitably stimulate the creative imagination of poets and liturgists who will seek to articulate the so-called feminine dimensions of humanity. Among the new voices will undoubtedly be many men. For feminism is not only about women. It is equally about how men perceive themselves. The latter cannot help but realize that they too can no longer be what they have been until now. It might be that the revolution in the self-understanding of males will be even more traumatic than the reordering of the female mind. As a consequence, we should expect some surpising developments in the next century in the theology, content, form, and esthetics of prayer.

NOTES

1. Susan Weidman Schneider, *Jewish and Female* (New York: Simon and Schuster, 1984).

2. Recently, Shalvi identified herself with the Masorati movement and became the rector of its school for the training of rabbis, cantors, educators, and laity.

3. Sylvia Barish Fishman, *A Breath of Life* (New York: Macmillan, 1993), p. 144.

4. Susannah Heschel, ed., *On Being a Jewish Feminist* (New York: Schocken, 1983), p. xxi.

5. Fishman, *A Breath of Life*, p. 177.

6. Arthur Green, "Bride, Spouse, Daughter: Images of the Feminine in Classical Jewish Sources," in Heschel, *Jewish Feminist*, pp. 248–249.

7. Fishman, *A Breath of Life*, p. 238.

8. Eliezer Diamond, "Image and Imagination: The Revealed and Hidden Faces of God in Jewish Liturgy," *The Reconstructionist* 59, no.1 (spring 1994), p. 64.

9. Tikva Frymer-Kensky, "On Feminine God-Talk", *The Reconstructionist*, p. 48.

10. Ibid., p. 149.

11. Ibid.

12. Marcia Falk, "Beyond Naming: Reflections on Composing *The Book of Blessings*," *The Reconstructionist*, p. 68.

13. Ibid., p. 70.

14. Ibid., p. 68.

15. Ibid., p. 70.

16. Diamond, "Image and Imagination," p. 62.

17. Ibid.

18. Fishman, *A Breath of Life*, p. 240.

19. Ibid., p. 241.

20. Rita M. Gross, "Steps toward Feminine Imagery of Deity in Jewish Theology," in Heschel, *Jewish Feminist*, p. 235.

21. Ibid., p. 237.

22. Judith Plaskow, "The Right Question Is Theological," in Heschel, *Jewish Feminist*, p. 231.

23. Ibid.

12

Can Prayer Be Revitalized?

THE BESHT IS QUOTED as having said, "If after you've prayed, you're the same as before you prayed, why did you pray?"[1] Dr. Louis L. Kaplan, who cites this passage, goes on to say, "This teaching of the Besht charges us to understand that we enter a synagogue not to appease the Divine or solicit his intercession, but to learn what we are to do after we leave the synagogue and make our way to where the action is." He adds that the real purpose of prayer ". . . is to stimulate, not sedate, to make us aware of new concerns and move us to new deeds so that we do not remain at ease in our little Zions."[2]

Louis L. Kaplan, a noted Jewish educator who at the time of this writing had reached the age of ninety-five, is an outstanding exemplar of those Jews to whom worship in the synagogue should be an adventure and a challenge. Like the Besht, Kaplan wants worshipers to emerge from their participation in the communal prayers as new beings, stronger in their faith, more steadfast in their commitments, more energetic and clearer in their vision. This is a tall order, but unless one sets one's sights beyond one's reach, little of worth can be accomplished.

Taking our lead from Louis Kaplan, let us ask for what purpose should men and women gather to pray together? The reader will recall that Kaplan's activistic approach is a dominant theme in the philosophies of the thinkers we have presented in this study. All want Jews to emerge from prayer as better and more complete human beings, ready to do battle for their ideals and more determined to serve God and their fellow men and women. However, beyond this important area of agreement, praying Jews differ radically as to the ideal human being who should be the subject and object of the worship experience. One can presumably pray to God without being certain of His essence, but it is pointless to pray for self-improvement unless one determines what kind of person one wishes to be. It is precisely here that the crisis in prayer is most manifest. As I have intimated, men and women can pray together without a common conception of God. They share the hope that in communal worship, they will be strengthened in their faith in the reality of God and in the hope for their salvation. Most worshipers realize that they might never succeed in fathoming the mystery of divinity. On the other hand, their destiny and that of the human race as a whole is to a large extent in their hands. They have to know where they want to go together. Therefore, their common prayer must be founded on a consensus as to what constitutes the complete human being and the ideal Jew.

At this point, we are confronted with a bewildering variety of visions of the honest worshiper and of the purposes, content, and form of group prayer. Among our thinkers, there are those, like Kook, Arele, Munk, Heschel, and probably Petuchowski, who, more than the others, believe that the traditional liturgy, piously recited and properly interpreted, suffices to inspire Jewish worshipers. But even were these men somehow to find themselves praying in the same synagogue, they would nonetheless occupy different spiritual spaces. For instance, it is unlikely that Arele would have been disturbed by the intellectual and social concerns that might occasionally have interfered with Kook's concentration. Kook, in turn, would have been less likely than Heschel to extend the reach of his prayer into the concerns of general human welfare that activated the latter. It would be pointless, of course, to press too hard on such differentiations, for sincere worshipers cannot avoid praying on behalf of all their fellows. Nor can they divest themselves of their mind or their emotions when they enter a house of worship. Nevertheless, each person employs his or her faculties in different degrees and with varied objectives. In this sense, all five of the "traditionalists" can be said to respond in his own idiosyncratic way to the classical liturgy. Five worshipers—five prayer moods.

The designation "traditionalist" belongs in one way or another to all the thinkers we have examined. They all travel with the heritage. I have placed Heschel and Petuchowski alongside three men whose traditionalism was clearly more austere than theirs. I have done so because Heschel's poetic vision and Petuchowski's latitudinarian approach to the text of the siddur enabled them to overcome whatever doubts they might have had about the meaning of the ancient prayers. They seem to have believed that the traditional words could cope with modern cosmology, anthropology, psychology, and universal ethicism. Apparently, they succeeded in breathing comfortably in the atmosphere created by the ancient Sages without inhaling any foul air or feeling any urgency about introducing fresh air. They could rest satisfied with poetry and reinterpretation.

The other philosophers also respected the traditional texts of the daily, Sabbath, and holiday prayer books but, in varying degrees, found it necessary to revise and supplement their contents. However, as I tried to make clear in my summaries of their philosophies of prayer, although they branched off in different directions, they were united in their common effort to accommodate the synagogue service to what they thought is spiritually compelling in modernity. We are thus left with the realization that there is and can be no single solution to the current crisis of prayer. All we can do is to indicate some of the options, identify their parameters, and assess as fairly as possible their potential contributions to the revitalization of public worship. In the course of this exposition, it behooves me to make my own recommendations. One must run the risk of error, particularly after being so free in criticizing others.

The traditional siddur is replete with prayers, meditations, and statements that constitute an excellent point of departure for exploring the nature of humans and the values for which they ought to live. For example, the benediction to be recited by women at the outset of the morning service praises God "Who has made me according to His will." This blessing, which deserves to be recited by men as well, prepares every person to seek self-understanding and self-acceptance. We are all born with differing capacities, and we all have to learn how to make the best of whatever gifts we have, without rancor at the fact that we may not be the equal of others in regard to certain talents. Furthermore, we all have to learn the hard lesson that the universe was not created in order to satisfy our egos and that many of us might have to struggle with adversity all our lives. The blessing under discussion calls upon all humans to resist bitterness and to maintain their dignity.

A few paragraphs later, the traditional Jewish prayer book instructs us always to revere God, whether in public or in private, to acknowledge the truth, and to speak truth in one's heart. No person can afford to forget for a moment this call to honesty and clear conscience.

During the *Pesukei D'zimra* (the selections, mostly from the Book of Psalms, that build up the mood for community worship), there are a number of references to the quality of all humans and to the destiny of humankind. At one point, the Psalmist offers advice to the person who wishes to live fully. The Psalmist says: "Keep your tongue from evil and your lips from speaking guile. Depart from evil and do good. Seek peace and pursue it" (Ps. 34:14–15). Ideal humans avoid misusing their power of speech, and they engage actively in the pursuit of peace and in contributing to the welfare of all humans.

Anyone familiar with the traditional prayer book could cite similar examples. Nevertheless, the siddur falls short of satisfying the need for clarity regarding the kind of person whom prayer should help to cultivate. In the first place, remarks like those to which I have referred are too scattered to stir worshipers to reflect on the quality of their own character. More importantly, the siddur offers here and there a picture that is a distortion of what enlightened opinion today considers to be an accurate portrait of what a human person is or might become.

For example, while women recite the blessing cited above, every halakhic-minded male thanks God for not having made him a woman. The customary explanation for this blessing is that since men are obliged to perform more mitzvot than are imposed upon women, they must express their appreciation for their special status. This explanation only aggravates the anachronistic Rabbinic view that is founded on the assumption that the psyches of men and women are essentially different. The time has come to revalue this and other perceptions of human nature on which the social roles of men and women have been based. The work of Carol Gilligan is helpful in revealing the disparate ways in which men and women perceive reality and how necessary it is for each sex to reappraise its perceptions and learn how to achieve a character that is both caring and responsible.[3] In the wake of such examination, it is essential that liturgical adjustments should follow.

Similarly, the sharp contrasts that are set forth between the spirituality of the Jews and that of the other nations are founded on an unacceptable morality of the responsibility of nations. Without denigrating the enormous contributions made by the Jewish people to theological and ethical maturity, I suggest that the emphasis on the comparative mood is a detriment to further advances toward full spiritual stature. The idea expressed in the reference to God as having "raised us [the Jewish people] above all tongues" is hardly calculated to encourage Jews to relate objectively to the spiritual resources of other nations.

To cite one more instance, the prayer for the annihilation of heretics, found in the *Amidah*, does not belong in a modern prayer book. Apologists for the retention of this prayer argue that it was composed under threatening circumstances. The sectarianism of the Jewish Christians weakened the morale of the people in its struggle against Rome. Deviations of a spiritual nature had—and continue to have—political consequences. Hence resistance to heresy is essential. However, a historical reflection of this type cannot justify the attitude toward heresy contained in this prayer. Who is to define heresy in a free society? And what should be the fate of a heretic, assuming that he could be located with justifiable assurance? Has not the moral development of man reached the stage at which mind control has become, or should become, an anachronism? Ismar Elbogen, in his magisterial study of the history of Jewish prayer, suggested that the most sensible change in this benediction ". . . is to eliminate it entirely."[4]

Moreover, the ideal human of the traditional siddur could not be expected to have attributes or capacities that have only recently been thought desirable. For example, it never entered the minds of the Sages that men and women ought to or could enter into intimate relations stemming from professional interests or simple friendship. Classical Hebrew knows no word for nonsexual intimacy. The concept did not exist. We humans have learned or should have learned to be more circumspect than ever in regard to our claims about our capabilities and limitations as human beings. For example, we have had to abandon the presumption that humans stand at the center of the universe and that all of nature is theirs to subdue. Just as the Copernican revolution deprived the earth of its centrality, so has the disclosure of the vastness of Creation given us pause as to the meaning and purpose of human existence or of existence itself. We can no longer be sure that we humans are the crowning achievement of the creative process. At most, we have a right to hold out hope that the human adventure may eventuate in something more magnificent than it already is. We can extract new meaning from the prescient cry of the Psalmist: "O Lord, our Lord / How glorious is Thy name in all the earth! / Whose majesty is rehearsed above the heavens / . . . When I behold Thy heavens, the work of Thy fingers, / The moon and the stars, which Thou hast established; / What is man, that Thou art mindful of him? / And the son of man, that Thou thinkest of him? / Yet Thou hast made him but little lower than the angels, / And hast crowned him with glory and honor. / Thou hast made him to have dominion over the works of Thy hands; / Thou hast put all things under his feet" (Ps. 8:2, 4–7). The Psalmist is right in his grasp of the sublimity of the universe. He is right about our ability to exercise considerable authority as God's creative assistant. But even as we explore the stars and outer space, we acquire or should acquire greater humility before the ever-expanding reality that flees from our grasp. This new realization is both daunting and inspiring.

The ideal Jew, like all men and women, should contemplate human life as but a passing phenomenon, which can nonetheless be worthwhile to the individual or of great cosmic importance. We can and should find satisfaction in our earthly existence, without expectation of reward in this world or in life after death. Not that we know any more about what happens after death than has ever been known. We do, however, observe that the disintegration of the human body seems more and more to be an inevitable incident in the reorganization of all matter, large and small. If it be argued that there is always the possibility that human souls survive, the surmise, at best, can only be a guess or a gamble. Mature human beings should want to base their life on the certainty that they have only a little time in which to work out a satisfying career. This is a more somber and tough-minded kind of expectation than is offered by supernatural religion, but it seems to me to be a more reasonable and therefore more spiritually rewarding assumption on which to determine the fulfillment of human destiny. Prayer should be one of the main instruments for enabling men and women to face life as it is, with dignity, courage, and determination to play the game zestfully to its end.

I realize that the foregoing paragraph will shock some readers and raise the hackles of others. The former will claim that were they to accept my view, they would have nothing to sustain them in hours of pain, despair, and disappointment. The latter will charge me with hubris in claiming to possess information about the reality beyond the grave, concerning which I can have no knowledge whatsoever. Better that I should remain silent. To both of these critics I say, "You are correct. But you, too, are in the same boat. We are all guessing and staking our visions of life on surmise. All I ask is that you credit the position I have stated with being a serious and honest attempt to contribute to human maturity. Our prayers should at least reflect the uncertainty that we should all feel about the future of humanity and spur us to try together to improve the human lot during our limited life span."

The human soul also needs comfort and revitalization in the face of the sorrows and moments of despair that inevitably befall it. Here again, by means of prayer, the individual can acquire the broad perspective that is a prerequisite for what has been termed "peace of mind" or "peace of soul." In some sophisticated circles, such an expression is derided, but the derision is undeserved. Human beings cannot survive creatively if they are always despondent or incapable of exerting an effort to carry their share of the social burdens. Of course, if prayer is conceived as an anodyne to soften the pain of reality but does nothing to strengthen worshipers' ability to cope with the truth of their condition, then it is misguided. But peace of mind or soul need not be a passive state. It can bespeak a courageous and wise resistance to a dangerous lapse into passivity. Peace of mind can be viewed as the healthy reaction of a person determined to survive against the hostile forces of environment. Like the man on the verge of freezing to death, who must resist a false sense of warmth, so the worshiper out of despair must seek the kind of mind-set that is at one and the same time alert to the peril of self-pity and sufficiently self-possessed to do battle against the temptation to surrender the will to live. This is no less a valid reason to pray than the desire to improve one's character or to commune with an undefinable God.

Perhaps the most important purpose of prayer, and the most difficult to accomplish, is to strengthen the sense of human equality in the face of existential inequality. Humans are born unequal. They are not endowed with the same gifts of body and mind. Some are granted strong and vigorous bodies; others are doomed to suffer physical disabilities, even to die prematurely. Some persons are accorded great intelligence; others are retarded. These inequalities are accentuated in the course of our daily existence. Our societies reward the gifted and condemn average and handicapped persons to a less than fair share of life's rewards. I can think of only one institution of human creation that is designed to overcome the natural, unequal state of all human creatures and make them conscious of their essential parity. Such equality is conceivable only when we see ourselves as servants of God. As such, we are brought to understand that there are no superior or inferior creatures. From the standpoint of divinity, nothing in our natural endowments or in our acquired status can raise us above any of our fellows. But it is only in prayer, when worshipers are conscious of their need to rely upon the power and grace of God, that they can understand how irrelevant are their intellect, their age, their wealth, or any of their assets as measures of their standing in the sight of God. Before God, all are equal—or so they must assume themselves to be.

The attainment of this level of self-understanding is extremely difficult; but if this purpose of prayer is acknowledged, it can at least serve as a criterion for the evaluation of our communal worship. Clearly, when this purpose is held up for examination, we have much to be ashamed of in the conduct of our organized worship. It is not difficult to compile a list of ways in which we carry into the synagogue the inequalities of the street.

At this point, the discerning reader will ask me to pause. The emphasis I have placed on prayer as an occasion for exploring various scenarios of human destiny and for self-examination and self-improvement seems too secular. After all, is not surrender to God's will at the heart of prayer, and not the assertion of human, generally self-centered concerns? Eugene Borowitz, one of the most cogent proponents of Covenant theology, raises the question with clarity. Borowitz writes: "If the modern Jew is to learn to pray as a Jew and not just as man in general, he does not need a better prayerbook but a better theology, not a different form of worship, but a deeper belief."[5] Belief in what? Borowitz answers that we must have faith that ". . . needs are best met in terms of God's will, his law, his purposes."[6] This rhetoric, which also characterizes Heschel and others who try to surmount the danger of exaggerating the power of reason and human assertiveness, cannot hide the fact that all talk about God's will, law, and purposes is projection of human imagination. However much we all want to bow to God's will, we have no means other than modest, disciplined use of our mind on which to base our claims of having apprehended it. Thus, prayer should be conceived as but another, albeit unique and indispensable, step in man's search for God. Simultaneously, prayer is also the instrument that is designed to tame humans' assertiveness and arrogance. In no way may naturalists divest themselves of the awareness that humans stand forever before the dauntless power of the universe. The humanistic point of departure, therefore, should not be dismissed as lacking in religious sentiment.

All of our thinkers highlight as another purpose of prayer the endeavor to foster the unity and the continuity of the group—in this instance, the Jewish people. Judaism is largely a family-oriented, rather than a synagogue-centered religion. More of the mitzvot are related to the home than to the synagogue. But it is through synagogue worship that the family ties can be strengthened and the family can sense its belonging to an inspiring tradition and to fellow Jews who share their ideals and their dreams.

Prayer is thus meant to be a way of lifting people out of the narrow confines of their egos and qualifying them to be caring, useful members of society. This overriding aspiration, however, can be approximated only if we attend seriously to other facets of the prayer experience. The main such consideration is the theological basis of prayer, which we shall discuss after examining one of the other purposes of prayer—satisfying the passion for Truth.

Truth, when conceived as a divine attribute or even as synonymous with Deity, is undefinable. Rationalists nonetheless pursue it, hoping that somewhere along the road, they will catch a glimpse of this unseen, mysterious siren. Even then, however, rationalists admit that they will have to find satisfaction in the glimpse alone, because they know that in following the trail of Truth, they are engaged in an endless chase after a real but ultimately elusive existent. Yet rationalists, in contrast to mystic-oriented pietists, are satisfied with this limited goal. They are exhilarated by the race; they enjoy the excitement of knowing that the object of their pursuit is truly desirable. Does not love itself always fall short of the ideal? But does that fact deprive love of its fascination and its joy? Having caught a momentary glimpse of the potential of the beloved, the lover will not be deterred from courting. Seekers of Truth are thus adventurers exploring the outer reaches of experience, never certain as to the significance of what they have discovered or the scope of what they might yet bring within their grasp. For such persons, prayer can play a twofold role. It can spur them to reach beyond the limits of today toward a more promising future; it can also remind them that Truth is indeed not their metier and that whenever they are tempted to apply uppercase lettering to their perceptions and conceptions, they had better examine their hubris and retreat to the lowercase mood.

There are those, however, the mystics in our midst, who believe that they are capable of piercing the veil. As Evelyn Underhill has written, the mystics are convinced that ". . . they have succeeded where all others have failed, in establishing immediate communication between the spirit of man, entangled as they declare amongst material things, and that 'only Reality,' that immaterial and final Being, which some philosophers call the Absolute, and most theologians call God. This, they say—and here many who are not mystics agree with them—is the hidden Truth which is the object of man's craving; the only satisfying goal of his quest."[7]

We have observed how the inclination toward mysticism or rationalism affected the expectations from prayer on the part of our thinkers. For some, prayer is indispensable in the education of human beings. For others, prayer is necessary to enable the individual to cope with the tensions of existence. Among these worshipers, there is also a tendency to flee from the reality of earthly existence to the Reality of the realm of Truth. Apparently, temperament conditions the choice of purposes. Inasmuch as mental dispositions are extant in different proportions in every group, we cannot dismiss any of the foregoing purposes of prayer out of hand. An all-encompassing philosophy of prayer will have to reckon with all of them.

TOWARD A THEOLOGY OF PRAYER

Purpose, if it is not to be illusion or arrogance, has to be founded as much as possible on verified experience. The desire of Icarus to fly was wishful thinking; it was unrelated to the then-known capacities of man or the facts of the natural order. Not so the pioneers of modern aviation, whose efforts were founded on steadily growing knowledge of the workings of gravity, wind currents, the potentials of various types of engines and the fuel that energizes their operation, etc. However, this observation has to be qualified. The human imagination cannot be constrained by the incompleteness or tentativeness of available information. A person's desire or vision is often a first step in causing something to happen, for whose attainment the dreamer has at present no reliable instrumentality. The purpose itself sometimes generates the actions that create the conditions for success.

Thus, the distinction between truth and Truth, empiricism and idealism, rationalism and mysticism, might not be as wide as described above. We might define truth as the conclusions about the relatedness of phenomena most warranted in the light of current information. Truth (with a capital T), on the other hand, demands that all truth claims be subject to revision whenever they fail to accord with expanded knowledge. At the same time, the belief in Truth makes worthwhile the pursuit of truth. Meliorism rather than perfectionism is the rule of mundane existence. But the search for perfection, for Absolute Truth, is what drives human beings to become more knowledgeable, better, and more mature than they are at any given moment.

Prayer is one of the most effective means of enabling a person to be aware of how far he or she has come along the path between truth and Truth. However, prayer, its form and content, is conditioned by the social and theological vision that motivates the worshiper's efforts at self-transcendence. Having examined theologies formulated by several twentieth-century theologians, I feel called upon to grapple with the problem from my own stand-point.

I start by describing the natural environment in which I believe humankind must try to define and fulfill its destiny.

I neither know nor can ever know any of the absolutes so dear to seekers of ultimate answers. I follow scientific cosmologists as they push back the frontiers of human knowledge about the gene-sis of the cosmos. The various branches of science have pooled their resources and succeeded in unwrapping some of the mystery of our vast cosmos. But although we are now able to speculate about the origins of our earth and other planets in our solar sys-tem and have discovered the existence of many more celestial systems, we cannot answer the question of Creation itself. To say that God created the universe is to give verbal form to the mys-tery. Wrapped in God-language, we gain emotional warmth but are no closer than before to unraveling the secret of Creation. Nor can we solve the problem by positing the eternity of the mate-rial universe and putting all our trust in its amazing degree of orderliness. The creationists have a point when they argue that it is unlikely that our cosmos is an accident and that some blueprint was involved in its formation. Honesty, however, demands that we admit our ignorance. The explanations of Creation (not cre-ation) are pure guesswork, and all of the sophisticated philoso-phizing and theologizing in which brilliant minds have engaged cannot hide that fact. We must all be humble agnostics in regard to Creation.

In spite of our ignorance, however, we need not despair. Our universe opens its arms to us and invites us to employ its many resources for the satisfaction of our needs. Our job is to identify those needs and, as Mordecai Kaplan has urged, to distinguish them from our greeds. We can then turn to our outer and inner worlds and search for ways to fulfill what is lacking in us. We do not always succeed, but our experience justifies our assumption that if we have correctly defined our needs, their satisfaction is available in our environment. However, we have to be realistic. As far as we can discern, the cosmos was not made for our instant satisfaction. Our very mortality should suffice to curtail our pride and lower our self-importance. We humans have to play the game of life without illusions. There is enough encouragement in our present accomplishments and in imagining a better future to make life worthwhile, but we must accept the fact that we shall always fall short of accomplishing all our purposes. We are, after all, mortal creatures, and we have to learn to find our fulfillment within that context.

Many men and women find this orientation to life too stark. They want to live eternally. Existence after death is more real to them than what takes place on earth. Indeed, for them, this world is a corridor to the world-to-come. Obviously, I repeat, no one can prove or disprove either of these visions of human destiny, and it is likely that humankind will always be divided about the subject. I believe, however, that the sober view is the better way to look at life.

In the first place, by bracketing the question of Creation and operating on the assumption that the universe is guided by unchanging laws of nature, we accomplish several things. We avoid the necessity of attributing to God the terrible unfairness of natural evil. We cannot, of course, deny the evil, but taking the universe's composition as it seems to be, we can hope that our efforts to overcome some of its deficiencies and discontinuities need not be in vain. This is a career worthy of our investment. By concentrating on the world as it is, rather than speculating about its First Cause or the God who created it, we make our natural environment more hospitable. We prove to ourselves that our efforts to probe the order of the universe are reasonable and a good basis for planning a better future for the human race. Can this view, however, in any way be called religious? Where is God? How can one pray to a natural process? Such questions, we are told, once brought Hermann Cohen to tears. Even those rationalists who might not easily be emotionally stirred must take up the challenge of prayer to a God who is not a Person or a Being, but who might be identified in terms of Process.

How is one to distinguish between religious and secular conceptions of reality? The usual, trite response to this query is to say that religion begins with a recognition of God's existence and rule, whereas secularism denies that this assumption is at all necessary for the conduct of life.[8] Both positions beg the question. The theist posits the very divine existence that he has to prove and that, to the best of my knowledge, remains the subject of faith rather than fact. The secularist too, in all of his varied manifestations as agnostic, atheist, or indifferentist, relies on his unproved assumption that God's presence is irrelevant to human concerns. In sum, all of us are forced to make the most fundamental decision of our lives, affirming, denying, or suspending belief in God, as a *response* to our experience but not as an *answer* to its riddles. Given this uncertainty, what response should be designated as religious and what secular?

Religion and secularism are united in raising the crucial question of the role and destiny of human beings. Moreover, their responses to the mystery of human fate leave unanswered many more questions than they answer. Both are filled with uncertainties. We have no choice but to stake our lives on a guess. Yes, we all beg the question, and we must all bear the consequences of our respective points of departure. We have to keep open minds about the evidence put forth in the positions of those who disagree with us. The secular-religious debate is pointless. The issue is not which answer is secular or religious, but which responses (not answers) offer the best chance for human beings to fashion their future.

Certain theists will immediately charge me with anthropocentrism, which, they maintain, is what secularism is all about. They will say that God, not human beings, is central and that humans were placed on earth to do God's will. I reiterate that this pious argument of God's centrality is a not too subtle way of hiding the fact that the assertion is a human speculation. The validity of such an assumption is to be judged in the same manner that we evaluate other workings of the human mind. What does the centrality of God mean other than that different men and women advance claims about God's attributes and will and what it is that God demands of us? The truth is that the theists and the humanists in all their varieties are groping in the dark. They affirm or deny a transcendent reality about whose essence any Truth claim is or approaches idolatry. For humans to define what is always beyond their reach is the height of hubris. This becomes especially clear when the definition of or denial of God is used to determine how humans should behave. How many crimes have been committed in the name of God and/or in the name of a world conducted solely by mortal beings!

This perennial controversy is beautifully described in two striking talmudic passages in Berakhot 7a. The first reads as follows:
"R. Yohanan said in the name of R. Yose, How do we know that
God prays? Because it states (Jer. 9:7), 'I shall bring them to My
holy mount and make them rejoice in My house of prayer.' The
text does not read the house of *their* prayer; it says *My* prayer.
From this we learn that the Holy one, blessed be He, prays. What
is the content of His prayer? R. Zutra bar Tovia said in the name
of Rav, 'May it be My will that My mercy will triumph over My
anger and prevail over My attribute of [strict] justice, so that I
may treat My children mercifully and judge them leniently.'" Immediately following this imaginative incursion into the mind of
God comes a no less remarkable aggadah. In it, we are told that
R. Ishmael ben Elisha [evidently a High Priest] is reported to have
said, "Once I entered the Holy of Holies [on Yom Kippur] to
offer incense, and I saw Akatriel, Yah, the Lord of Hosts [it is
uncertain whether R. Ishmael is referring to an angel or to God
Himself], sitting on a high, exalted throne. He said to me, 'Ishmael, My son, Bless Me!' I said to Him, 'May it be Your will that
Your mercy conquer Your anger and that it prevail over Your attribute of [strict] justice, so that You may deal mercifully with Your
children and judge them with lenience.' "

To whom is prayer addressed? In these two Rabbinic homilies,
we learn how troubled the Sages were by this question. Their perplexity is all the more fascinating when we consider that their
theological bent was toward the concept of God as a Being or
Person. However, along with this vision of God—without which
the whole structure of God's revelatory power and of the divinity
of the Torah would have collapsed—the Sages had a highly sophisticated view of the workings of the human mind. They understood the phenomenon of meditation, of talking to oneself, and
of the complex nature of reflection. They were receptive to some
forms of worship in which prayer is addressed to transcendent
elements in the human makeup. There are many prayers in the
traditional siddur that are addressed to the Jewish people as a
whole or to the individual Jew. The classic example, of course,
comes from the Bible, when Israel is told to reflect on God's
unity—*Shema Yisrael.* In essence, prayers that are addressed to
God indicate what is going on in the minds of the worshipers.

We humans have no choice but to shape our lives according to the values we conceive. We must try to avoid the sin of pride by recognizing our creaturely limitations, but we must also use as wisely and as responsibly as we can the enormous power conferred on our minds. This balancing act is a prime duty of humankind, and it makes no difference whether the act is dubbed religious or secular. Once this premise is accepted, we can then conduct the semantic argument as to what we mean by affirming or denying God.

However, beyond the semantic issue, there remains the question as to whether or not human consciousness is graced with other means besides the intellect for capturing the meaning of life. Martin Buber (1878–1965), for example, viewed true prayer as an experience of the whole being rather than as the expression in words of human aspirations or as reflection on the meaning of divinity. "To teach how to pray," he wrote, "means above all forms of words: to teach how to turn one's self thence."[9] That is to say, a formal liturgy and even a spontaneous verbal prayer fall short of the vital worshipful experience. Prayer for Buber is turning to God, and that is not to be accomplished through reflecting analytically or synthetically upon the lived concrete. "Meaning is to be experienced in living action and suffering"[10]—that is, man at prayer is the object of the impact of life and not only the subject that comprehends life's unreduced immediacy. Buber continues: "Of course, he who aims at the experience of experience will necessarily miss the meaning, for he destroys the spontaneity of the mystery. Only he reaches the meaning who stands firm, without holding back or reservation, before the whole might of reality and answers it in a living way. He is ready to confirm with his life the meaning which he has attained."[11]

It would take us far afield to enter into an in-depth consideration of Buber's theology. Important for our treatment of prayer is to note the virtual eclipse of reflection in what Buber calls "living action and suffering." Experience of God and of life's meaning is immediate and direct. Maurice Friedman describes Buber's conception of prayer as ". . . not spirituality floating above concrete reality but lived concreteness. Prayer is the very essence of the immediacy between man and God, and praying is, above all words, the action of turning directly to God. In true prayer, no matter what else the individual asks for, he ultimately asks for the manifestation of the divine Presence, for this Presence's becoming dialogically perceivable."[12] Thus, prayer occurs when the individual feels that he is confronted by God and is able to respond in kind.

Buber senses the risk in his version of prayer. He is quick to utter a word of reservation and precaution. "That one accepts the concrete situation as given to him does not, in any way, mean that he must be ready to accept that which meets him as 'God-given' in its pure factuality. He may, rather, declare the extremest enmity toward this happening and treat its 'givenness' as only intended to draw forth his own opposing force. But he will not remove himself from the concrete situation as it actually is; he will, instead, enter into it, even if in the form of fighting against it. . . . He knows no floating of the spirit above concrete reality; to him even the sublimest spirituality is an illusion if it is not bound to the situation. Only the spirit which is bound to the situation is prized by him as bound to the *Pneuma,* the spirit of God."[13]

It is hard to see how Buber can escape the analysis that he rejects but that is essential if one is to determine when one has turned to the *Pneuma* and when to the evil inclination or to an idol. Buber is either powerless or unwilling to describe when we have been confronted by one or another of these forces. While there is much that is suggestive in his insistence on rooting prayer in specific experiences, he has not, in my opinion, clarified what he understands as experiencing the meaning of existence. Experience devoid of cognition is a tautology—experience is experience—and can make no claim about meaning. Emotion, it is true, cannot be reduced to intellection, but a bare emotional experience can only provide the raw material on which the mind must eventually perform its task of rational interpretation.

Furthermore, Buber's whole orientation is beyond the scope of this study, whose concern is not limited to individual prayer. Buber was not involved in group worship. He did not attend the synagogue, nor did he seem to be impressed with the liturgical aspects of Jewish tradition. Prayer for him was highly personal, an individual achievement. I do not deny the possibility and desirability of personal prayer. Indeed, as I have argued throughout this study, all those who affirm group worship hope that it will contribute to the ability of the individual to feel close to God. Buber, however, evidently saw nothing in the synagogue that could contribute significantly to the interaction of the individual with God.

Let us now return to the main thread of our theological argument. I believe that the reality experienced by man is composed of both immanent and transcendent elements. Hardly anyone disputes the evidence of the senses, although many of us are cognizant of their unreliability. Some of us, the philosophical idealists, look upon the world of the senses as a pale reflection of the true reality of Ideas. But our skepticism is mild; we have learned how to minimize and correct the misleading propensities of our physical faculties. At the same time, we have traveled beyond immanence and comprehended or created a realm of transcendence by which we explain or judge the events of our concrete experience. I refer to the natural laws and the moral standards by means of which we determine the connectedness of physical phenomena and the forms of behavior most likely to advance human welfare.

Religionists and secularists can, I believe, travel together on the road just described. Some of them part company over the question as to whether the transcendent is equivalent to the supernatural. But even here, the denial of that equivalence is no indication of the ideological camp, religious or secular, to which one belongs. Both sets of ideologies are guided by assumptions that transport them beyond the gravitational hold of the immanent. The division between them comes at the point at which the religionist conceives this transcendent reality as favoring the possibility of human fulfillment and the secularist considers it to be irrelevant to human destiny. Indeed, says the secularist, as I define him, the human race is doomed to extinction as the irreversible, destructive force of entropy grinds our planet slowly to its end.[14] At best, the secularist seems to tell us, humans can trust only themselves and their resources.

I must now confront the question as to where God is to be sought. Religionist and secularist alike enter the theological arena the moment they accept the reality of transcendence in the sense described above. Those who perceive transcendence as essential to the disclosure and fulfillment of what is possible in the realm of the immanent will perforce find God in the workings of the transcendent order. They might adopt either a naturalistic or supernaturalistic interpretation of transcendence, but in either case, they will be unable to escape the necessity of grappling with the God-idea. Secularists will most likely express their view by stressing their faith in Man or Woman. But that faith too carries them into transcendence. For what is trust in humans if not unprovable confidence in the process of human improvement and in the climb to a superior level of existence? Can one hope to reach that peak unless the human makeup and the nature of the environment are so constituted as to assist or at least not stand in the way of human endeavor? Whether one names this attitude faith in God or natural piety is of small moment. What counts is how one ought to relate to the transcendent factor. Religionists will worship; secularists are likely to confine themselves to the study of humankind and nature, perhaps in a spirit no less pious than that of worshipers. As we shall try to demonstrate, worship in the future will have to travel along some of the path followed by sensitive secular humanists, just as the latter, if they are to be candid, will find their way to some point of contact with worshipers.

Finally, it comes to this: Yes, one can pray to a God who is not a Being but a Process that comes to consciousness in the human soul. The Psalmist long ago showed us this possibility when he not only addressed God, the Other, but turned to his inner self in frequent meditation. In his very first contemplation on the human condition, the poet concludes that happiness and proximity to God are attained by avoiding association with wicked, sinful, and scornful men and by meditating day and night on God's law (Ps.1:1–2). The entire psalm is clearly an appeal to the better self of the poet. It is, at the same time, a prayer in every sense of the term, in which God is addressed only as the inferred guarantor of happiness to the worthy person.

I cite just two other examples of the Psalmist's meditative prayer. In one, he proclaims again his conviction that "Happy is the man who has made the Lord his trust, / And has not turned to the arrogant, nor to the treacherous" (Ps. 40:5).

In the next psalm, the poet declares, "Happy is he that considers the poor; / The Lord will deliver him in the day of evil" (Ps. 41:2). Once again, the soul discovers God's saving grace—and this without doing more than naming the redemptive Power. For many of us moderns, that Power might well be the natural order of the universe. Calling that order nature is equivalent to the Psalmist's identifying the object of his faith as God or Lord. For in both instances, the namer is expressing his faith in his salvation, whose fulfillment is dependent on the workings of an orderly universe.

In other words, it is reasonable for a person to probe the soul for its ideal possibilities. In so doing, the person realizes that without the support of the force or forces that control the universe, all human aspiration would be idle fancy. What is this effort at self-transcendence if not prayer? Who is the God to whom the Psalmist refers in his meditations? Must God be conceived only as the totally Other, the supernatural Creator, Legislator, and Judge of all the earth? Or may we not conceive of an alternate belief, namely that the name "God" should refer to the natural but mysterious order that the worshiper piously acknowledges. Cannot "God" be a proper designation for the unknown and untapped resources of the transcendent laws of existence? Is one not praying when one articulates reliance on this inexhaustible process? Is not the search for the source of human fulfillment tantamount to a quest for God? That source can be only partially uncovered by mortal beings, but is not this limited achievement an indication of the indispensability of prayer in the intellectual and moral refinement of humankind?

PRAYER AND WORSHIP

How does one pray to a God who is not a Being or a Person? Or, to state the question more accurately, how does one worship a God to whom one has given a Name but about whose existence one can do no more than express confidence? This problem does not bother the believer in a supernatural God, but it is crucial to the philosophy of prayer of anyone, like myself, who wants to arrive at a more satisfying encounter with God than can be experienced in the synagogue of today. I have dealt briefly with some of the theological concerns that must engage a naturalist. I turn now to some of the practical implications of such an orientation.

First, we have to distinguish between worship and prayer. Long before prayer became customary among our ancestors, they worshiped God in other ways—by song and dance, by offering sacrifices, and by observing a variety of rituals and other mitzvot. Evidently, they felt that they could be made to feel God's presence in ways other than prayer. Prayer was and is only one of the methods by means of which mortals hope to feel God's presence and remind themselves of how much they are dependent on forces beyond their ken.

There are many persons who react casually to the life process into which they are born. As Heschel repeats time and again, they are often blind to the wonder of life itself, are incapable of appreciating the sights and sounds that impinge on their senses, and are governed only by their inner drives. These are not the people, no matter how legion they be, who are admired by those of us who are cognizant of the dual greatness and smallness of humans. Once we have become aware of our creative potential and learned to respect the limits of our ability, we have no choice but to accept our creatureliness. When we concentrate on exploiting our native talents, we treat the environment as our possession and our tool. But when we step back and look honestly at our situation in the universe, we cannot help but acknowledge our reliance on the cosmic order. The fact that this order is pliable to our manipulation cannot override our having to behave according to its rules. With this recognition, we put ourselves into a mood of worship—a mood of pious gratitude for the gifts of nature, of determination to learn what is expected of us during our short span on earth, of refusal to knuckle under to the cruelties in Creation, and of struggle to maintain human dignity against the temptation to be bitter about our mortality.

Worship is the manner in which we humans go about searching for and relating to whatever it is in the cosmos that can help us to cope successfully with all these reactions. This "whatever" is "God." Note that the word "God" is in quotation marks; for all we can do is to try and extrapolate the divine in nature. We can never claim to have approximated its Truth.

Worship, however, cannot be confined to the intellectual dimension. A religious service is not another class in philosophy, psychology, or history, although these and other disciplines are necessary ingredients in worship. In some way or other, worshipers have to feel that they are not only talking *about* "God" but *addressing* Him. This is the great problem of the worshiper of a God who is not "wholly Other" but whose reality is experienced in the awareness of the natural world and to Whom the worshiper responds in gratitude, love, awe and fear, doubt and protest.

Worship under such a theology calls for incorporating into the ritual of the synagogue some elements not ordinarily thought to belong in this context. We humans are already in the midst of a long period of trial and error, during which we shall make many mistakes, travel in wrong directions, and do many silly things in regard to prayer and worship. But freedom is often accompanied by waste, and we must not fear the prospect of failures. In this spirit, I offer the following agenda for the revitalization of Jewish communal worship. The reader, I hope, will find traces below of the thinkers whom I have brought together in this volume.

1. The focal point of Jewish worship can and should remain the framework of the traditional prayer service. As we have seen, some profound thinkers are convinced that the form and content of the traditional prayers should be left untouched and that we need only educate Jews to extract as yet unrealized meanings from the ancient text or interpolate new thoughts into its emotionally satisfying wording. Since this approach is advocated by noted spiritual personalities, it undoubtedly satisfies a need for many Jews. I surmise, however, that this is a blind alley, at whose end we shall arrive sooner or later. The end has already been reached by the mass of Jews whose absence from the synagogue speaks for itself.

In recommending thoughtful examination of the prayers and courageous change and enrichment of their content, I do not delude myself or the reader into believing that the outcome of such textual revision will be to bring hordes to public prayer. It will, hopefully, engage the interest of those current worshipers for whom the synagogue service has become an uninspiring, mindless habit. The obligation to pray keeps many such persons in the pews, but in moments of honest reflection, they know that their worship is in the doldrums.

I shall not recommend here specific changes and additions. What is needed is to set in motion in every synagogue a process in which rabbis and laity will study the siddur, examine its rich

treasure of Jewish thought, poetry, and spiritual musings, and together with recommendations from national commissions on
worship already operating in the various denominations, experiment in liturgical reform. Inasmuch as every congregation has
members who would strongly oppose such "tampering," it might
be advisable to establish *havurot* (fellowships) in every synagogue
that would meet separately for at least a part of the regular service
and rejoin the main body of worshipers to complete the service in
unity. After a reasonable period of experimentation, the pioneer
group should report its experience to the more conservative
members of the congregation in order to determine whether the
latter might now be open to a reconsideration of their unbending
opposition.

2. Mind and soul, intellect and emotion, articulation and silence, meditation and study are all necessary components of worship. I have said that a service is not and should not be a class in
philosophy or any other academic subject. But it should contain
the kind of study and reflection that will add to the self-understanding of the worshipers and to their ability to cope effectively
with life. Worship should contain the kind of study whose purpose
it is to enlighten men and women about what it means to be
human and Jewish. Thus, instead of rote reading of the Torah,
the study portion of the service should examine how the tradition
and the modern mind address themselves to the spiritual problems that disturb the worshipers. In this endeavor, the rabbi will
inevitably turn to members of the congregation whose expertise
can supplement the wisdom of the tradition or, whenever necessary, correct the mistaken ideas of the past. Underlying this form
of study should be the search for satisfying responses to the questions of God, humankind, and the universe.

3. Communal worship can succeed only if the interpersonal
relationships of the congregants are warm and caring. Human
beings need to be sustained by their fellows in their sorrows and
their sufferings. They want to share their joys and to express their
concerns to caring friends and fellow worshipers. They have to
feel wanted and to empathize with those who need their understanding. They need their fellows to support them in their efforts
to sharpen their spiritual and moral sights. These are among the
elements that bring about the formation of congregations. The

ancient Sages understood that the prayers of a congregation divided by dispute cannot succeed. There is a horizontal dimension to worship that is as essential to emotionally satisfying worship as the effort to commune with God. Indeed, if the unity of humankind is one of the divine demands, then its manifestation in the act of communal worship should be paramount. It follows that when Jews or any other religious group meet to pray together, they must have already been united by shared experiences of *gemillut hasadim,* acts of mutual loving-kindness, such as visiting one another in times of illness or comforting one another in days of bereavement.

This closeness is difficult to foster in synagogues whose membership involves many hundreds of families. However, there are methods to establish bonds of friendship, such as forming small *havurot* or dividing the congregation into small units. The latter would be obligated to perform these services of friendship for part of each year for families with whom they have had no previous contact. God is manifest among humans in their behavior toward one another. Communion with God, which is confined solely to a person-to-Person relationship, may offer some emotional satisfaction, but ultimately, it overlooks the fact that the sense of at-homeness in the universe is dependent on satisfying interpersonal relationships with one's fellows. The experience of God is channeled through the values and purposes that we acquire through association with other humans. It might be that we can come to God in solitariness, but even then we bring with ourselves all that we have learned in society. Worship occurs whenever we try to be sensitive to the transcendent implications of what we have learned about life from our social heritage.

4. Worship should engage the whole person. In the spirit of the Psalmist, we can say, "All my being declares, / Who is like Thee, O Lord?" (Ps. 35:10). It is this total dedication to God of the body and mind that should inform public worship. A service in which the worshipers are passive spectators is alien to the tradition of the synagogue as understood by all our thinkers. Lawrence Hoffman most clearly presses for a Jewish worship that engages all the senses. The architecture of many modern synagogues is both a reflection and a cause of the passivity mentioned above. The revitalization of worship will depend, therefore, not only on attention

to the wording of the prayers but also on the physical setting in which worship takes place. The abandon of Purim and Simhat Torah cannot and should not be repeated daily or on Shabbat, but these occasions should serve as examples of how the most staid congregants can and should be galvanized into active participation in worship.

5. Of critical importance is the music of prayer. A religious service will not stir the heart unless it is filled with melodies that clothe the words of prayer with esthetic sound. Attention must be given in the choice of melodies to the rhythm of the spoken language and to the content and intent of each prayer. Much contemporary synagogue music is an imposition of folk and popular tunes that are foreign to the spirit of the liturgy.

These are some of the considerations for the agenda of those who would renew the spiritual interests of Jews. There is no easy answer to any of the problems delineated in these pages, but we have to ask ourselves what would happen if the synagogue were to disappear as a focal point for Jewish spirituality. Perhaps a replacement can be manufactured, but until it is invented, we have no alternative but to try and shore up the foundations of the traditional structure.

THE LANGUAGE OF PRAYER

The most crucial issue in regard to the language of prayer in our time is, as I have suggested in the previous chapter, that raised in the wake of the feminine revolution. There can be little doubt that the male bias of the traditional prayer book needs correction. If only to set the historical record straight, proper mention should be made of the role played by the matriarchs and other women who have helped to weave the fabric of Jewish life. Some feminists tend to overlook the fact that women do receive recognition in the historical references of the Jewish holidays and the prayers, but apologetics cannot erase the masculine mood of traditional Jewish prayer. That bias must be eliminated.

More serious are the theological questions that have arisen. Until the emergence of feminine consciousness, hardly anyone paid serious attention to or was disturbed by the gender of *Shekhi-*

nah, God's Presence. Only the kabbalists gave concentrated thought to so-called feminine manifestations or traits of the Deity, and their views were generally considered to be aberrations. Now we are being challenged to reexamine both the theological and semantic presuppositions of our prayers. It is a challenge that cannot be ignored.

Some of the feminist responses to the challenge are deceptive, because, in my opinion, they detract our attention from the major theological issues. What should concern us is not the feminine attributes of God's essence but the nature of God's immanence and transcendence. By adopting kabbalistic, feministic terminology and by alternating He with She when referring to God, we dissuade worshipers from confronting the contradictions that are entailed in treating God as a Person or other type of Being. The theological problems of the moment arise from the possibility of believing in God as a Process and the implications of such a belief for the language of prayer. Again, how can one pray to a Process? That problem is only compounded by accentuating the poetry of femininity. I need not add here to the comments on feminist approaches to God-language that I have already made in chapter 11.

Unquestionably, many of the traditional prayers can and should be incorporated in our worship today. We must not lose touch with the piety of our ancestors. At the same time, we also have to express our own needs and convictions in new prayers and in a contemporary language. We must strive, no less than our forebears, to be poetic and to be emotionally involved in our worship. In doing so, we shall have to reckon with the insights of the latest high morality and physical and social scientific endeavor. God is still merciful in any acceptable theology, but can we accept today the concept of a vengeful or punishing Being? Is mercy a feminine trait or vengeance an expression of masculinity? Can we clarify what we mean by each of these traits of Process and find an appropriate, gender-neutral terminology? What do or should we now mean when we address Him or Her as the Giver of Torah? Is either pronoun a poetically adequate way to express our understanding of and the reasons for our dedication to Jewish tradition? Quite obviously, we have a lot of homework to do before we can prepare the kind of worship appropriate to the sophisticated minds of educated men and women.

CONCLUSION

I have tried to convey an approach to prayer that confronts its many complications. I consider prayer to be indispensable to our growth as spiritual creatures, but I see no easy solution in the offing that would convert the masses to its practice. How could it be otherwise? Prayer is, after all, not only a means to self-transcendence. It is one of the very goals of human development. For it is only in prayer that men and women deliberately acknowledge the limits of their creatureliness, the greatness of their creative gifts, and the responsibility that they have as a result of these two features of their nature. Men and women will dispute among themselves about whether their prayers fall upon a listening ear or whether they are a form of introspection or meditation. But both one who turns to "God" and one who seeks one's better self are united in the realization of their dependence on one another and on a reality into which all creatures are born and whose origin and ultimate fate neither can ever know. In prayer, humans accept with gratitude what they are and what they have. It is their way of proclaiming with humility the values by which they propose to live. It is the opening of their minds and hearts to the voices of experience and integrity that, from time to time, call upon them to retreat from their overbearing certainties. The task of spiritually alert Jews is to bring together under one roof of worshipful search and dedication men and women who have different visions of God, humankind, and the universe but who are united by their love of Israel and of their fellow human beings.

NOTES

1. Louis L. Kaplan, "An Educational Credo for Our Time," *Jewish Education* 60, no. 2 (summer 1993), p. 41.

2. Ibid.

3. See, for example, Carol Gilligan, *In a Different Voice* (Cambridge: Harvard University Press, 1982).

4. Ismar Elbogen, *Jewish Liturgy,* trans. Raymond Scheindlin (Philadelphia: Jewish Publication Society; New York: Jewish Theological Seminary of America, 1993), p. 46.

5. Eugene B. Borowitz, *How Can a Jew Speak of Faith Today?* (Philadelphia: Westminster Press, 1969), p. 128.

6. Ibid.

7. Evelyn Underhill, *Mysticism* (New York: Meridean Books, 1955), p. 4.

8. A classic example of this pessimistic view is Bertrand Russell's essay, "A Free Man's Worship," in his *Why I Am Not a Christian* (New York: Simon and Schuster, 1957), pp. 104–116.

9. Martin Buber, *Two Types of Faith* (New York: Harper, 1961), p. 157.

10. Martin Buber, *Eclipse of God* (New York: Harper, 1952), pp. 49–50.

11. Ibid.

12. Maurice Friedman, *Martin Buber* (Chicago: University of Chicago Press, 1955), p. 136.

13. Buber, *Eclipse of God,* pp. 52–53.

14. Friedman, *Martin Buber,* p. 136.

GLOSSARY

Ahavat Yisrael—Love of one's fellow Jews.

Amidah—Literally, standing. This prayer is also known as Hatefillah, the prayer par excellence, and is recited three times a day. In the normal weekday service, the Amidah contains eighteen benedictions and is known as the Shemoneh Esray (18). On sabbaths and holidays, there are seven or more blessings, as well as a number of piyyutim (religious poems).

Ashkenazi (plural, Ashkenazim)—Jews who live in or whose families originated in one of the countries of Europe. Ashkenaz is the pre-modern Hebrew designation for Germany, but Ashkenazim came to be used as an identification for the Jews of Eastern, Central, and most of Western Europe. There are notable exceptions, such as the Jews of Spain, Turkey, and Bulgaria, who are recognized as Sephardim (see below).

Berakhot—The first tractate of the Gemara.

Besht—Abbreviation of Baal Shem Tov (Bearer of a Good Name), generally credited with founding modern Hasidism. R. Yisrael Baal Shem Tov lived from 1700 to 1760.

Beth Hamidrash—Literally, house of study. It ranged and ranges from a single room to a whole institution for research, individual study, schooling, and training of rabbis and scholars.

Daven—The origin of the word is in dispute, but it refers to the mechanical reading of the liturgy. Daveners are worshipers who piously recite the prayers but who do so without attention to their meaning.

Devekut—Mystic union with God, an objective particularly sought by those under kabbalistic influence.

Haggadah—The text containing the ritual conducted in Jewish homes on the eve of the Passover festival.

Halakhah—Traditional Jewish law that has developed from the biblical period until our day.

Hasidism—Hasidism features an emotional pietism that goes beyond the intellectual study of the traditional classics. See Besht.

Kabbalah—The mainstream of Jewish mysticism, based mainly on the medieval classic, the Zohar, and the theology of R. Issac Luria (sixteenth century) and his followers.

Kaddish—A doxology recited in different forms as an introduction to or a close of sections of the synagogue liturgy, as a prayer for mourners, or as a conclusion to the study of a classic text.

Kavvanah—The term applies to the criteria for measuring true prayer—sincerity, devotion, attention to meaning, elimination of self-centeredness, humility, directing oneself to God's will, and so on.

Kiddush—A prayer for the sanctification of a holy day, mostly recited in the home on the eve of the sabbath or a festive holiday.

Mahzor (plural, Mahzorim)—Literally, cycles. The prayer book for each of the holidays. Each holiday has a mahzor containing special prayers relating to the theme of the occasion.

Midrash—Homilectical interpretation of biblical verses. There are a number of collections of these interpretations, each of which is called a midrash. The midrashic literature is rich in theological, philosophical, moral, and psychological insights.

Minyan—A quorum necessary for public worship. The tradition calls for at least ten adult males, but in today's liberal religious streams, women are also counted in the minyan.

Mitzvah (plural, Mitzvot)—Literally, commandment(s). The mitzvot are the moral and spiritual directives and ritual practices that Jews are expected to observe. Traditional Jews believe that the mitzvot are expressions of God's will that were revealed at Mount Sinai and later elaborated by the rabbis. That process continues to this day. Free-thinking Jews tend to be selective about the observances and their underlying spiritual, intellectual, and moral foundations. In popular parlance, a good deed is called a mitzvah.

Neilah—The final prayers of the service on the day of Yom Kippur.

Pesah—The Festival of Passover, commemorating the exodus from Egypt as recorded in the Bible.

Pesukei Dezimra—Literally, verses of song. The first section of the daily morning worship. It is composed of selections from Psalms and other books of the Bible, the Mishnah and Gemara, and benedictions and prayers of the ancient sages.

R.—Abbreviation for rabbi, usually when referring to the sages of the talmudic and post-talmudic periods, for example, R. Akiva instead of Rabbi Akiva.

Rosh Hashanah—New Year in the Hebrew calendar. A holiday on the first two days of the month of Tishri devoted to exploring the meaning of God's sovereignty. See Yamim Noraim.

Sephardi (plural, Sephardim)—Jews who come from non-Ashkenazic European countries, North Africa, and Asia. See Ashkenazi.

Shabbat—The Sabbath.

Shavuot—Literally, weeks. The Feast of Weeks, Pentecost. Coming seven weeks and a day after Pesah, Shavuot celebrates the theophany at Mount Sinai and the giving of the Torah to the Israelites.

Shema Yisrael—Together with the Amidah, the core of Jewish prayer. It consists of passages from Deuteronomy 6:4–9 and 11:13–21 and Numbers 15:37–41.

Shemini Atzeret—Eighth Day of Solemn Assembly. A holiday that follows the last day of Sukkot. It brings out some of the universal concerns of the Jewish people for the nations of the earth and also highlights some of the theological questions involved in prayer.

Siddur—Prayer book. Short for Siddur or Seder Hatefillot, the order of the prayers. The term Siddur is applied to the prayer book used in the daily and sabbath services. See Mahzor.

Simhat Torah—The Joy or Celebration of Torah. A holiday that, in Israel, occurs on the same day as Shemini Atzeret. In the diaspora, Simhat Torah comes a day after the latter. The holiday is devoted to the completion of the annual cycle of the reading of the Pentateuch from the special handwritten scroll.

Sukkot—The Feast of Tabernacles, commemorating the forty-year wandering of the Israelites after their exodus from Egypt. It features the building of temporary huts to serve as symbols of the uncertain life of the Israelites before they entered the Promised Land. During the week of Sukkot, the families eat their meals in the sukkah, or hut.

Tallit—Fringed prayer shawl, draped over the shoulders during worship.

Tefillin—Phylacteries worn on an arm and the forehead during worship. They symbolize the need to bring both mind and heart together in the worship of God and in trying to perfect the human spirit.

Teshuvah—Literally, return. Repentance and atonement for one's sins. According to Jewish belief, both the individual and the people as a whole are required to ask forgiveness for their sins.

Tikkun Olam—Repairing the world. Derived from the mystic belief that through adherence and obedience to the laws of the Torah, the Jewish people will effect the mending of the present reality of disruption and corruption.

Tirha Dezibbura—Troubling the congregation by slowing the pace of the service unnecessarily. Prayers in public worship, whether silent or verbalized, are optimally recited in unison.

Torah—Literally, teaching, but frequently translated as Law. Specifically, the Pentateuch, the first five books of the Bible. However, the word is applied to the whole range of classical and modern tradition and has a normative thrust. That which becomes crucial to the spiritual welfare of the Jewish people is ultimately placed under the category of Torah. Talmud Torah (the study of Torah) is the study of the old and new Jewish classics.

Yamim Noraim—Days of Awe. The ten-day period of penitence at the outset of the Hebrew month of Tishri, featuring the holy days of Rosh Hashanah and Yom Kippur.

Yibadel (for a woman, Tibadel) l'hayyim arukim—A blessing on behalf of a living person, wishing him or her a long life.

Yom Kippur—The high point of the Yamim Noraim. A day of fasting devoted to prayer and meditation on sin and repentance, both of the individual and the whole society.

Index